PRODIGAL SONS

THE VIOLENT HISTORY OF
CHRISTOPHER EVANS AND JOHN SONTAG

"As reverence for the past dies out in the breasts of a generation, so likewise patriotism wanes. In the measure that the love of the history of the past dies, so likewise do the higher aspirations for the future. To keep the flower of patriotism alive, we must keep the memory of the past vividly in mind."

Ezra Meeker: *Personal Experiences on the Oregon Trail.*

PRODIGAL SONS

THE VIOLENT HISTORY OF
CHRISTOPHER EVANS AND JOHN SONTAG

BY

WALLACE SMITH

WITH A NEW AFTERWORD

BY

WILLIAM B. SECREST, JR.

Craven Street Books
Fresno CA

PRODIGAL SONS
The Violent History of
Christopher Evans and John Sontag

By
Wallace Smith

Cover art by James Goold

© 2005 Linden Publishing

135798642
ISBN: 0-941936-89-9

Printed in United States of America

Smith, Wallace, 1895-
    Prodigal sons : the true history of Christopher Evans and
    John Sontag / by Wallace Smith.
        p. cm.
    Includes bibliographical references and index.
    ISBN 0-941936-89-9 (pbk. : alk. paper) —
    ISBN 0-941936-90-2 (alk. paper)
    1. Evans, Christopher, 1847-1917. 2. Sontag, John, 1861 or
    2-1893. 3. Outlaws—California—San Joaquin Valley—
    Biography. 4. Train robberies—California—San Joaquin
    Valley—History—19th century. 5. San Joaquin Valley (Calif.)—
    History—19th century. 6. San Joaquin Valley (Calif.)—
    Biography. I. Title.
    F868.S173S7 2005
    364.15'52'092279455—dc22   2005006006

A Craven Street Book
Linden Publishing Inc.
2006 S. Mary, Fresno CA
www.lindenpub.com • 800-345-4447

TO

EVELYN, PATRICIA, AND LUCIA

ACKNOWLEDGEMENTS

I found the following books, manuscripts, and persons useful in the collection of data pertaining to the life and times of Christopher Evans.

William Elsey Connelley: *Quantrill and the Border Wars.*

Emmett Dalton: *When the Daltons Rode.* Quotation reprinted with the permission of Doubleday & Company, Inc.

Carl B. Glasscock: *Bandits and the Southern Pacific.*

Al Jennings: *Through the Shadows With O. Henry.*

Robertus Love: *The Rise and the Fall of Jesse James.*

Eva Evans McCullough: *An Outlaw and His Family* (an unpublished manuscript). Mr. and Mrs. Perry McCullough were guests at our house in September, 1940. Shortly after their return to their home in Laguna Beach, Mrs. McCullough wrote to me in part as follows:

> "A thought occurred to me while reading your account of Lew Draper in *Garden of the Sun:* Why don't you collect legends of Chris Evans for a book to write in the future? . . . . You could call it *The Robin Hood of the San Joaquin* . . . . I do not mean Robin Hood in the sense that Chris Evans robbed the rich and gave to the poor, but that feeling that I have gotten from the old-timers that the years have added glamor to his name. . . . You are close to the source, and would enjoy doing it. . . . In your revision you may use any of my material you choose, because if my story is ever published your having it would aid instead of detracting. . . ; I am not in a hurry for the return of my manuscript. I want you and your wife to read it at your leisure, and then tell me if he (Chris Evans) is not more real to you. The enclosed photo is the only good one we have because that mutilated eye detracted from the nobility of his face and head. My sister, Ynez, made this one in the dining room of her home at Marshfield, Oregon. It is yours to keep and use, and you might be able to get a fairly good copy of it. . . . I feel that if you write a story about Chris Evans from my point of view I would benefit by it if my book is ever published, and that, to me, would be ample compensation. . . . My father has had little justice, but I am sure you will grant him that."

Ed. Morrell: *The 25th Man.* Permission to quote granted by Mr. Raymond S. Ward, former secretary-treasurer of the now defunct New Era Publishing Company.

Frank Norris: *The Octopus* (a novel).

Pioneers: The scores of old-timers whom I have interviewed from time to time during the past eighteen years cannot all be listed here. Those whom I have quoted directly are named in the *Appendix.*.

　　　ACKNOWLEDGEMENTS

Dr. George Hammond, Director of the Bancroft Library, the University of California, Berkeley, had photostatic copies made for me of the various old newspaper articles which I needed.

Mrs. Mabel R. Gillis, State Librarian, Sacramento, sent me typewritten copies of certain newspaper articles, and the poems by Ambrose Bierce.

Mrs. Pauline Nordstrom, Kingsburg, presented me with her collection of old newspapers dealing with Evans and Sontag. They aided me greatly in my research.

Mr. James Paulson, Fresno, made valuable suggestions with respect to form and organization of my material.

My wife, Evelyn, was patient with me as I stayed up into the wee, small hours of the morning trying to unravel the testimony which kept accumulating from books, court transcripts, manuscripts, newspapers, personal interviews, and personal letters. Her sister, Mrs. Helen Driedger, helped me in the typing of the original manuscript. My mother-in-law, Mrs. Daisy Buller, proficient in both High and Low German, and my wife's sister, Mrs. Belle Ross, put into German dialect the conversation between Johnson, the ex-convict, and Eva Evans. My daughter, Patricia, played Tchaikovsky's *Nutcracker Suite* softly for me during the long winter evenings while I tried to lead three outlaws into and out of trouble. I lost two of them early in the book, but managed to take the most important of them through the gloomy shadows of impending disaster and death out into the bright light of a happy old age.

PREFACE

I SPENT my boyhood along Kings River in Tulare County, California. As a lad I listened wide-eyed to the pioneers as they talked about the adventures of Chris Evans and John Sontag. No two stories agreed, but they were all thrilling to a youngster. I have found that my interest in these two men has not subsided with the advancing years, and so I decided to do something about it. The result is this book.

It has not been my intention to write a wild-Western thriller or a story suitable for a pulp magazine. Rather I have tried to show how the lives of Evans and Sontag were interwoven closely with their times. The San Joaquin Valley has been the scene of many heroic episodes, stirring deeds, new inventions, and amazing developments. No section of a similar area in the United States can show a greater variety of happenings. In the struggle to conquer the arid plains and the insolent railway, Chris Evans and John Sontag were destined to take prominent parts. Were they heroes, villains, or ordinary citizens catapulted into sudden strife by forces which they could neither understand nor control? A part of the purpose of this book has been an attempt to answer this question.

Wallace Smith
Fresno State College
Fresno, California.

TABLE OF CONTENTS

11

Prodigal Sons

CHAPTER 1

GO WEST, YOUNG MAN

"I'M LOOKING for Chris Evans." This was the tearful remark of a four-year-old boy lost on the corner of Fifth and Harrison Streets in San Francisco. The policeman, who had picked him up, thought this was very funny. Almost everybody in those days was looking for Chris Evans.

But unlike most people who were then looking for Evans, the little boy was not filled with homicidal intent. He was lost in a large city, and needed his father. That evening, after he had been rescued from the police station, he explained his statement to his family:

"Everyone talks about Chris Evans. He is my papa, and I thought if I talked about him too, you would hear about it, and then maybe you would find me."

The presence of little John Christopher Evans in San Francisco in 1893 was the result of many things, and a lost four-year-old boy was reaping the harvest sowed by greed, lawlessness, and corporate control.

The chief character in this drama, the man for whom the child and scores of man-hunters were then searching, was being impersonated nightly by a professional actor in a San Francisco theater in a lurid melodrama entitled *Evans and Sontag*. He was also

15

appearing in real life down in the San Joaquin Valley in a drama even more spectacular than the one then being shown on the stage.

Just who was Chris Evans? Why was he attracting nation-wide attention in 1893? It will require the rest of this book to answer these two questions.

Christopher Evans was born in 1847 at Bell's Corner, a small hamlet located twelve miles from Ottawa, Canada. His father, small and dark, was Irish; his mother, large and blonde, was German. Chris, as he was always called, was small like his father, and fair like his mother. He was a towhead, and remained one until his late twenties. The children in the Evans family, four boys and four girls, were reared in the Roman Catholic faith. The family was large and the times were hard and so, at the age of sixteen, Chris ran away from home and crossed the boundary line into the United States.

This was early in the summer of 1863, and the American Civil War was approaching its climax. For many decades the American people had celebrated their national holiday, the 4th of July, with spectacular pyrotechnical displays. Firecrackers by day and fireworks by night were considered evidences of patriotism. No doubt it was blatant and adolescent, but the people liked it. Twisting the lion's tail was the order of the day, and the 4th of July orator in the park or auditorium always ended his address by roaring:

"We have licked the British twice and we can do it again!"

In time the exploding giant firecrackers had killed

or maimed enough children and adults to equal the entire combined casualty lists of the American Revolution and the War of 1812. Leaders in the movement for a safe and sane 4th of July argued that we were in danger of losing our third war with Great Britain. But never did the American people equal the noise and the fury they achieved on July 4th, 1863. The previous day had seen the fall of the fortress at Vicksburg in one last tremendous crescendo of gunfire, and the defeat of the Confederates after three days of furious fighting at Gettysburg. The Union was saved!

Stepping across the line from a peaceful Canada, Evans must have thought he had entered a madhouse. No doubt it had a psychological effect on him. He promptly enlisted in the Union Army at Buffalo under an assumed name. Years later a Visalia paper was to print this about Evans:[1]

"It is said that Chris Evans is used to the smell of gunpowder. He served in the Civil War when a mere boy, and was wounded in the foot at the battle of Winchester. He also served against the Indians after the war, and was under Reno at the time Custer was killed. He says he heard the firing at the time of the Custer massacre."

It is regrettable that the foregoing quotation cannot be accepted entirely as fact. Evans' daughter[2] stated that her father saw no action in the eastern theatre of operations, either with the main Army of the Potomac or any portion thereof. He did see active service, but it was with a detachment of troops sent to western Minnesota where the Sioux Indians were on the warpath in the Kandiyohi country. The boys in blue subdued the redskins, and finally reached the Dakota prairies where Evans won fame as a scout.

Late one evening Chris, who had been out on patrol duty in advance of the troops, lay down on his blankets in a small thicket. A Sioux Indian had been trailing him cautiously and, in the early dawn, sneaked up on Evans and swung his tomahawk at the sleeping scout, cutting through three of his ribs. This annoyed Evans very much, who did not like to have his slumber disturbed in such a rude manner. He felt that a remonstrance, a reprimand, or even an argument would not meet the situation. After thinking the matter through, which didn't take him long, he decided that this was a time for action and that steps must be taken to remove his assailant from this mundane sphere. Evans hurriedly assembled his weapons, and employed them in the execution of the techniques learned in the school of the soldier. This led to the demise of the noble red man. Chris wanted his girl-friend in Canada to appreciate his prowess, so he carefully removed the scalp from his late opponent and mailed the Indian's hirsute adornment to her. The stench from the uncured souvenir led postal inspectors to open the package somewhere en route and Evans received a severe reprimand from Washington, D.C.

Evans never became a naturalized American citizen. As a Canadian he may have resented the American philosophy that "the only good Indian is a dead Indian." He said years later that he felt that the Indians were being wronged and soon lost all interest in fighting them. Evans admired his commanding officer, General George A. Custer, and agreed with the latter's contention that it was the graft prevalent during Grant's administration which was leading to Indian troubles. When Custer was unable to prove his charges against Secretary of War Belknap before a Congressional investigating committee, he was penalized by removal from command, and Evans was disgusted. The latter's family always suspected he deserted.[3] At any rate, in 1873, after ten years service with the United States Army, most of it as a trooper in Custer's Seventh Cavalry, Chris Evans, accompanied by his army "buddy," Jack Egan, went for a walk along the rails of the Union Pacific Railway. When they stopped they found that they were in California. Evans had enlisted under an assumed name and his army moniker always remained his own deep, dark secret. When his daughter wanted to know under what name he had soldiered, he asked her confidentially:

"Can you keep a secret?"
"Yes," she answered eagerly.
"Well, so can I."
She never interrogated him again.

In subsequent years Chris Evans never joined the Grand Army of the Republic, or ever permitted his family to apply for a pension in his behalf. There was probably a good reason why he refused both the fraternal association and the financial aid which meant so much to other veterans.

Evans and Egan brought their hike to a halt in San Benito county, because they did not know whether to go north or south. They decided to leave it to Fate. Evans set a trigger stick in the road and it fell south. But Egan did not want to abide by its decision after all. So he marched north and out of the ken of history. Evans went south.

In 1873 the only town of any importance in the San Joaquin Valley was Visalia. Many years later fantastic stories were to be printed in the Visalia papers stating that Evans had escaped the massacre of the Little Big-horn River because Custer had ordered him across that stream with Reno's battalion just before the battle. This was not true, but it made a good story. Custer met Crazy Horse and his Sioux and Cheyenne warriors in 1876, and that year Evans, a married man with one child, was the engineer on a lake steamer making regular runs on Owens Lake. Anyone could have found that out by looking at the record.

The first man in California to give Evans employment was a Visalia lawyer named Daggett. The latter encouraged the young man in his endeavors to improve himself. Chris bought books and studied at night and in this way managed to secure an education which was in later years to astonish men with better opportunities and more formal training.

The next spring, Hudson Barton, owner of a large lumber-mill located at Cedar Springs in the mountains northeast of Visalia, employed Evans as one of his teamsters. He was given a wagon and trailer and eight horses, and set out for the mill. The one-way trip required three days. The few isolated ranch houses along the way served as wayside inns and sold meals to the freighters. And it was the evening of the first day when Evans reached the Byrd ranch and met his fate.

The Rattlesnake Ranch, as the Byrd place was then called, was located twenty-five miles northeast of Visalia. Some time after Evans made his first stop there, a postoffice was established and the name changed to Auckland. Today, when a motorist enters the mountains by driving due east from Orosi, he will climb a steep incline known as Boyd's Grade, and a few miles beyond this point he will pass the building still bearing the name Auckland. Here Mrs. Byrd and her daughter, Mary Jane, always called Molly, operated an eating house.

Mrs. Byrd was originally a McCullough, and her parents had come from the mountains of Tennessee. She was a person of strong convictions and little formal education, but had taught herself to read remarkably well by a constant perusal of the only three books in her possession; the Bible, a dictionary, and Dr. King's *Doctor Book*.

Molly Byrd's father was a very dignified man. Even his wife never called him anything but "Mr. Byrd." He was a handsome, aristocratic, fine looking man, a native of Virginia, and a member of the family which has since produced Harry, a United States Senator from Virginia, and Richard, an aviator and rear-admiral, whose exploits in the Antarctic and at the South Pole have made him known to the entire world.

Some years before this the Four Creeks near Visalia had overflowed their banks and destroyed the Byrd improvements and most of the livestock. The impoverished owner was forced to leave and settled twenty-five miles to the northeast in the foothills at the place already referred to as the Rattlesnake Ranch. But Byrd was unhappy there, and brooded much over his financial losses. He began to drink to excess. When he had occasion to go to Visalia to sell a few cattle he would usually spend most of the proceeds for liquor, then he would ride toward home singing raucously, and upon his arrival he would pick up his rifle and fire at random in the general direction of his home and family. When the wife and children fled, as they always did, there remained only the house and furniture on which to wreak vengeance. He would fire through the walls and smash the furniture until he felt better. Thus far no member of the family, miraculously enough, had sustained injury.

But Mr. Byrd was not the only member of the family who knew how to shoot. In order to supply meat for the table Molly spent much time shooting cotton-tail rabbits. One night she anticipated her father's belligerent arrival by getting to the rifle first, and she met him with the announcement that henceforth she would do all the shooting around the Byrd household. She was twelve and he was drunk, but he had seen her shoot. So he took a walk and did not return for five years. There was never a dull moment in that family. After her marriage Molly was presented with a .32 calibre Ballard rifle. It was equipped with special sights and cartridges and she often astonished hunting companions by shooting hawks on the wing. So her father was no doubt wise when he left home that night.

This was the unhappy state of affairs when Chris Evans entered the Byrd eating place for his first meal, and met Molly. She was fifteen then; he was twenty-seven. It must have been love at first sight, because they were married that fall on November 4, 1874.

The newlyweds went to the mountains immediately where they spent their honeymoon. The mill owner for whom Evans had freighted that summer was impressed with his reliability and had hired him to stay at the mill all winter to keep the snow off the roofs of the various mill buildings to prevent the excessive weight from causing their collapse. A wagon brought in a load of groceries and housekeeping necessities, and Molly and Chris spent the entire winter alone in the mountains. They were literally snowbound. It was a portent of things to come. Chris was destined to spend other winters in the snow-clad hills, but happiness was not to be his portion later. Now Molly and he were happy, and enjoyed the winter immensely. Years later Evans, who loved poetry, would recite to his children stanzas written by Frank Stanton:

> Never'll fergit it as long as I live—
> Don't keer what blessin's I know;
> The hills standin' white,
> Skeery ghosts of the night—
> An' Molly an' me an' the snow.

The next spring Evans bought a large tract of land some miles from the Barton mill which contained a large grove of Sequoia gigantea redwoods. He appropriately named this place the Redwood Ranch. His brother Tom and the latter's wife and small daughter arrived from Canada that spring, and Tom helped Chris build the cabin in which the family later resided. Tom was a fraternal (not identical) twin brother, and was tall and dark.

Shortly after the two brothers had completed the cabin, tragedy entered the lives of Chris and Molly for the first time; more was to follow. On the morning of June 15, 1875, Chris was saddling a fractious horse. He asked Molly to hold its bridle while he tightened the girths. A sudden lunge threw Molly to the ground. As a result of this accident she gave birth prematurely to a baby boy. He lived only two hours. Chris made a little coffin out of redwood boards and buried their first-born child at the Redwood Ranch.

Molly's recovery was slow and finally Chris placed her on a mattress in a wagon and drove slowly down to the old Byrd ranch at Auckland. Leaving Molly to convalesce in her mother's care, Chris returned to his Redwood Ranch. Shortly thereafter Brother Tom's wife gave birth to a baby daughter, who died within a few weeks. Chris helped his brother make another little coffin and the baby girl was buried under the big redwood beside her little boy cousin. There they rest to this time. Chris then went over the mountains to Inyo County and secured a job. Tom's wife, grieving over her lost child, and homesick for relatives and friends in Canada, wanted to leave California. So Tom Evans bought a mule, placed his few belongings and surviving daughter on it, and then Mr. and Mrs. Tom Evans walked over the Sierra into Inyo by way of the Kearsarge Trail. From there they went by stage coach to the nearest railway and thence back to Canada. Years later it was said that Tom had helped Chris hold up trains and also that he had joined the Dalton gang just before it was wiped out at Coffeyville, Kansas. Such stories are false. Tom went back to Canada with his family and stayed there.

The second child born to Chris and Molly was christened Eva. At birth she weighed two pounds and was twelve inches long and so tiny that she wore her mother's wedding ring as a bracelet. Her diminutive size also prevented her from using all of her mother's milk. Grandmother Byrd solved that problem by finding a new-born pup which was used to help relieve the pressure. In those days, when expert medical help was not available, women could not afford to be squeamish. Mrs. Byrd recalled her own experience when Louis Napoleon, Molly's brother, was an infant. She was living in an isolated region in the northern part of California. No pups were available, but her husband shot a bear and brought home one of the small cubs which was used to give relief when needed. Molly's mother, who will play an important part in this history, was a forthright pioneer woman who never minced words or hesitated to take action when she thought it necessary.

But to complete this bear story. Louis Napoleon and the cub, his foster-brother as it were, grew up to be inseparable companions. They had shared the same mother's milk. But the bear grew faster than the man-child, and its strength became a menace even in play. Therefore it was given to a miner who happened to pass that way. Sometime later Mrs. Byrd had occasion to go to Sacramento. A large crowd had gathered at a street corner and when she stopped to learn the reason for the commotion she saw a street musician with a performing bear. The poor mangy animal recognized his former foster-mother and she had a hard time getting away from the poor creature.

When Molly's baby was six months old both mother and daughter were strong enough to travel by stage-coach over the mountains to Inyo. Chris saw Eva for the first time. This child was destined to be closer to him, perhaps, than any other mortal.

The steamboat on Owens Lake on which Evans was the engineer was named the *Bessie Brady*. It made daily trips between Cerro Gordo and Cartago Landing. This was the summer of 1876 and, years later, Visalia reporters were to state that this was the time that he had been fighting Indians with Custer in Montana. As a matter of fact there was entirely too much fighting in Owens Valley to suit the Evans family; Chris did not have to go to Montana to find it. A Mexican shot and killed a popular peace officer there, and he and several of his race were lynched and the rest driven out of the valley. One morning Molly opened the door and screamed. A dead Mexican, grimacing horribly, was hanging from a branch of the tree directly in front of the Evans house. Molly was expecting another baby

and felt that such an environment might have evil pre-
natal influences and lead to disaster. So Evans resigned
as engineer, took his family to Visalia, found no work
there, and went on to San Francisco.

At that time Seattle was booming. Evans decided
to take his family there. They went by boat. As they
steamed out through the Golden Gate they found on
board the famous midgets, General Tom Thumb, his
wife, and his sister, Minnie Warren, and a famous circus giant, Colonel Goshen, over eight feet tall. The
latter, to amuse the ship's passengers, would place Mrs.
Tom Thumb on the palm of one open hand, Eva
Evans on the other, and then hold them both out at
arm's length. When they reached Seattle, Evans
planned to file on a homestead of one hundred and
sixty acres which has since become the heart of the
present city of Seattle. However, the excessive rainfall
got on Mrs. Evans' nerves, and the Evans family, after
a six weeks sojourn in the wet state of Washington,
returned to sunny California and Visalia. Here Evans
bought some lots at the edge of the town and began to
build a house.

The plot of any story involves getting the characters
into and out of trouble. The setting of the plot must
include the time when, the place where, and the conditions under which the plot unfolds. The "little gray
home in the West" which Chris Evans was now building was the place where he both was to begin and end
his struggle with duly constituted authority. On it and
him was to be focused national attention. Here was
to be the scene of spitting gun-fire in the night, the

shedding of tears, loud lamentations, and mental anguish. The time when and the conditions under which these turbulent manifestations come to pass will be the theme of subsequent chapters.

CHAPTER 2
GANG-PLOW, SCRAPER, AND COMBINE

THE MAN in the street would call it bad luck, a philosopher skilled in the ways of the occult would discourse learnedly about metaphysical insecurity, and the astrologer who charts human affairs by reading the planets would say that there were very few beneficent aspects in the Evans horoscope.

Christopher Evans and his family were fated to experience extreme measures of both joys and sorrows. Happiness came to them in the form of a baby boy, christened Elmer, who was born in June, 1878. He was a source of pride to them for eighteen months. Then both Eva and he were stricken with diphtheria. The family physician, Dr. Henrehan, promised to save the sturdy little man-child, but felt dubious about Eva's chances for survival. However, they both recovered. One day when Elmer was toddling about the room he suddenly went into convulsions and died. Eva never forgot her emotions when she climbed up on a chair a day later and looked into a small box standing on the table in a corner of the room. The little waxen face staring up at her with unseeing eyes was to haunt her for many years.

This was the second son that Chris and Molly had lost under tragic circumstances and, again, Molly was to find it hard to recover from the shock. Her husband decided to take his wife for a visit to her parents. Five years had elapsed since Molly's father had walked out on his family, more or less by request. He had been too proud to make any overtures toward peace, but in time the influence of the children had brought about a reconciliation between Mr. and Mrs. Byrd. The ranch at Auckland had been traded for another near Adelaide in San Luis Obispo county. When misfortune once more became the portion of Chris and Molly, it was to this place that their thoughts naturally turned. In the years that lay before her Molly was to find herself on numerous occasions desperately in need of her mother.

The trip from Visalia to Adelaide was made in a buckboard drawn by two horses. Evans, his wife, and small daughter Eva, rode through Hanford, along the north shore of Tulare Lake, over the Coast Range, and finally arrived in Cholame Valley. The journey took one week.

Chris found work in the Clau quick-silver mine in the immediate vicinity[1] of the Byrd ranch. The new environment helped Molly to recover and the Evans and Byrd families lived together in amity. Peace so seldom came to them that it is worth recording. Eventually a fourth child was born to Molly and Chris, who was named Ynez after one of the Franciscan missions along the coast.

Eva, who had become used to being the only child in the family, resented and feared the little redhead. She did not want to share her dishes and other playthings with the new arrival, so she hid them in a squirrel hole. Some days later she went to get them, and they were gone. When she confided in her father and told him the cause and result of her planning, he refused to help her look for them, chided her for being selfish, and comforted her by saying that Ynez would not want any of her toys for many years to come. In the fall of 1882 the Evans family returned to Visalia, and a third daughter, Winifred, was born there in November.

Many years later it was asserted that Chris Evans was a Mussel Slough settler, and had engaged in the battle fought there on May 11, 1880. Any honest searcher after truth can easily verify the fact that from 1878 to 1882 he was employed in the mine in San Luis Obispo County. He was not even a resident of the San Joaquin Valley at the time of the fight.

In the spring of 1883, Evans, his wife, and three daughters moved to their Redwood Ranch in the mountains. This was to be their summer home for many years. There were no moving pictures or radios to amuse people then, and Chris taught his children to memorize poems. Evans had no particular musical ability, but he loved the swing, rhythm, and the message of great poetry. He was especially fond of Scott, Swinburne, and Tennyson, and when he had occasion to walk the floor with the baby at night he often recited from memory all of *Locksley Hall*. Elmer Perkins of Sultana told the author that to hear Evans either read prose or recite poetry was a rare treat; few professional impersonators could surpass him.[2]

During the long winter evenings he tutored his

children in a strict code of ethics: Never lie, steal, carry tales, or invade the rights of others, and fight your own battles. Bart Patterson of Dinuba, for many years a director of the Alta Irrigation Company, whose father was a personal friend of Evans and one of the five Mussel Slough settlers who, with his family, spent eight months in the San Jose jail, told this writer that Evans set a high moral standard for his family and was a good neighbor. Patterson recalled that on one occasion he and some of his young friends from Grangeville drove to Visalia and, after sundry experiences, decided to raid Evans' melon patch. The latter caught Bart, whom he knew well, booted him earnestly, and then read him a lecture on the evils of stealing which he never forgot. Chris ended his harangue by saying:[3]

"Next time you want a melon come and ask for one and I'll give it to you, but don't steal."

Years later, when other agencies and men were to accuse Evans of stealing, Patterson was to remember the dissertation on honesty he had heard that night. Even if Evans were guilty of train robberies, he would have been justified in the following rebuttal:

"I asked the railroad company for a melon and it patted me on the back, but those pats were forcefully delivered and peculiarly located!"

While living at the Redwood Ranch, Evans selected a huge Sequoia gigantea tree and told his daughter Eva that he wanted to be buried in it. In picking a tree for a tomb, he revealed his profound love of nature. He requested that a slab of bark be removed, and then enough wood chiseled out to leave ample space for his body placed there in a perpendicular position. Then the bark was to be replaced. Since the wood of the Sequoia gigantea is not subject to decay such a tomb would have had a unique advantage. This was one of the few requests his daughter Eva was unable to grant her father.

The Evans family spent the winters and springs in Visalia. The growing children loved flowers, and became interested in the Decoration (Memorial) Day programs, and the great masses of flowers placed on the graves of the Union veterans. This celebration infuriated Mrs. Byrd and she told her grandchildren in no uncertain terms to stay away from it. The Byrds of Virginia and the McCulloughs of Tennessee had suffered terribly during the Civil War; most of their menfolk had been killed while serving with the Army of North Virginia under Robert E. Lee. Grandmother Byrd had become a confirmed Yankee hater. She would permit no bluecoats on her property, even though they were only members of the local Home Guards, whose uniforms were also blue.

One day Eva proudly waved the Stars and Stripes in Grandmother Byrd's face, and the latter promptly burned it. She admonished Eva:[4]

"Never wave that bloody rag in my face again!"

On another occasion, the grandmother discovered Eva reading *Uncle Tom's Cabin* and, although the latter had finished only half the book, it too was relentlessly burned. It was Mrs. Byrd's contention that Harriet Beecher Stowe and her book were to blame for the War between the States. Abraham Lincoln had

expressed a somewhat similar opinion when he met the
creator of Uncle Tom and remarked in his droll way:

"So you are the little woman who caused this big
war!"

Grandmother Byrd even carried her partisanship
into the realm of religion. Chris and Molly sent their
children to the Sunday School of the Methodist
Church, South. This denomination had broken away
from the Methodist Episcopal Church in 1844 as a result of the bitterness caused by the argument over slavery. This breach would not be healed until 1939 when
the two factions were once more to be united. Both
the northern and southern branches of this denomination had churches in Visalia at this time. Mrs. Byrd's
hatred for all "damyanks," as she called them, included
even those who were affiliated with the northern group
of Methodists; she considered them schismatics, guilty
of heresy, and not within the true fold. When the
Evans children had occasion to go to the main part of
Visalia, their grandmother told them to walk on the
side of the street opposite from the edifice where the
Yankees worshipped; on Sundays the presence of the
congregation would be a source of contamination, and
on week-days the sanctuary itself might possibly be a
means of pollution.

Chris, who had served in the Union Army, was no
doubt amused by all this, but he tolerated his mother-
in-law's vagaries. Her people had suffered greatly, and
he told his children to obey their grandmother, who
was always good to them, and to respect her whims.
While she forbade them to attend the Memorial Day

exercises, he ruled that they be allowed to go to the cemetery the following day to view the flowers.

Evans, as breadwinner for this large family, had to look for work upon his return to Visalia in 1882. He was to find it in connection with three new inventions. During the rainy season the Stockton gang-plow and the Fresno scraper were to receive his attention; in the early summer he was to spend long, hot days on the platform of a combined harvester. The rest of the time he worked for the railroad, the Bank of California, or in his mine at Sampson's Flat.

During the Civil War period Westley Underwood, Henry Mills, and Lowell A. Richards,[5] all wheat growers in the northern part of the San Joaquin Valley, collaborated in the invention of the Stockton gang-plow, and then sold their patent rights to Matteson & Williamson, implement dealers at Stockton. The first factory-built plow was sold by Matteson personally to Ransome McCapes, a former schoolmate of Matteson in Grant county, Wisconsin. This was in 1868, and that year McCapes, together with his two brothers-in-law, Henry W. Lander and Stephen V. Porter, operated a large wheat farm which included the present site of Manteca. In order to handle expeditiously the long string of horses needed to pull the large Stockton gang-plow with its many shares, Irwin S. Wright,[6] employed as a teamster by McCapes, devised the so-called jerk-line method of controlling his animals. In 1870 McCapes moved to Fairview, north of present Sanger, and that fall he and his son, Eugene L., sowed the first wheat ever to be grown in Fresno county. They prepared twenty acres for planting, but could secure seed for only fifteen acres. Australian white wheat was used and, after the harvest in the summer of 1871, buyers, chiefly miners from the foothills along the San Joaquin River, paid McCapes a hundred dollars a ton in gold-dust weighed out on the steelyards. The next year Charles Lohse harvested his first crop on the Easterby holdings surrounding the present city of Fresno. Irrigation for this wheatfield was furnished by Fancher Creek which flowed through the McCapes ranch at Fairview.

One day, shortly after his return to Visalia, Evans placed his saddle on his favorite horse and rode to Fairview. Although Chris was a sociable person and well liked by his neighbors, he was not prone to spend his time visiting them. There was always work to do and so little time in which to do it. Therefore this visit had a purpose; it was to learn from McCapes, an expert in the matter, all he knew about the merits of the Stockton gang-plow and the jerk-line method of handling horses. As a result of this visit, Evans bought a Stockton gang-plow and secured contracts for plowing land. He used six horses until noon and another six during the afternoon which enabled him to do a prodigious amount of work in a day. On the frame of the plow he placed a little box in which eight-year-old Eva rode from morning until night. The smell of the freshly turned, moist loam; the singing of the melodious Western meadowlarks; and the companionship of her adored father made this experience one of the glorious episodes of her life. Sometimes the mother worried over the little daughter's absence from home all day; it annoyed her, but Eva and her father were becoming increasingly inseparable. This mutual attachment was to last throughout life.

During the 1880's there was much activity in the San Joaquin Valley with respect to the construction of canals and ditches to carry irrigation water from the rivers out on the open plains. Chris Evans, who owned good work horses, and was an excellent teamster, secured work operating a four-horse Fresno scraper, invented shortly before this by Abijah McCall[7] of Selma. During these years there was work for all, and no question of unemployment. Besides the various projects being sponsored by irrigation companies, the Southern Pacific was hiring local men to construct fills and lay new grades. Even if Evans cherished a bitter hatred in later years for that corporation the fact fact remains that he often worked for it, at times as construction foreman. When eventually Evans found himself in jail at Fresno he was to verify this:

"I am now forty-six years old, and have worked for the railroad company for years, overseeing Chinamen. I was not coming to the plains last Sunday to rob a train, but just to see my family and get fresh clothes. People living in Visalia cannot believe, knowing me for twenty years, that I would rob a train."[8]

A third invention, the combined harvester, made its appearance in the valley during the 1880's. Evans was a personal friend of a Tulare county farmer named Andrew Y. Moore, the central figure in the development of this huge machine. The latter's father, Hiram, a resident of Michigan, secured a patent dated April 4, 1836, on the first combine to actually operate in a wheatfield. Then the son built another combine which was an improvement on his father's machine and its successful harvesting of grain near Kalamazoo was vividly portrayed by James Fenimore Cooper in his novel *Oak Openings*, printed in 1848. However, conditions of climate, terrain, and small acreage prevented the combine from winning popular acclaim, and Andrew Moore, hoping to find more favorable conditions elsewhere, shipped his machine to California in a windjammer. It was operated successfully in the wheatfields surrounding Mission San Jose but, after some years, was destroyed by fire, due to lack of lubrication.

When bonanza wheat farms began to develop in the San Joaquin, Moore moved to Tulare county where some of his relatives and friends were to utilize his "know-how" in the development of combines which were to come into general use first in the San Joaquin Valley, and were ultimately to replace reapers and headers throughout the nation. Improvements were made by many men, all of them wheat growers in the San Joaquin, and chief among them were Richard Wilson, Rufus R. Moore, Daniel Houser, and David Young. Actual tests in the grainfields eliminated many models and by 1881 the Houser & Haines combine was leading all competitors.[9] Chris Evans knew personally most of the men who had labored to perfect this gigantic machine, and possessed enough mechanical ingenuity to appreciate the genius of men who could invent such a juggernaut and make it work.

These combined harvesters, intended to solve the shortage of labor, were, and remained, expensive. Therefore it was customary for one machine to harvest the wheat for several growers. Haste was unnecessary since the peculiar climatic conditions in the San Joaquin eliminated the fear of either rain or shelling. Hence it was possible for these large, cumbersome, and awe-inspiring machines to travel leisurely and ponderously from ranch to ranch during the long drawn-out harvest season. Since neither the elements nor nature threatened his crop, the valley wheat grower awaited his turn with relative patience, but it was nevertheless a big event in his life when the big harvesting monster arrived. For both the rancher and his family it was a magnificent spectacle to watch the combine cut, thresh, and sack the wheat as it proceeded majestically down the field. The Houser & Haines harvester could gather the crop from thirty to forty acres a day, and the size of the wheatfield determined how long the rancher's wife would have to cook for a crew of six or seven ravenous, hard-working men. She was understandably the only member of the family who saw the combine arrive at her home without too much enthusiasm.

The first Houser & Haines combine to operate in the fields between Traver and Visalia was drawn by thirty-six horses. The teamster who could handle that many horses and make them do his will must needs be an expert. Molly Evans' brother George, who had become a cowboy at the age of eight, and who certainly knew horses, was given the assignment. Chris Evans, who had by this time won local fame for strength and willingness to work, was employed to sew and buck sacks. This meant that Evans, as well as the other men assigned to similar duties, was required to sew each sack as fast as it was filled with wheat, and throw it off the platform to the ground, from where other men would pick it up, place it on a wagon, and haul it to the warehouse for shipment. It was a continuous, all-day performance, and permitted neither rest nor loafing.

Elmer Perkins of Sultana, who knew Evans well, is authority for the statement that Chris was amazingly strong for a welterweight. His daughter said that he was only five feet, seven inches tall, and weighed one hundred and forty-five pounds. The proclamation calling for his arrest described him as five feet, eight inches tall, and weighing one hundred and sixty pounds. In either case, he was not a large man, and yet, when he stacked wheat in the warehouses, Perkins said he always carried one sack under each arm. Since the sacks then in use on the combines would weigh not less than one hundred and twenty-five pounds, there can be no doubt that Evans was an abnormally strong man.[10]

Chris usually went home to Visalia every Saturday night during the threshing season. Sometimes this involved a walk of from ten to fifteen miles, depending upon the location of the wheatfield then being harvested. One week-end he failed to appear. His only explanation later was that he had been too tired. His family learned later that there had been a good reason for his extreme weariness.

When the threshing crew had reached the Luke Hall ranch, located near present Yettem and not far from Stone Corral, the three small Hall children were in bed with scarlet fever. The mother, obligated to cook for a harvest crew in addition to her other household and nursing duties, had secured the help of a neighbor's fourteen-year-old daughter, the only assistant available in that sparsely settled community. The additional burden of taking care of the sick children at night had brought Mrs. Hall to the verge of a nervous breakdown. When Evans became aware of conditions, he offered to help, and stayed up with the children at night, tended them, placed cool damp cloths on their foreheads during the hot nights, gave them their medicine on scheduled time, and placed water as needed on parched and swollen tongues. He did this for one week with the following time allotted to sleep; thirty minutes at noon, and an hour's nap after supper. No wonder Evans was tired, but the children and the mother were saved.

Evans owned twenty acres south of Visalia. In the fall of 1885 he planted beans on the entire tract. That may sound like a prosaic deed[11] to be listed here, but many old-timers have insisted that the terrific explosion which was later to shake the entire State of California had its inception in connection with beans. Before embarking on this horticultural program, Evans took the precaution to visit the depot agent at Tulare and inquire about shipping rates to market. The excessively high short-haul rates then prevalent on branch roads, such as the one from Visalia to Goshen, prevented him from shipping his crop from his home town. It was more economical to haul the beans by wagon to the main line at Tulare. Then he signed a contract to sell his entire crop on consignment to a firm at Oakland. When his crop was ready for shipment, the agent looked in his new book on freight rates, and blandly informed the astounded Evans that the price was now five cents a pound. Evans' contract with the bean merchants at Oakland was ironclad, and he was forced to ship his beans at a loss; the railroad company was under no compulsion to quote a reasonable freight rate; Evans was ruined; and the railroad had made another enemy. Aside from losses sustained through later robberies, it was to cost the railway and express companies more than $30,000 to fight Evans. Decent treatment would have paid even if measured only in monetary terms.[12]

An interesting episode took place in the summer of 1887 which was to test the resourcefulness of Eva and Ynez. At that time the Evans family was living at the Redwood Ranch. Louis was born there on February 5, 1887, and thereby hangs a tale. That summer the father left his mountain home and worked in the valley wheatfields on a combine, but returned after the harvest. Shortly after his arrival home in August, Molly decided to go down to Visalia to can peaches. To take a seven-months-old baby from the cool mountains to the valley where the temperature often rose to 110 degrees in the shade was deemed unwise, and so Molly went alone. Louis, still unweaned, became very irritable.

Molly Evans' brother, Perry Byrd, a resident of Visalia, had a neighbor named Wilson, who had a mining claim some miles above Evans' Redwood Ranch. Wilson offered Perry's wife, Jane, and her nine-year-old daughter, Edith, a ride to the mountains. They went. At that time of the year the weather at Visalia was uncomfortably hot, and the cool mountains beckoned. Jane did not know that Molly had already left the Redwood Ranch for the valley and was then travelling toward Visalia by a different road. Hence they did not meet along the way. Evans, who had planned to go to Sampson's Flat as soon as Molly returned, suggested to Jane, upon her arrival, that she care for the children. Then he told Eva:

"Now that your aunt is here to help with the children, I need not wait for Mamma's return. That two-mile walk for the milk won't hurt you, for you won't have much else to do."

Assuming that everything was under control, Evans left for his mine early the next morning. He was apparently assuming too much. The reason for Mrs. Perry Byrd's subsequent actions cannot be explained now; the chronicler can only tell what happened. It may be conjectured that Jane did not relish the idea of caring for six children, including her own; it was hardly her idea of a pleasant and restful vacation. She may have resented Evans' cool assumption that she would accept the obligation. Who was he, to tell her what to do? In modern slang, it wasn't "her baby." She may even have promised him, in a moment of generosity, to relieve him of the responsibility, and then, after sober reflection, she may have recoiled from the task. Perhaps she became apprehensive and was afraid to be alone in the mountains without an adult companion. At any rate, shortly after Evans had left that morning, she intercepted Wilson, on his way back to Visalia, and Mrs. Perry Byrd and her daughter returned home. Molly was to say later in a fit of anger that her sister-in-law was an arrant coward. Left at the Redwood Ranch all alone were five children: Eva, aged eleven; Ynez, seven; Winifred, five; Joe, three; and Louis, a seven months old baby in the process of being weaned. It was a difficult problem for a little eleven-year-old girl to solve, but she did it.

Eva had to walk two miles to get the milk for the family. She had neither bottle nor nipple, and tried to feed the baby with a spoon. At night the myriad-voiced coyotes yowled outside the chicken house, and failing to make a forced entry, their angry chorus sounded as if hundreds of little werewolves were singing out of tune, and baby Louis, with raw cow's milk in his stomach, furnished the obligato. Any pediatrician, or other person informed as to the modern conception of the nature and needs of a child, must be horrified at the conditions surrounding Louis during the next two weeks. Yet it left no apparent ill effects, because in time he developed into a powerful, tall, handsome, blonde six-footer. Either this infant was not like other babies, or one is led to suspect that the modern world is going soft. At the end of two weeks Molly returned confident that everything was calm and serene at home. When she learned the true state of affairs, she stormed so furiously at Chris and Jane that their ears must have burned, although neither was within miles of the irate mother. When the father finally came home, he looked grave and a trifle sheepish, and could only say:[13]

"Why, Mamma, it didn't hurt them. There was nothing to be afraid of, was there, Eva? What's a two-mile walk for a big girl?"

Then he turned to Ynez, and told her:

"You were a fine little mother, helping with the other children. There was plenty of food and fuel, so there was no harm done, was there?"

Molly was not mollified; at least not then. But Eva, who knew her father better than anyone else, even at this early age, knew that the sympathy he felt for her predicament during the preceding fortnight was equalled only by the admiration he had for the fine, womanly way in which she had met a difficult situation.

Thirty days later Eva was to meet a man. It did not seem important then. But it was!

CHAPTER 3

HE TILTED WITH THE IRON HORSE

THE BANK of California during the 1880's occupied a place in the financial affairs of the state
somewhat analogous to that of the Bank of America
at a later date. It lent money to ranchers and farmers
throughout the state which they needed to buy livestock, seed, and machinery for the sowing and harvesting of grain. Chris Evans worked as a laborer
in one of the bank's warehouses for some time. Later
he was appointed superintendent of the three warehouses maintained by this bank at Tulare, Pixley, and
Alila. Evans was expected, in his new position, to
check on all wheat shipped by growers who owed
the bank money, and was authorized to collect money
from these farmers after their wheat was sold.

At that time much bitterness existed between the
wheat growers and the Southern Pacific Railway Company. On May 11, 1880, a gun battle had been fought
between rival groups which had resulted in the death
of eight prominent men of the community. It had
been caused by a contest over land titles and the anger
engendered by the eviction of many farmers still
smouldered. As the ranchers delivered their grain,
Evans could not help but hear the tales of injustice
related by them. Aside from the loss of land, there
existed a violent objection to the discriminatory short-

haul rates and the custom of always increasing freight rates just before harvest time and lowering them when the farmers had nothing more to ship. In this way the corporation could always show the Railroad Commission that the *average* rate for the year was low. Another source of irritation was the rule that all freight from the East must be billed to Los Angeles or San Francisco. Therefore many a rancher at Tulare could see his machinery, which he desperately needed for the preparation of his seedbed or for his harvest, as the case might be, roll merrily past his place to San Francisco. Then he had to pay for its unloading, storage, and reloading at this terminal, and be "socked" in addition the exorbitant short-haul rate from San Francisco back to Tulare. Oftentimes his equipment came too late for its intended use. Such a misuse of a public carrier was common then, and the resulting emotions may well be left to the imagination.

By a judicious mixture of force, funds, and finesse the so-called *Octopus* managed to dominate the two major political parties in California. The "Iron Horse" had entered the valley a hero; now it threatened to become a villain. Crocker, Hopkins, Huntington, and Stanford had been small-town Babbitts originally, who are prone to consider "the rustic cackle of their burg the merriment of the world." Suddenly they had been transformed into glorified and enlarged copies of village merchants with the same attitudes and ethics as of yore. They were conducting an establishment which sold a single form of goods. That commodity was transportation. They argued that the sale thereof was governed only by the law of supply and demand. In fixing freight and passenger rates, the standing order of the directors was: "All the traffic will bear."

The Southern Pacific was not intended to be an altruistic organization or a philanthropic society. It sold transportation, but no one was forced to buy. If a customer disliked the service or objected to the price he was told to go elsewhere. But where could he go? The teamster was forced, in order to realize a profit, to charge $40 a ton for transporting goods from Oakland to Visalia; the railway did it for two dollars. The river-boats were excellent for bulky articles, but not available to all. The pack-mules were useless for transporting cattle or wheat. The first farmers in the valley were wheat growers. Their grain needed a market, and the road to that market lay by way of the Southern Pacific rails. The farmer knew it; so did the Southern Pacific.

In 1887 there lived at Tulare a man named John Sontag. He was employed by the Southern Pacific as a brakeman and the end of his run was at Fresno, about forty miles to the north. One day when his train was switching in the yards at Fresno the engineer confused his signal for "Go" with the one for "Back" and when Sontag stopped between two cars to uncouple them the cars bumped together instead of coming apart. The two flat-cars he was trying to uncouple were loaded with iron rails and the projecting end of one rail pierced his right lung from the back. He fell down and crawled out on his hands and knees with

blood gushing out of his mouth. He caught the upright of an adjacent switch and tried to stand up, but
fell in a faint. For two weeks he hovered between life
and death. His right lung bled away and he spent
two months in the railway hospital at Sacramento.
When the wound in his back healed the scar tissues
pulled his heart over toward the right side, and left
a cavity in his back into which a clenched fist[1] could
be inserted. Years later, Sontag, while lying on his
death bed, told a reporter from the San Francisco *Examiner*:[2]

"You know I once worked for the Southern Pacific,
and some time ago I got seriously hurt in Fresno. I
was sent to the company hospital in Sacramento, where
I laid for some time, suffering a great deal. One day
the doctor came and told me I was all right. I wasn't,
but a few days later they threw me out, still sick, and
refused me an easier job with the company. They
treated me as though I was asking them to make me
a present of the road and the rolling stock. Naturally
I had no love for them and I didn't hesitate to say so.
They had no love for me either, and I knew it."

When Sontag was discharged from the hospital he
was so weak he could not walk a block without sitting
down to rest. The railway company promised him
light work as soon as he wanted it, but later told him
the only job available was the one he had previously
held as brakeman. This he could not handle any longer, and so he was left without means of support. In
those bad old days of "sin and gin before Volstead
took our breath away," there was no form of accident,

health, or unemployment insurance to tide a man over a rocky stretch in the road of life. Naturally Sontag was bitter and often, to his own detriment, expressed his hostility toward the corporation. The hotel in which he lived was occupied by other railway workers and they took up a collection and provided him with board and room. There were no unions then to fight for his rights. The other workers could not be expected to support Sontag indefinitely, and so this arrangement was a temporary one.

One day Chris Evans was in Tulare on business for the Bank of California. He happened to meet a friend in front of the railroad hotel and stopped to chat with him. Sontag, still weak from his accident, was sitting with some other men in the front of the hotel. He was introduced to Evans by a man who remarked:

"Chris, we have been telling Sontag here about the Mussel Slough tragedy. Sontag's been badly hurt in an accident and the railroad company won't do anything for him. I want him to know that he ain't the only one that's suffered from the injustice of the Southern Pacific. You know a lot about it, don't you? Wasn't one of your folks mixed up in it?"

"Yes, in a way," answered Chris. "My wife's uncle was one of the settlers, and was beaten out of his land, and years of hard work. But he was not there the day the men were murdered, and he wasn't one of the seventeen men arrested and tried in San Francisco, though several of the men who were arrested and sent to jail were not there either."

"How many settlers were killed that day?" he was asked.

"Six settlers and two railroad men. The six farmers were all killed by one man, that dirty renegade, Crow, blackhearted as his name. I knew him. He was one of the settlers, but he was getting railroad pay long before any one knew of it."

The low opinion which Evans had of Crow was not necessarily a true estimate of the latter. Crow was a fine man, a good citizen, and had many friends in the community, but tension had mounted between purchasers of railway land and those who had pre-empted claims and later refused to vacate them. Even men not actually involved in the dispute, such as Evans, had felt impelled to take sides.

Several men sitting on the porch of the railroad hotel had arrived in the San Joaquin Valley after the fight at Mussel Slough. They were not familiar with the details, and asked Evans to tell them the story of this famous battle.

"Well," said Evans, "it is rather a long story. The Big Four who owned the Central Pacific Railway Company were Charles Crocker, Mark Hopkins, Collis P. Huntington, and Leland Stanford. They built a road from Lathrop to Goshen without government aid, although they demanded land and money from landowners and communities along the way. For example, when Visalia refused to donate land to the company for its railway yards, a junction was built out in the salt grass country and named Goshen, and

Tulare's county seat was left stranded many miles from the Southern Pacific main-line. At Goshen the the "Big Four," by hook or crook, and I suspect mostly by crook, got control of a small company called the Southern Pacific, and by taking the name of this organization inherited its rights to land-grants along its proposed route to Los Angeles. These amounted to twenty odd-numbered sections,[3] or 12,800 acres, for each mile of track laid. With this land-grab to help pay the way, a railroad was built into Los Angeles. Then a branch-line was constructed from Goshen westward through Lemoore to Alcalde. The directors promised that they would connect this point with the Southern Pacific railroad previously built from San Francisco by way of San Jose to Tres Pinos, but they never did."

"I wonder why?" muttered John C. McCubbin, talking more to himself than because he needed any information on that subject. McCubbin, a trained civil engineer, and at that time an official with the 76 Land & Water Company at Traver, was a master in the regional history of that time and place.

"You know the answer to that better than I do," suggested Evans, who respected McCubbin for his erudition and other good qualities. For the benefit of the others, Chris added:

"The land between Alcalde and Tres Pinos is arid, and it takes about twenty acres to feed one sheep. The "Big Four" were too smart to build a railway line between these two terminals, even though the law on which the land-grants were based specified that this must be done. What did those bloated moguls care for any law?"

This was in the days before the drilling for oil had transformed much of this territory into one of fantastic wealth. The time was to come when the railroad company would regret that it had failed to complete this short stretch of one hundred and ten miles; failure to do so had caused the land-grants in that area, then deemed worthless, to revert to the government. Twenty sections per mile between Alcalde and Tres Pinos would have amounted to 1,408,-000 acres, and such an area in the oil-fields would have yielded lucrative returns in subsequent years.

Approximately forty years after the discovery of oil, another amazing development would take place in the same region. Scientific agriculture combined with free enterprise would make possible, on a large scale, the growing of flax, wheat, cantaloupes, and especially cotton, which would transform the barren wastes into an incredible empire of opulent farmers. Their holdings would vary in size from small plots of 30,000 acres up to relatively large farms of 250,000 acres. Big capital and huge acreages would be necessary due to the excessive cost of lifting water for irrigation purposes, and the big farms, measured in square miles rather than in acres, would need, for successful operation, fleets of trucks and tractors, hundreds of laborers in season, costly deep-water wells, airplanes for supervision, and automobiles equipped with telephones and two-way radio sets.

The landlords destined to rise to the top in the mad

scramble for wealth and power prior and subsequent to the Second World War would be as far removed from ordinary dirt-farmers as Dan is from Beersheba. They were promoters, comparable to the wheat-growers who had developed the Tulare Lake bottom in a previous generation, gamblers by inclination, open-handed, generous, daring, wild-spending, extravagant, adventurous, and thoroughly admirable in their willingness to win or lose in a big way.

The workers on these huge estates were to be drawn from all walks of life, from many races, and would represent as many different culture patterns and social levels as there were to be found in the nation. During their free time in the evenings and over the week-ends the melon-pickers and cotton-choppers and their families would make "whoop-pee" in their community and shopping centers at Huron, Firebaugh, and Mendota in a manner which would remind old-timers of the riotous days in the rollicking gold-mining camps and shrieking cow-towns of the Old West. "Wild Bill" Hickok would have felt right at home; he would also have been useful as a peace officer.

Angry reformers, often endowed with more sensitivity than sense, and fearing all things big, would be horrified by the difference in living standards between the cotton-pickers and their employers, and would write scathing denunciations about the west side of the valley and its "factories in the field." However, in 1887, all this lay far away in the future.

Chris Evans, not wishing to monopolize the conversation, turned to McCubbin and said:

"John, you're a surveyor, and know land conditions in this valley better than anyone else. Will you tell us just what started the trouble between the settlers and the Southern Pacific?"

"Well, just before the Southern Pacific had received its patents to public lands, settlers were invited to take up filings on the odd-numbered sections with 'a privilege of purchase' effective as soon as the railway had received final patent rights. The price as specified in the circular advertising the land was set at from $2.50 to $5.00 per acre. Land was to be appraised *without regard to improvements*. With this understanding, the wheat growers spent $400,000 in dredging and irrigation projects. When the land was finally appraised by the company's land-graders, the average price exceeded $35.00 an acre. This figure proved ruinous, and the settlers brought suit in the federal courts for 'specific performance of contract.' While these cases were still pending in the Supreme Court at Washington, D. C., the Circuit Court at San Francisco issued writs of ejection which were served by a United States marshal. This officer, A. W. Poole, accompanied by one of the land-graders, W. H. Clark, disliked facing the disgruntled and belligerent settlers at Hanford, and so they got off the train at Kingsburg, hired a team and livery rig at that place from Josiah Draper, and appeared in the Mussel Slough country early in the morning of May 11, 1880. That is now seven years ago."

"Did anyone know they were coming?" asked one of the listeners.

"Yes," said Chris. "The wheat growers, who were to lose their homes, knew nothing of the marshal's arrival, but two men were waiting for him. They were Walter Crow, and M. J. Hart, both of whom had bought land from the railroad company, land already occupied by other settlers. These were to be dispossessed by the marshal."

"What kind of a man was this marshal?" Sontag asked Evans, not knowing that at a future date United States marshals were to play a part, not only in his life, but in his death as well.

"I don't know; never saw him. The men who were there that day have told me that he seemed to be a nice, gentlemanly sort of fellow. He talked reasonably with the settlers, and told them that he was sorry to bring them bad news, and that he was there merely to carry out orders."

"What happened after the marshal met his two clients?" asked a young lawyer, who had recently hung out his shingle at Tulare, and was addicted to legal terminology.

"They met at the home of Crow's father-in-law, a man named Louis Haas.[4] From there Crow and Hart drove in a spring-wagon to the home of a bachelor named William Braden; the marshal and land-grader followed them there in their buggy. Finding no one at home, the Braden furniture was carried out into the road, and Hart placed in possession. The two parties then drove to a ranch operated by Brewer and Storer. Crow claimed this property by right of purchase from the Southern Pacific Railroad Company, and while the matter was under discussion a group of farmers on horseback arrived from Hanford, where a big community picnic was in progress. The fight started as soon as they reached the marshal and his party."

"Who fired the first shot?" asked a brakeman who worked the night shift.

"A rancher named Jim Harris. He was a hot-tempered fellow, and had had some trouble with Crow before this. Crow, with all his faults, was afraid of nothing and you couldn't push him around."

"What happened then?" This question came from Sontag, who by now was much interested in the story.

"Well," replied Evans, "just what did take place is hard to say. No two men who were there have told it exactly the same way. From what I can gather it went something like this. Crow, sitting in the wagon with Hart, may have been guilty of some dirty crack or gesture which Harris couldn't take. That is what some settlers said afterwards. At any rate, Harris rode his horse up to the wagon and fired at Crow, but his unruly horse threw the shot out of alignment and it hit Hart in the groin. Crow picked up his shotgun and sent a load of buckshot into Harris' thigh, then jumped out of the wagon and gave him another load square in the chest. Ivar Knutson's horse, startled by the three shots, was bucking hard to unseat his rider when a blast from Crow's shotgun did the job for him; Knutson was literally blown out of his saddle. Crow and Knutson were friends; it was assumed later that Crow, in his excitement, had mistaken Knutson for

Mike White, a personal enemy of Crow and similar in appearance to Knutson. Dan Kelly, another settler, got in Crow's way and had his entire side blown off by a load of buckshot. Archibald McGregor, detailed to guard the marshal, received a load of buckshot in the back which perforated his lungs. A stray bullet from Crow's revolver creased Edwin Haymaker's scalp. Then another settler, John Henderson, went mad with grief and rage and charged Crow on horseback, fired, missed, fired again, and received Crow's bullet in his brain. All of the men hit that day died, either on the field or some time later."

"Why didn't someone shoot Crow?" was asked.

"Oh, I don't know. Not all the men had guns, and I suppose they were all so shocked at the sudden uproar that they let Crow get away into a wheatfield where he hid. Other settlers soon arrived but no one cared to go into the wheat after Crow. He was a dead shot, and it was sure death to go after him."

"What finally happened to Crow?" asked Sontag.

"That evening Crow was climbing over a fence on his way to the home of his father-in-law when someone shot him. The man who did it was using Crow's own Winchester which he had left in his wagon. It was rumored that the man who killed Crow was named Flewelling. This led to the arrest of Dr. James B. Flewelling, a dentist practicing here in Tulare; I'm sure most of you know him."

Several of the men nodded. Evans continued:

"The doctor was taken to San Francisco with the farmers from Mussel Slough, but he had a perfect alibi. He easily proved that he was neither a land-owner nor a wheat-grower; that he was not involved in the land troubles in any way, and had been in his office during the entire day of the fight. So he was exonerated and released."

"Then why had the name of Flewelling been bandied about?" asked the discerning young lawyer with a legal gleam in his eye.

"Because Flewelling did kill Crow," retorted Evans with equal keenness of perception and a twinkle in his eye.

Noticing that some of his listeners, including the young would-be legal expert, appeared somewhat puzzled, he added:

"Oh, no, James Flewelling, the dentist, didn't kill Crow. It was another man by the same name.[5] Dr. Flewelling had a cousin, a wheat grower, similar in appearance but not so well known in the community, and when detectives overheard the name of Flewelling mentioned in sibilant whispers they arrested the only person they knew by that name, and got the wrong man."

"Was the man who killed Crow ever tried?" asked a weather-beaten old rancher, who already knew the answer. He was merely prodding Chris to get on with the story.

"You know as well as I that he wasn't," snapped Evans. "For a few days he was a hero among the few who knew he was the man who had avenged the death of their friends and neighbors. However, when it became evident that the federal government took a dim view of the whole affair, and was getting ready to indict and prosecute all concerned, this other Flewelling quietly left the state, assumed a new name, and located near Spokane. He was never suspected or troubled by any officers of the law."

"How did the settlers come out in their law suits over their lands?" queried the young lawyer, still trying to show his grasp of matters juridical.

"The Supreme Court, then composed of nine reactionary old men, upheld the rights of the Southern Pacific. The high price already fixed on the lands in dispute was retained and the settlers could take it or leave it. Most of them had to leave it, and that explains why today you will find few old-timers in this part of the state who love the Southern Pacific."

A newly arrived merchant at Tulare, wanting to get all the packing out of the case, asked Chris a pertinent question:

"Why were the settlers tried at San Francisco, and what luck did they have?"

"The Federal Court which had issued the writs of eviction was located in that city, and they were tried on two counts. First, for a conspiracy against the nation, which was ridiculous. Forty men on forty mustangs were not going to try to overthrow the United States government. Second, they were accused of resisting a federal marshal in the performance of his duty. Five men were found guilty on the second charge. They served eight months in the San Jose jail.

"Three of these men, James Patterson, Wayman

Pryor and John Pursell, brought their wives and children along, since they had no other place for them, and refused to leave them alone and unprotected down in the valley. The law made no provision for feeding their families, but rooms were set aside in the second story of the penitentiary for housekeeping purposes. J. C. Black, founder of a chain-store famous throughout California, supplied groceries free of charge, and the St. James Hotel management donated breakfasts for the wives and children for the entire eight months.

"John Doyle had married after the trial and before sentence had been pronounced, and his bride and he spent their honeymoon in jail. William Braden, whose furniture had been carried out into the county road under the federal marshal's orders, was a bachelor at the time. He courted the jailer's daughter, Susie, and they were married the same day he was let out of the pen. This whole mess started out as a tragedy, but it finally turned into a comedy with a wedding at the end.

"The jail sentence turned out to be a farce. The sheriff, John Fitts, and the jailer, William Curtis, had been notified that five prisoners were arriving for a long stay, but these officers were astounded when they were confronted with the problem of caring for several women and children as well. They were still further flabbergasted when four hundred fellow church members of Patterson called on him during his first day in jail, which happened to be Christmas Eve. Then came cables of sympathy from Europe, telegrams from all parts of the United States, and letters by the hundreds. The officers quickly decided that these people were no ordinary prisoners. The wheat-growers from the San Joaquin made a fine impression on the guards at the prison and were soon permitted to go to the postoffice, the church, and the lodge whenever they chose. They actually enjoyed an eight months vacation with all expenses paid. They acted like paying guests at a hotel, and were allowed to entertain visitors at all hours. This riled the directors of the Southern Pacific, and both jailer and sheriff were to lose their jobs because of their lenient and unorthodox treatment of their so-called convicts."

It was getting late in the afternoon, and after Evans had finished his story the group broke up and the men began to wend their various ways homeward. Sontag had no home. Evans noticed a haunted look in the young man's eyes. He lingered to speak sympathetically to him. From this chance meeting was to spring a rare and unusual friendship, but that is another story.

CHAPTER 4

THE WAY OF A MAN WITH A MAID

JOHN SONTAG had listened intently to the story
of the Mussel Slough fight. He was tremendously
impressed by Evans, and the latter liked John. They
clicked! Perhaps Chris subconsciously identified John
with his first-born son, who had been deprived of life
because of an accident, and whose little body had
by now been reposing for many years in the solitude of
the Big Trees at Redwood Ranch. Evans impulsively
offered John a home and light work. He explained his
offer thus:[1]

"I am away from home much of the time as manager for the Bank of California's wheat warehouses.
I need a man who is reliable and gentle. He must
not swear before my children, or at my horses. The
work will be easy, but I want someone I can trust."

Incidentally Evans had a perfect obsession about
profanity. He would tolerate no one on his premises
who cursed, with one big exception, and that was his
wife's brother, "Uncle George" Byrd. Even the latter's sister resented his swearing, and asked Chris to
take action against George. But Evans excused George
on the grounds of ignorance. He reminded Molly of
the unhappy conditions in her home when George was
a little boy. Instead of being sent to school, he was
placed on the back of a cow-pony at the age of eight,

and sent out to herd cattle. This no doubt gave him the worthless distinction of being the youngest cowboy in the state, but it had left him woefully ignorant. He had been the recipient of no education whatsoever, and his vocabulary was so limited that he had to fall back on the only safety valves he knew. Like many other under-privileged persons, George had an engaging personality, and some of his verbal efforts were droll rather than sinful. One of his favorite expressions was:[2]

"Hell's afloat, and the devil can't swim."

And he always made the Evans children laugh when he roared:

"The devil's to pay, and there's no hot pitch."

There was no doubt that his little nieces and nephews loved "Uncle George" very much.

When John Sontag walked into the parlor at the Evans home that evening in 1887 he met Eva, aged eleven; John was then twenty-five. She saw before her a man who was tall, dark, and handsome. Five years after this Evans and Sontag were destined to be interviewed in their mountain hide-out by Henry Bigelow, a sophisticated and experienced newspaper reporter from the San Francisco *Examiner*. When he met Sontag, the latter was without the benefit of a shave, a haircut, or a bath. Bigelow wrote:[3]

"The proclamation (calling for the arrest of Evans and Sontag) states that Sontag is rather good-looking. It is not enough; he is *very* good-looking."

This was the verdict of a man used to the best and most highly cultivated society to be found in California. If John Sontag's good looks merited the high praise bestowed on them by Bigelow, then it is self-evident that he must have made a favorable impression on the young girl named Eva.

John Sontag was born in Connecticut, Minnesota, and Missouri. At least each of these three states has been cited as the true birthplace of Sontag by men and women who knew him well. They can't *all* be right. Scores of letters[4] addressed to the proper county officials and other agencies have brought the invariable answer that no birth certificate, records, or other documentary evidence existed with respect to one John Sontag, or John Contant.

John's real name was not Sontag. His father, Jacob Contant, was born in Holland, and came to the United States where, according to one story, he found work in the cotton mills of Aspetuck, Connecticut, located about twelve miles from Bridgeport. He married a German immigrant girl by whom he had two sons, John and George. Contant died, a victim of tuberculosis, shortly after the birth of George. The widow supported herself and her two children by selling milk from the four cows that she owned. When her younger son was three years old, the mother married a German named John Sontag. He proved to be one of those rare persons, a loving and understanding stepfather. The Contant boys took his surname. Mr. Sontag, accompanied by his new wife and two stepsons, returned to the hotel which he owned at Mankato, Minnesota, and this became home to them. The mother was a devout Roman Catholic, and wanted her son John to become a priest. He was sent to the Brothers' Day School, and served as an altar boy. But he was not interested in the priesthood as a vocation and, at sixteen, in order to avoid friction at home, he left for the Far West.

Since John Sontag came to California from Minnesota, it was generally assumed that he was a native of the latter state. The members of his immediate family resided there, and he told Eva Evans, his fiancee, that he had been born on a farm near Mankato.

However, many pioneer residents of California refused to accept this statement as final evidence with respect to John's place of birth. William Work, who owned a ranch in the foothills east of Visalia, and who often gave food and shelter to Evans and Sontag after they had become outlaws, was absolutely certain that Sontag was, like himself, a native of Missouri. In the first place, Sontag told Work confidentially that he was born in Missouri; and second, in long conversations with Sontag, Work was convinced that John knew every nook and cranny of the region which had been Work's boyhood home. The latter always insisted that Sontag spoke the language of "the show me state."

Whatever the truth of these conflicting stories may be, the fact remains that at this time the exact spot where Sontag first saw the light of day is of more interest than importance.

Although John Sontag (Contant) was of German and Dutch extraction, he looked more Mediterranean than Nordic. This often led new acquaintances to ask him if he was of Spanish or Italian descent, and he always laughingly replied:

"No, I'm black Dutch."

He was gentle in manner, soft-spoken, wide in the shoulders, narrow in the hips, six feet tall, and endowed with a clear olive complexion. The children in the Evans family liked him forthwith, and the horses placed in his care responded to his unique treatment. He loved horses, and learned to ride superbly. But he never became a bronco-buster in the Western sense of that term. He liked horses too much to abuse them, or break their spirits. He learned to rule, not by force, but by kindness.

John's love of good horse-flesh was both inherited and the result of his association in youth with the horse-loving men of Mankato. This admiration of well-bred animals was to give a peculiar twist to the history of banditry. On the afternoon of September 2, 1876, when John was fourteen, eight strange men rode into Mankato mounted on magnificent thoroughbred horses. Four of the men, all distinguished in appearance, registered at the Hotel Sontag. The other four men stayed at the only other hostelry in Mankato. One of them called at the First National Bank and changed a fifty dollar bill. A native of Mankato saw the stranger and blurted out:[5]

"That is Jesse James!"

His fellow citizens laughed scornfully at his statement. Why would a nationally known figure like Jesse James visit their little city? But the man was right; it was Jesse James! And the other seven men were his brother Frank; his three cousins, Coleman, Frank, and Jim Younger; and three comrades, Clell Miller, Samuel Wells, and William Stiles. Robertus Love, who wrote an authoritative and fascinating biography of Jesse James, stated that measured in terms of horsemanship, revolver work, and all-around outlaw efficiency, this double-quartet was undoubtedly the greatest outlaw band ever assembled in the history of mankind.

These eight strangers spent the next day, which was a Sunday, resting quietly in their hotel rooms. About noon on Monday they all rode down to the bank, which was the reason for their presence in Mankato. But it so happened that the building next to the bank was undergoing repairs and, as is usual in such cases, idle men were standing in groups watching the carpenters at work. When the would-be bank robbers noticed the intense interest which the citizenry, including the workers, showed in them they became suspicious and rode away. They returned later in the afternoon and when the men and boys, among the latter John Sontag, turned to watch them intently, the Missourians became disgusted and left town. They headed for Northfield, forty miles away. What happened there the following Thursday is another and a bloody story. It gave the Mankato man, who had recognized Jesse James, a chance to remind his fellow citizens: "I told you so!"

What had saved the Mankato bank from being robbed was not any special alertness on the part of the local citizens. It was learned later that the men of Mankato were fond of good horses, and when the eight bandits rode up to the First National Bank, the lounging men and boys, as well as the workmen on the job, were staring, not at the strangers, but at the finest saddle horses they had ever seen.

Regardless of the exact place of John Sontag's birth, it has been well established that he and his brother George had spent their adolescent years in the city of Mankato. Therefore they were products of the sidewalks rather than of the wide, open spaces. Their background was urban rather than rural. Hence John found the wild western aspects of Visalia and its environs a new and thrilling experience. In 1887 this town was not only the center of the cattle industry in the San Joaquin, but also the home of the Visalia Saddle Works. The owner, Juan Martarel, had settled in Visalia in 1869, and had won fame and fortune largely because one of his workmen, Ricardo Mattley, was a genius in building stock saddles. Sontag spent much of his spare time in the saddle shop watching the various skilled artisans at their tasks. They intrigued him, because in manner, dress, and speech these men of Spanish-California ancestry were different from the genus *Homo sapiens* he had known in the East, and the railroad men with whom he had worked in California. On one occasion his deep sympathy for the under-privileged almost led him into a brawl in the Visalia Saddle shop. One of Martarel's workers was young Alsalio Herrera, gifted in making fancy silver-mounted bits and spurs. He was shrewd in many ways, but his deceptively naive appearance soon attracted the attention of the ignorant loafers of the type which often infest small towns. While they consider themselves worldly-wise, they are generally stupid. Youths of this calibre derived a mild sadistic pleasure in offering Alsalio the choice of a nickel or a dime; he always took the nickel. To Sontag this ancient and "corny" trick seemed insulting, but before he committed any overt act in behalf of his new friend, he learned that this daily rite was mutually satisfactory to both parties. It amused the "wise guys" and made them feel superior; it also pleased Herrera, who thus had a fairly steady source of revenue aside from his regular work. When John asked him why he always took the cheaper coin, Alsalio replied:[6]

"If I took the ten cents they would not give me any more nickels!"

This answer no doubt showed great profundity of thought and sound economic reasoning, but Sontag, who had never expected to see this old trick in real life, could not resist retorting:

"When I first heard this yarn of the dimes and nickels I thought it was so funny I almost kicked the slats out of my cradle."

During the summer of 1890 Chris Evans and his family camped under the redwoods in what is now Grant's Park. Before they left, Evans assigned to Sontag the task of breaking some of his colts. His methods of handling them aroused the ridicule and hilarity of the old-timers. One of the latter, a native of Pike county, Missouri, told John, after watching him handle a young stallion in a corral:

"Wal, perhaps that is the best way effen a man has got the patience. Lookee here, young feller, ain't you a terrible hand with the women?"

Sontag confessed his lack of experience as a lady's man.

"Wal, you'll be pretty bad when yer turn comes. I allowed from seeing ye handle that there hoss, that you had got yer hands in on women more than once; —they is the wust devils to tame I ever seed."

Whether or not John Sontag learned about horses from women is immaterial now. The fact remains that the way of a man with a maid is instinctive rather than acquired. Growing up in the Evans home was a young lady destined to become famous for her vibrant personality and petite beauty, not only in her own community, but as an actress on the stage in San Francisco and elsewhere. Sontag's method of courtship was gentle but firm. Three years after he had become a resident of the Evans home the fourteen-year-old Eva and he became engaged.

Chris and Molly heartily approved of the proposed match, but Evans felt that Eva was still too young to have dates, and she was not permitted to go buggy riding with her fiance. When she had occasion to go to parties, her father[7] took her there and brought her back. But it was understood by all concerned that when Eva had reached the age of seventeen, she and John were to be married. But they never were!

CHAPTER 5

FIRE! FIRE!

THE SUMMER of 1890 was a relatively happy and care-free one for Chris Evans and his family. Several weeks were spent camping in the grove of Big-Trees which included the General Grant, in recent years made doubly famous as the Nation's Christmas Tree. During the later part of the summer Dr. James L. McClelland, a physician practicing at Selma, decided to go bear hunting. He took several friends along, among them James M. Leslie, a young man who was serving as foreman of the doctor's ranch south of Selma. McClelland and Evans had married sisters. The doctor was well aware of Evans' skill as a guide and hired his brother-in-law to serve in that capacity. Therefore the hunting party proceeded to Grant's Park, where Evans assumed command.[1]

One of the things which impressed Leslie at that time was the fact that the members of the Evans family were all fond of reading. After Eva Evans, then fourteen years of age, had completed her light chores about the camp, she was constantly perusing a book. The same was true of the father.

The Evans family remained in the camp while the father led the valley men and a train of pack-mules to Cedar Grove in Kings River Canyon. Here they camped one night near a permanent post maintained

by two old professional hunters. The latter had flour
for sale and Evans, in charge of the expedition, bought
what seemed to the other men a very small amount.
The two old-timers, trying to boost their sales, insisted
that there was no flour to be had in the mountains
beyond this point. However, Evans was unimpressed
and said he would get along with what he had. From
Cedar Grove the party went up Bubb Creek and along
this stream, surrounded by awe-inspiring mountains
and far from all human habitations, the men ran out
of flour. But Evans did not seem worried. That
evening he disappeared and when he returned he had
a sack of flour. This made Leslie suspicious, and when
the next shortage occurred the young man followed
Evans to learn the source of his supply. To Leslie's
amazement, he saw Evans dig into a pile of leaves
under a ledge and come out with a small sack of flour.
The ledge was formed in such a fashion that no bear
or other animal interested in such a type of food could
get at it. No human being would have discovered it
without fore-knowledge. Why had Evans hidden
flour and other supplies along the Kearsarge Trail
which runs from Kings River Canyon over the mountains to Owens Valley? Leslie assumed that even then
Evans was preparing for a possible retreat in case of
pursuit.

Two things impressed the men in that hunting party
with respect to Evans. First, he was an avid reader
and carried several books with him. He was not interested in the yellow-backed "penny dreadfuls" of
the period, or the Nick Carter stories. He is probably

the only well-known outlaw in history whose favorite authors were Swinburne, Scott, Shakespeare, Huxley, Darwin, and Spencer. He read the first three because he loved poetry of a high order and committed to memory much of what he read. The other three satisfied his longing to learn about things scientific. When the valley residents, fatigued by scrambling over steep mountains after bears, found it necessary to rest in camp, Evans would lie down on his back under a tree and read all day. The other men, active in business and professional pursuits, learned to their amazement that Evans was by far the best read man in the group. He was remarkably well-informed and an excellent conversationalist when the spirit moved him. At times, to enliven the party, he would recite poetry or long passages from Shakespeare with deep feeling and rare interpretive skill.

The other accomplishment which won the admiration of his companions on the trail was his amazing skill with either rifle or revolver. It has often been stated that shooting from the hip is merely a figment of the fiction writer's imagination, but Leslie said that Evans proved to them on this trip that it could be done. This uncommon ability was partially the result of naturally swift reflexes and keen eyes; it was also a product of his training as a trooper with Custer's cavalry in the days when, measured in terms of shooting, there were only two kinds of men, the quick and the dead. Thereafter a lifetime of practice had kept him from losing a true gunman's feel for his weapons.

He came close to being a combination of Hopalong Cassidy and Red Connors.

James Leslie was destined to become a prominent man in the San Joaquin Valley in civic, fraternal, business, and religious affairs. He was affiliated with the Presbyterian Church and was often sent to its national convocations as a delegate. Serving in that capacity he often met William Jennings Bryan. Leslie felt that there were many points of similarity between Bryan and Evans; charming personalities, vibrant voices, uncommon abilities, and qualities of leadership. On one occasion he used these two men as the subject of an address to a Y.M.C.A. convention, showing how men of unusual powers must avoid detours as they move along the main-travelled road of life. One of these men became a noted statesman; the other, a great outlaw. Was it predestination, or is a man the master of his own fate?

One of the largest livery stables in the San Joaquin Valley was owned by a man named Wallace and located at Modesto. Chris Evans, who liked horses and everything connected with them, began during the summer of 1890 to dicker with Wallace concerning its purchase. Since a series of train robberies occurred during that same time it was asserted later that Evans must have secured from these hold-ups the money which made possible this purchase. His supporters maintained that he raised the money by mortgaging the twenty-acre ranch he owned south of Visalia. His house in town was already encumbered. The holder of the new ranch mortgage was S. Sweet & Company of Visalia, a firm which dealt in everything from needles to combined harvesters, from handkerchiefs to circus tents.

Evans sold his cattle and all of his horses excepting twelve roadsters which he sent to Modesto in a railway car. His wife canned two hundred half-gallon cans of fruit which went in the same car. Wallace transferred to Evans his stable, horses, harnesses, buggies, and feed together with a $1,000 fire insurance policy. Evans neglected to secure any additional insurance. This was to prove a mistake.[2]

After installing his family in a little house around the corner from the livery stable, Evans decided to go to Stockton to purchase additional buggies, robes, and harnesses. Eva went along.

After completing his business in the Delta City, Evans and his daughter decided to take a vacation. They went to San Francisco by river-boat. While Evans was in no sense naive, or a bucolic character, he was not familiar with the vice of that city which has since been so powerfully depicted by Herbert Asbury in *The Barbary Coast,* nor was he prepared for the enticing way in which it could be presented.

In looking for a place to eat Evans saw a beautiful entrance marked "Cafe" and assumed it was a first-class restaurant. He and his daughter entered and were led through a beautifully illuminated hall to an elevator which was the first one that Eva had ever seen or ridden in. They were whisked up several flights to a private room with a dainty table set for

two. While they were waiting for their meals to be
served, Eva noticed a curtain drawn apart slightly, and
beyond it a bed prepared for two occupants. When
she called her father's attention to it he gasped, and
said:
"This is no place for us!"
Grasping his young daughter firmly by the hand,
he hurriedly left the place, not even stopping to use
the elevator. They ran down the stairs. They found
out later that they had inadvertently entered the in-
famous Poodle Dog Cafe, a notorious place of assig-
nation. Evans soon found a less ornate but more respectable eating place.
That same evening they decided to visit Chinatown.
Here again they encountered life in the raw. A Chinese
accosted them and asked:
"You likee see China Mary? One look-ee two bittee,
one feel-ee flo bittee, one do-ee six bittee!"
Evans decided it was time to take his daughter
home.
The Evans family had left Visalia for Modesto in
September, 1890. The trip to San Francisco took place
during the latter part of that month. From then until
December the members of the Evans family were to
enjoy prosperity and happiness. These things were
never again to be their portion in life.
Some time during the latter month a man hired a
horse and buggy and said he wanted to make a leisurely trip to Newman and would not return until
some time the next day. For some reason known only
to himself he returned early the same evening and

Paddy O'Neill, one of Evans' favorite trotting horses from Visalia, showed the effects of over-exertion. With the help of his daughter Eva, Chris tried in every way to save the horse, but at midnight the beautiful animal died. Evans sank down beside his horse and cried. He loved animals, especially horses, and could not condone or endure cruelty to them. The next day he located the man who had mistreated Paddy O'Neill and beat him unmercifully. The man was taken to a hospital. Whether the battered man planned revenge or took his beating submissively no one now knows. But what happened later led many to believe that it was a repercussion from the fist fight between the two men.

About two o'clock of a morning in January, 1891, Eva Evans was awakened by the glare of lights in her window and saw a sheet of flame enveloping the adjacent livery stable. She ran out of the back-door and, as she circled the house, she met her father rushing down the front steps. Together father and daughter ran to the stable, but found the heat too intense for them to reach the front doors. The night man was trying to get out through a side window, and Evans managed to break out the glass with his bare fists and assisted the frightened caretaker to safety.

While the members of the fire department stood impotently by, Evans was galvanized into sudden furious action. He remembered Jacob Claypool. The latter was an eighteen-year-old orphan, who supported himself and his ten-year old brother by freighting goods from Modesto to La Grange. Evans always had a soft spot in his heart for the under-privileged and admired the struggles young Jacob was making to care for himself and his dependent. Claypool always kept his teams in the Evans stable, and had been told by Chris that, in order to save hotel bills, he could sleep in a small bedroom up in the loft of the barn during the nights he spent at Modesto. He was there now!

Measured in terms of human values, Claypool was worth more to Evans than all of his horses, much as he loved the latter. As a result of Evans' fierce urgings, the fire department quickly threw ladders against the wall and an entrance was made through a small window. Some boards in the flimsy wall were hacked out, and a mattress, partly burned, was brought out and deposited on the ground. On it lay the horribly disfigured body of Jacob Claypool. He had evidently been suffocated.

At this inopportune time Mrs. Evans appeared on the scene. When she saw the body of the dead boy, she went into hysterics. Her husband, aided by neighbors, carried her back to the house where she gradually quieted down, aided by soothing sedatives administered by a physician. It was feared for a time that she might suffer a miscarriage, but the baby, christened Carl, was born on May 21st at the expected time.

After leaving Molly safely in the hands of friends, Evans went back to the smouldering ruins of his livery stable. The spectacle was over, and those who had come to help or to be entertained, had become weary and had gone home. Even the members of the fire department had left. Evans sat down on the curb with Eva and his thoughts. For a time he merely stared, with glazed eyes, at the ruins of his hopes. Practically all of the equipment was gone, and twenty-two horses were dead. Sontag had taken two bay trotting horses and a buckboard to La Grange that day. A stranger had hired two gray horses and a carriage for a trip to Oakdale. These were saved. And that was about all. Even the fruit which Molly had canned with so much labor that summer, and which had been stored in the barn, was gone up in smoke.

For a long time Chris and Eva simply sat on the curb. Then the father began to cry. There is nothing more pitiful than when a strong man weeps. Over the soft hissing of the clinkers which shrouded his dreams could be heard the dry sobs of a man broken in spirit, weak with fruitless anger, whose shaking body revealed how absolutely helpless he felt in the grip of a malicious Fate.

CHAPTER 6

EXCURSE

EVANS was broke. Sontag, who had invested his few meagre savings in the livery-stable enterprise, had been forced to go to Fresno to look for work. Chris collected the $1,000 fire insurance policy and paid off some of his outstanding debts. Andrew McGinnis, a bill collector, was assigned the task of securing the money which was owed to Evans by former patrons of the livery-stable. Then word came from Fresno that John Sontag was in bed with pneumonia. Chris went there to nurse him. With only one lung, Sontag found the fight for survival a severe one, but finally managed to regain his health. He then went back to Mankato to visit his mother who had not seen him since he had run away from home years before. Soon after Evans had returned from Fresno and John, his children went to bed with a severe attack of scarlet fever. Fate seemed to hand him one wallop after another.

Chris Evans was an unusually affectionate father. He never forgot the welfare of his children. When they had regained sufficient strength to endure travelling, he decided to take them to the seacoast for a vacation. Chris told his wife:

"Eva is the only one of my children who has seen the ocean. A few weeks along the coast will be good for them. It won't cost more to live there than here in Modesto. We have to eat wherever we are, and so do the horses."

Due to his constant reading Evans was well versed in the history of California and planned to make this trip educational as well as recreational.

Four horses had escaped the holocaust in January. They were used to provide transportation for the large family. A happy group of vacationists left Modesto early one morning in August, 1891. Eva drove the gray horses, Gray Eagle and Joe Eagle, that were hitched to the buckboard. On it was loaded the camping equipment. Winifred went along as swamper. The father drove the bay team hitched to the carriage. In it rode the parents and five children: Carl, Joe, John, Louis, and Ynez.[1]

Eva, with good reason, fancied herself quite a horse-woman, but she had an experience the first day of the trip which would have shaken the nerves of a robot. While they were crossing the bridge over the San Joaquin River one of the horses looked down and saw the water underneath through a crack between two planks. He decided to go back home and the team made what is known today by automobile drivers as a U-turn, and headed for Modesto at a quick run. Eva tried desperately to check their speed, but was not strong enough. The father, ever alert, looked back, saw what was happening, stopped, unhitched his bays, mounted one of them, and in a mad gallop caught up with the runaways, and stopped them. After the excitement had subsided, the journey was continued and the little caravan reached Byron, forty miles from Modesto, that evening.

In a family where bad luck seemed to hold full sway, it is refreshing to note that Dame Fortune decided to do the Evans family a good turn for a change. Evans wanted to place his horses in the livery-stable at Byron that night. He argued that they were tired after travelling forty miles with heavy loads on a hot summer's day. They were in need of a good feed of grain and comfortable stalls. But Molly was obdurate. She had developed a complex on livery-stables. So they camped along a creek some miles from Byron that night, and the weary horses picked up what food they could by grazing. Shortly after midnight Evans was awakened by a fire in the town, but did not know until next morning that the Byron livery-stable had caught on fire and all the stock had been destroyed.

During the second day the Evans party made a detour west of Brentwood, and visited the former home of Dr. John Marsh. Evans told his family:[2]

"I want you to remember the name of this man. You have heard a lot of old-timers down in Tulare county boast about how long they have been in California. Not one of them can equal Marsh in that respect. He was the first American to practice medicine in California, and the very first English-speaking settler in the San Joaquin. In the latter part of 1837 he paid Jose Noriega $500 for a tract of land twelve miles long and nine miles wide, containing 69,120 acres, and moved out here among the Indians in the spring of 1838. He wanted the United States to acquire California, and as a result of his publicity the first prairie schooners set out for California. Bartleson and Bidwell led these covered wagons to the east side of the Sierra; here they packed their belongings on the backs of horses and oxen and hurried over the mountains to avoid being snowed in, and arrived safely at this ranch in the fall of 1841. Perhaps more than any other man, Marsh did the spade-work which led to California becoming American."

At the end of the second day the Evans party reached Martinez, and camped in the hills at a spot where they could look out over Carquinez Strait. The next day they set out for Oakland.

As they drove along San Pablo Avenue they passed the former home of Luis Peralta. He had come to California with the Anza expedition which consisted of thirty married couples and their children sent from Sinaloa to colonize Alta California. Luis was then twelve years old. In time he became a California cattle-king; his original grant included the land now occupied by the cities of Richmond, El Cerrito, Albany, Berkeley, and Oakland. His home, which Evans pointed out, lay directly in front of the Golden Gate.

Eva asked: "Why did they come, and when?"

Her father told her: "The Anza party arrived at Monterey in 1776, the same year that our Declaration of Independence was signed at Philadelphia. The settlers were sent here by the viceroy, Bucareli, to establish an outpost of empire for the Spanish king. You may be interested to know that in this group of colonists were children, many of them younger than you are, who travelled more than 2,000 miles on horse-back. One of them, a chum of Luis Peralta, was Gabriel Moraga. He was to win fame as a soldier and explorer, and gave the name to our biggest river down in Tulare county. On an exploring trip he and his troopers rested along its banks during the 6th of January,1805, which is the day of Epiphany. So he named it Rio de Los Santos Reyes (the River of the Holy Kings)."[3]

The third night was spent in Oakland, and the following morning the two teams were driven onto the ferry-boat, and the vacationists crossed San Francisco Bay for a sight-seeing tour of "The City." They drove by the Bank of California, headquarters for the institution which then owned wheat warehouses in most San Joaquin Valley towns. Evans explained:

"This is the bank I worked for while living in Visalia. William C. Ralston was the genius guiding its destinies, and was drowned under very peculiar circumstances some years ago. It was he who promoted the building of the Palace Hotel, and his community spirit was so great that he is now known as 'the man who built San Francisco'."

The Evans family enjoyed a picnic lunch in the military cantonment known as the Presidio. While resting in the shade of some beautiful trees, Chris told his children the following story:[4]

"If you look where I point now, you will see the home of the former commander of the Spanish troops stationed here in 1806. His daughter, Concha,[5] was the heroine in California's most famous love story.

This girl, a bewitching beauty,[6] was born for history, and possessed uncommon intellect. She proved immune to the blandishments of the guitar-strumming caballeros who swarmed under her window. She vowed to marry a man who could take her out of her narrow sphere to the great capitals of the Old World. Unfortunately, most people born for history are not born for happiness."

Evans summed up her subsequent career:

"In April, 1806, when Concha was fifteen, one of the most influential men in all Europe arrived in San Francisco. He was Nicolai Petrovich Rezanov, Privy Councilor[7] and High Chamberlain to Czar Alexander I, ruler of all the Russias. It was a case of love at first sight, and the California girl and the Russian nobleman were betrothed. Rezanov left for Russia to arrange for the wedding, and died suddenly while crossing Siberia. The girl was left to wait and wonder for ten long years. In 1816 she first heard about the tragedy,[8] and thereafter took the veil and devoted her life to religious service."

The next day the tourists drove down the Peninsula toward Santa Cruz. As they passed the stately country homes of the prominent socialites[9] from San Francisco, Evans was reminded of an incident which had occurred fifteen years before this. He greatly amused his family with the following yarn:

"Mr. and Mrs. Milton S. Latham, whose house we just passed, had invited a wealthy and aristocratic group of their friends to meet his Grace, the Duke of Manchester. A duke was a duke in those days, and the members of our democracy awaited the English nobleman's arrival with palpitating hearts. When the butler, in his most haughty manner, announced "His Grace, the Duke of Manchester," a veritable apparition[10] stalked into their midst. He was wearing boots up to his thighs, similar to those worn by General Custer and Buffalo Bill; his flannel shirt was a fiery red; there was a big pistol stuck in his belt; and he was minus coat and neck-tie. No one fainted, but the blood pressure of the immaculately groomed and sophisticated group went up to a dangerous point and reached an all-time high. Fortunately the Lathams were self-contained, poised, and gracious hosts, and the poor duke, whose face had turned as red as his shirt, blurted out that he had read the stories by Bret Harte, and had thought that he was dressed in the true California fashion."

The Evans family spent three weeks at Santa Cruz. The Sequoia sempervirens did not impress them; they were familiar with the Big Trees of their native mountains. Another week was spent in Monterey, where they visited the historic Custom House, the home of Thomas O. Larkin,[11] and strolled along the Calle Principale. At Carmel they saw the sarcophagus of Father Junipero Serra, the first father-president of the Franciscan Missions in Alta California. Evans pointed out that Father Crespi[12] was shown as one of the mourners at the bier of Serra, an understandable inaccuracy, although actually Crespi had died two years before Serra. The seventeen-mile drive around the sand dunes and through the famous Monterey cypresses, at one time thought to have been identical with the cedars of Lebanon, took one day. After a week of sight-seeing at Monterey, the Evans finances were running low, and it was time to go home.

Evans and his family returned to Modesto by travelling over the road made famous by the stage-coaches of John Butterfield's Great Southern Overland Mail; this was the first transcontinental line to operate in the United States. Between 1858 and 1861 this company sent two Concord stage-coaches, each drawn by six horses, from San Francisco eastward each week, and on the same days two stages also left St. Louis for the west; the average speed was one hundred miles a day. The two Evans vehicles rolled along this road by way of Pacheco Pass into the San Joaquin Valley and across the holdings of Miller & Lux,[13] at that time the owners of the largest cattle ranch in the world. It took two days of hard driving to cross it.

Modesto was reached some time in the early days of September, and the members of the Evans family began to pack their possessions for their return to Visalia. Evans still owned his house and ranch there, and that fall he and his family re-occupied their old home. Evans lived quietly there that autumn and winter and, if there were any grumblings about railway robberies and guilty men, there are no reports extant to show that he was in any way suspected. However, it was noticed both by his family and outsiders that he was nervous and worried, but this was to be expected from a man whose experiences during the past months had been shocking and bitter.

The exact date of Evans' return to Visalia in the fall of 1891 became a subject for dispute the next year. After Chris had become involved with the law, a Visalia paper printed the following article:[14]

"Chris Evans was one of the most indefatigable attendants during the trial of Grattan Dalton for complicity in the Alila train robbery. The trial took place in the court-house here, and day after day, Evans sat outside the railing, drinking in every word. He had little to say, however, to the general public concerning the evidence.

"But after Detective Smith's testimony had been given, the usual taciturnity of Evans was overcome by his manifest hatred of the detective, whose testimony proved so damaging to Dalton's cause. Evans declared to an acquaintance that Smith's story was a pack of lies. 'I would not hesitate a minute to shoot down a —— like that detective if he'd lie on me as he's lied on Dalton,' Evans growled out, an evil gleam discernible in his eye."

After Evans' daughter, Eva, had read the foregoing, she insisted that it was both untrue and unjust. She maintained that Evans and his family did not arrive in Visalia from their ill-fated Modesto venture until after Grattan Dalton's trial. She asserted that her father was never present at any time as a spectator. Here is her statement:[15]

"It did not occur to me to make it clear that my father was not in Visalia at the time of Dalton's escape, but I can remember that we were still in Modesto when this happened, and we did not return to Visalia

until October or November of that year. I know because I objected to starting school as soon as we returned. I wanted to wait until after the Christmas
holidays. I was always looking for an excuse to stay
out of school. This is the first time that I had heard
the story of Dad attending Grat Dalton's trial, though
I had heard the rumor before this of his aiding in
Dalton's escape. I feel sure this wasn't true either, not
that he would not have enjoyed 'aiding and abetting,'
because I can remember that he thought it was a good
joke that Dalton escaped so easily from their new
jail, but he just happened not to be there."

During the summer of 1891, while the Evans family
was travelling over parts of the Spanish king's Royal
Highway (El Camino Real), John Sontag had
paddled his birch-bark canoe over the lakes of northern
Minnesota, and had carried his packs over portages
made famous by the French Canadian coureur-de-bois
employed by the Hudson's Bay Fur Company. He
had left home a slim, sixteen-year-old boy; he had returned a decade later, a six-foot, one-hundred and
eighty-five pound athlete who, in spite of the injury
received at Fresno, was still a man to attract attention
in any company. Old-timers who knew him in his
prime, men as well as women, have paid enthusiastic
tribute to his fine features and perfect physique. His
mother gloried in her older son, and his brother, George,
proved to be an excellent companion on the hunting
trail and on fishing trips. The two brothers attended
a round-up in Canada and John, to his younger
brother's surprise and satisfaction, won the bronco-

busting contest. His victory in open competition was
due in part to his skill; he rode in the graceful and
approved loose-jointed California manner. However,
the odd thing to the spectators was the fact that the
roughest buckers and wildest pitchers did not show
much enthusiasm in trying to throw Sontag. This
hypnotic power over broom-tail mustangs was not to
be seen again until the rollicking and cock-sure Tom
Minor came riding out of Idaho's purple sage-brush
some twenty years later to astonish the western horse-
lovers at Cheyenne.

John stood at the cross-roads of life that summer;
a slight nudge either way could have sent him on to
fame or infamy. Like many other sensitive men, he
resented insults and injuries, and anyone he hated was
hated by an expert; by the same token he loved deeply.
There were no half-measures about him. Anger or
fear will corrode a man's soul, and Sontag suffered
from unpleasant childhood memories which an extrovert might have shrugged off in a short time. The
thought that two men had harmed him as a youngster
disturbed him until he was virtually ill; in this modern
era he would have developed ulcers of the stomach.
The desire for revenge kept incubating in his mind,
and finally he would feel impelled to demand retribu-
tion. Even a more gentle soul than John Sontag might
have felt righteous indignation over the following jolt
to body and spirit:

Once when he was seven, John's mother sent him
to the meat-market. As he leaned over the show-case
looking at the meat display, the butcher, a huge brute

in human form named Bole, brought his ham-like hand down hard on the little boy's head, mashing his face against the heavy glass. A female customer, hardly to be classed as a lady although she was a wife and mother, joined the beef-selling bully in laughing at the crying child's bloody face. Either she was afraid to have the clown with the cleaver arrested, or she enjoyed cruelty inflicted without danger of reprisal. Whether her name should be printed in the hope that it will live in infamy, or omitted in the equally sincere hope that it will be forgotten, is hard to decide.

Another juvenile experience involved persecution at the hands of an older boy of the sadistic type who inflicts pain on smaller children because they are unable to fight back. The hoodlums of his own gang had dubbed this repulsive specimen of humanity "Corva-Wheat" Berg, which is strictly barnyard Norwegian.

Just how much childish woes will affect human behavior in later years may be debatable, and to what extent John Sontag's sufferings as a boy would be responsible for the intolerance he showed as an adult toward injustice, his defiance of oppression, and his hatred for brutality, whether meted out by a person or a corporation, must be left to those who specialize in such problems.

During the summer of 1891, after an absence of more than ten years, John decided to pay Bole and Berg a visit; the time had come to balance the budget. His mother tried to dissuade him from taking a walk along the path of unrighteousness. She pointed out the fallacy and futility of leaving the main-travelled road of life for a detour of hate which would lead to a dead-end street and destruction. The mother quoted a passage from the *Bible*, well known to John from his early training for the priesthood: "Vengeance is mine, saith the Lord, I will repay!" As she reasoned with her son, she pointed out that what a man thinketh in his own heart, so is he, and concluded her exhortation by saying:

"John, I dedicated you to the Lord when you were a mere infant. At sixteen you refused to continue your studies leading to ordination and, like the prodigal son, you ran away from home and went to a far country. You have lost your way, and I pray that you will turn back before it is too late, and re-trace your steps to that symbolic community where you will find a little red schoolhouse and a white church with a high steeple and a cross; when you reach that place, turn to the right, and then go straight ahead."

John, in no mood to heed his mother's advice, went to the vicious butcher's house only to learn that the latter had just passed away, a victim of his own excesses. John felt frustrated. He continued his walk along the road of revenge, and met his other evil genius of boyhood days, but the bullying Berg proved a snivelling coward and wouldn't fight. So, in sheer disgust, John slapped his face a few times and walked away. Sontag had expected to feel much refreshed after his two interviews; instead he felt blocked in his endeavors, and a trifle let down.

Many years before this, the Sontag family had spent a vacation at a summer resort in northern Minnesota.

John had attended a parochial school there for a few weeks. It had proved a happy time for him; the last day of the term had come all too soon, and a lovely schoolteacher and friendly schoolmates had bidden him fond farewells. Now, in 1891, George and John went back to this place to fish in the big lake. One day John told his brother he wanted to be alone; this time he was going for another solitary walk, but on this particular promenade he was not motivated by hatred or fear.

In a letter written this same day to a personal friend of long standing, a Fresno blacksmith named Andrew McClain, he recounted his happy adventures during the past summer with his family and friends. He mentioned his visit to the little schoolhouse, now deserted and falling into ruins, where he had spent a few short and happy weeks, and stressed his emotional reactions, which had burst through the flood-gates of his inhibited nature, when he stood beside the sagging gate in front of the dilapidated old building and recalled from the far fields of memory the parting scene at the end of that last day at school:

"Most vividly of all do I remember a very pretty girl, vivacious and high-tempered, who lingered after all the others were gone. I was eleven then; she was ten. With all the seriousness of a little man and a little woman, we built a beautiful house of dreams, and I solemnly promised to return and marry her. As we were making our vows I recall that gentle breezes toyed with her lovely hair. Our beautiful house of childhood dreams has been in ruins for many years now, and this afternoon for a little while—I sat and watched similar breezes toy in a similar fashion with the flowers which grow on a little mound."

John Sontag, like all other mortals burdened with a secret sorrow and obsessed with the haunting spectre of the might-have-been, was eventually obliged to resign his visions of the past, and in the early spring of 1892 he returned to California to greet with eagerness and rapture the living presence of the gracious little lady who was waiting for him at Visalia.

In the summer of 1892 Chris Evans and Clarke Moore went up to Sampson's Flat to work in the Evans mine. Moore was and remained, through thick and thin, one of Evans' best friends. While trimming timber for use as a tunnel support, Chris cut his foot with an adze, and had to return to Visalia. He did not know it then, but he was returning to face the most hectic experience in his life. His injured foot prevented his wearing a shoe, and so he walked around in a carpet slipper.

This old carpet slipper was to be of historic significance at a not distant date. August 5th was to be that date!

CHAPTER 7

WHO ROBBED THE TRAINS?

DURING the days when Spanish and Mexican governors ruled Alta California there was relatively little lawlessness. Some evil men, mostly mixed breeds without pride in ancestry or hope for posterity, congregated along Nigger Alley just off the plaza in the pueblo of Los Angeles. Fights to the death with knives were nightly occurrences but, since these homicides affected only the dregs of society, the *gente de razon* were undisturbed. In the northern part of the San Joaquin Valley a mission-trained Indian named Estanislao carried on a desultory warfare for a short time. But in general California from 1769 to 1846 deserved the name Spanish Arcadia, and its closing decade was well described by Gertrude Atherton as "the splendid, idle forties."

The first outbreak of lawlessness came as a result of the racial prejudices aroused by the war between the United States and Mexico and the influx quickly thereafter of thousands of gold miners. The worst of these newcomers were the Sydney Ducks from Australia and the self-styled Hounds from New York's Bowery. All forty-niners, regardless of their place of origin, seemed to resent the presence of the Spanish-Californians, and the customary nickname applied to them was "yellow-bellies." Out of this turmoil emerged the picturesque Joaquin Murieta, the sadistic Three-fingered Jack (Manuel) García, the handsome Tiburcio Vasquez, and the charming Procopio.

The second outbreak was the heritage of the evil passions aroused by the Civil War and the entrance into the valley of the Southern Pacific. While the connection between a railway company and the War Between the States may seem far-fetched at first glance, yet there was a correlation between the two. From these two affluents was to flow a general stream of lawlessness.

When the land troubles between the Southern Pacific and the settlers in Mussel Slough came to a head it was often mentioned that the directors of the corporation were of New England birth or descent, while many of the wheat growers were Southerners by birth or extraction. The latter, reared in the political faith of Patrick Henry and Thomas Jefferson, valued liberty above life, and justice above law. The written law favored the railroad, but that law had been unjustly drawn and interpreted. The settlers had no desire to rob anyone; they simply refused to be robbed. The railroad land agents and station masters were arrogant and officious. Had they kept out of the light and off the toes of the settlers, the latter would no doubt have remained polite. But they resented anyone, even a corporation, biting a thumb in their general direction, and were willing to fight without wages.

The owners of the Southern Pacific, Charles Crocker, Mark Hopkins, Collis P. Huntington, and Leland

Stanford, were all of Yankee stock, and sectional hostility had not died down during the decade which had elapsed since the Civil War. The settlers may have felt that *The Octopus* was doing to them what the Reconstruction program was doing to their kinsmen in the Old South. Then, too, the entire nation was permeated with hostility toward the railway corporations. No doubt the railway was coarse, crude, and to blame; it is equally true that many of the settlers were of an emotional type, willing to join the Settlers' Land League, or any other mysterious organization, if it only promised fun, excitement, and immunity from detection.

In the days before the Civil War, Kansas had been the scene of border warfare. Fanatical Abolitionists like John Brown battled for free soil with equally cruel Border Ruffians. William Clarke Quantrill, a native of Ohio, moved to the Kansas prairies. For a time he was a teacher in a little log schoolhouse. He soon became skilled in the border warfare then raging. Though born in the North, he aligned himself with the other side and opposed the Free Soilers. Then came the Civil War, and Quantrill became a notorious guerrilla leader. He remained neutral, and killed the boys in blue as well as those who wore the gray with equal pleasure and impartiality. His ferocity led his biographer to describe him as the "bloodiest man known to the annals of America."[1]

Many of the partisan leaders ignored the official surrender at Appomatox Court House; they had private reasons for continuing the horrors of guerrilla warfare. One excess led to another, and a new generation grew up in an atmosphere charged with hatred and fury. In this region lived the James, the Younger, and the Dalton families. During the days when Quantrill was a schoolteacher Jesse James, Frank James, Cole and Frank Younger had been his pupils. If we are to judge a pedagogue by his success in molding students during their plastic years, undoubtedly "Quantrill was a good teacher out on the Kansas plains before the war."[2]

Jesse James and Cole Younger were first cousins. Adeline Younger, an aunt of the outlaw Younger brothers, married and in due time became the mother of the boys who were to achieve notoriety as the Dalton gang. The Daltons were respectable people[3] in their community. The boys in that family were not inherently vicious; they were merely high-spirited and the product of their environment. Francis Bacon claimed that "a man's nature runs either to herbs or weeds." From the inside out, the Daltons were like other boys; from the outside in, there was much at that time and place to make them different.

Bob Dalton was made of the stuff out of which heroes are created. While in his early twenties he was appointed a United States deputy marshal. In those days deputies were not paid salaries; they worked on a fee basis. The law specified that if a deputy marshal or other officer killed an outlaw he was responsible for a decent burial. The cost of planting a corpse then was eighty dollars. If an outlaw killed an officer he was under no obligations. Bob found it hard to collect his fees, and when he had run into debt fulfilling his obligations, he became disgruntled and resigned. His brother, Grattan, also served as a deputy marshal in Oklahoma when conditions in that Territory required unflinching resolution and dauntless courage. But he learned that public officials are not always honest; he also learned to his sorrow what many a man has since learned, that when a subordinate attempts to expose cupidity and peculation in a superior officer it is generally fatal—to the honest subordinate! When Grattan's pay was withheld, he tried to collect, was framed, resigned, and started for the West. His superiors, fearing exposure at his hands, naturally tried to defame him. In New Mexico he and his brother Bob entered a poker game in a saloon. It was crooked and they soon said so. The result was a shooting scrape and more trouble for the Daltons. They fled to the San Joaquin Valley.[4]

When Grattan and Bob arrived in California, a brother named Littleton resided on a ranch near Clovis; another brother, William, owned a ranch in the foothills near Paso Robles. A cousin, Sam Oldham, was a wheat grower residing a mile due east of Kingsburg.

Reports had come to California concerning the pugnacious proclivities of the Dalton boys. The United States Marshal back in Oklahoma, who had cheated Bob and Grattan and therefore hated and feared them, sent word to California officers that they would bear watching. Grattan, especially, was a combative individual, and willing to fight for the sheer

joy of the battle. In the San Joaquin he found men
who were willing to accommodate him. For a time
Bob and Grat remained with Sam Oldham. At that
time the latter employed two teamsters named Charles
Flewelling and Eugene Curtis. One evening these
two men and the two Daltons attended a dance at
the Brick Hotel in Kingsburg, located on the present
site of the Ford Agency garage. Curtis told the writer
that before entering the hotel the Daltons removed
their revolvers from their arm-pit holsters and placed
them under the front porch. Noticing his look of
amazement, one of them said:[5]

"We want to place our guns where we can find
them in a hurry in case we need them. They would
be in our way while we danced."

No one else noticed this little precaution, or suspected that the Daltons were in any difficulty with
the law enforcement officers, and so a pleasant evening
was had by all.

In the 1880's the robbing of trains was still a novelty.
The first locomotives, small as they were by modern
standards, were still so fast and powerful that men
stood in awe of them. No one with any understanding
of steam cared to wrestle with them. When the Union
Pacific began sending its first transcontinental trains
across the plains shortly after 1869 some Indians decided to hold up a passenger train. They secured a
stout rope of braided buckskin and held it across the
rails with ten warriors on each end. The engineer,
astonished at what he saw, entered into the spirit of
the occasion, and struck the rope with full steam

ahead. The result, in more than one sense, was side-splitting.

The first well-planned attempt to rob a train was made by Tiburcio Vasquez in 1873, a few miles north of Tres Pinos. He piled logs across the rails hoping to cause a wreck, but the engineer saw them in time, and stopped the train. When men began to get off the coaches, Vasquez decided that discretion is the better part of valor and that he had better *vamos*; Western men at that time and place were always armed.

At 8:30 in the evening of July 21st of the same year Jesse James invented train robbery.[6] He and his companions pulled the spikes out of the ties holding one of the rails in place and tied ropes to it. When the Rock Island train, west of Adair, Iowa, came round the bend, the engineer, John Rafferty, was astounded to see the rail mysteriously slide out toward the fence. He slammed on the brakes, but was unable to stop in time to avoid a wreck. The locomotive rolled over, and the engineer was killed. The bandits removed $3,000 from the express coach, and then moved leisurely through the other coaches collecting donations from the frightened passengers. Twelve hours later a train passed over the same route loaded with $75,000; the Jesse James gang had made a serious miscalculation in time.

One important distinction between train robberies in the Middle West and the San Joaquin must be noted. In the former, passengers were molested; in the latter, never.

The first train to be robbed in the San Joaquin Valley was No. 17,[7] the Southern Pacific southbound passenger train. It left Pixley at 7:30 in the evening of February 22, 1889, with two masked men riding undetected in the tender. They crawled down into the cab and forced engineer Peter Boelenger to stop his engine. While the latter and his fireman, C. G. Elder, were guarded by one bandit, the other went back to the express coach and ordered the express messenger, J. R. Kelly, to open the door to the safe. He refused. A dynamite bomb was then detonated under the coach, and the concussion caused it to heave convulsively. This was the first recorded attempt in history to use explosives in connection with train robberies. It was suggested that its use indicated a man familiar with certain kinds of mining. When the train came to a halt a brakeman named Anscon started to walk down the east side of the coaches to investigate. He carried his lantern and his approach was visible to the waiting bandit. Anscon was followed by a railway employee named Henry Gabert. A split second before the bandit fired the brakeman hurled himself to the ground and the blast from the shotgun passed over him and caught Gabert in the chest.

The conductor, James Symington, and Ed. Bentley, a deputy-sheriff, who happened to be a passenger, ran down the west side of the train toward the express coach. The conductor also carried a lantern. The deputy, hearing steps on the other side of the coach, stooped to peer under the rods of the car, and the bandit, who had decided to peek at the same moment, hastily fired a load of buckshot, which careened crazily off the rods and brake-beams, and made the sparks fly. Bentley, severely wounded in the face and hands, ran to the rear of the train, but was out-distanced by the conductor, who ran the entire two and a half miles back to Pixley. He explained afterwards that he had run back to town to make a telegraphic report of the hold-up to headquarters. Rumors that the loot amounted to $5,000 in greenbacks were received with glee by many residents of the valley, who generally referred to the Southern Pacific in those days as *The Octopus.*

However, their emotions were not entirely unmixed. Not all of the settlers approved of lawlessness, and when the train rolled into Delano, the next stop to the south, and the dead body of Gabert was unloaded, it cast a gloom over the community. Even if robbing the railway corporation was excusable in the opinion of some, no one was willing to condone the killing of good neighbors and useful citizens. That made it a different matter.

The trail of the bandits was followed for some distance toward the Sierra Nevada, but was soon lost. The skill shown in effacing their tracks led officers to believe that these bandits were not thugs trained in big city stick-ups, but frontiersmen trained to hunt big game, stalk Indians, and to travel without leaving any tell-tale marks.

When this hold-up occurred, the Dalton boys had not yet arrived in California, and Chris Evans was still working for the Bank of California. His detractors were to maintain later that he knew when the bank shipped gold destined for the grain warehouses at Goshen, Tulare, and Pixley. Hence it would have been easy for him to intercept these shipments. The bank, toward which Evans was friendly, would not suffer any loss. As public carriers, the railroad company and Wells, Fargo & Co. would sustain the damage. His supporters argued that he was in financial straits during the years the Southern Pacific and Wells, Fargo were assertedly losing huge amounts of money. There should have been some evidences of wealth at that time in the Evans home. Either the public carriers were magnifying their losses, or Evans was hiding the money and not using any of it. Chris, to the day of his death, denied that he had ever robbed a train, and the charge was never proved. When he was finally convicted and sent to the penitentiary it was on other charges. However, someone was enjoying an open season on the Southern Pacific express coaches. Stories of buried treasure still persist in the San Joaquin Valley. It is based on the fact that thousands of dollars were reported stolen and apparently never put back into circulation. Men with doodlebugs (divining rods) have traversed the salt grass area of Traver and Goshen. In their search they have been guided by secret information handed down from a previous generation. Their success is unknown; a leprechaun should be imported.

The second hold-up took place on January 20, 1890, two and a half miles south of Goshen. The southbound train, No. 19, was stopped by two masked men, who employed the exact technique used at Pixley. The engineer, S. R. DePue, and the fireman, W. G. Lovejoy, were marched to the express coach. Each had a revolver stuck in his back. The express messenger was told to throw down the strong-box. What should he do? If he complied he would be called a coward; if he refused his two fellow workers would no doubt die forthwith, and his own life was likewise in jeopardy. When one of the bandits fiercely reiterated the demand and tightened his finger on the trigger, the messenger remembered the words of the popular song of the period he had been singing just before the train had been brought to an abrupt halt: "Shall we believe what we are told, or shall we surmise?" He decided that the first clause in the sentence was the correct answer on this occasion, tugged at the heavy box, pushed it out through the door, and the bandits took it. It was quite a treasure chest; in it were $20,000 in gold.

While the bandits were struggling with the heavy box a tramp dropped from the brake-beam where he had been riding and started to run away. He was drilled between the shoulder blades. He lived long enough to tell the trainmen that his name was Christiansen. The raiders left an indistinct trail which again led toward the Sierra.

It was in September of this same year that Chris Evans bought Wallace's livery stable and moved to Modesto. Later men would say that it was the Goshen gold which had financed this purchase. His friends said he raised the money by mortgaging his twenty acres south of Visalia; his detractors argued that a laboring man with a wife and seven children would normally lack the capital needed in the big undertaking he essayed that fall. His little farm would not have been sufficient security for the big loan required to swing the deal.

The disastrous and heart-breaking fire which destroyed Evans' barn occurred in January, 1891, and shortly after this, on February 6th, the southbound train out of Alila was stopped half a mile south of the town. Alila, now non-existent, was located a quarter of a mile south of present Earlimart. Engineer Thorne and fireman Radcliff were marched out of the cab toward the express coach. Brakeman F. W. Langdon ran toward them to investigate, and miraculously lived to tell the tale. Instead of being shot down, he was merely halted and added to the procession. The express messenger, C. C. Haswell, profanely told the bandits to go to that place from whence no man returneth, and had his scalp creased by a single buckshot from the bandit's shotgun. He returned the fire through the grating of the coach-window and twelve or fifteen shots were exchanged. While the two shotguns of the bandits and the single revolver of Haswell roared and crackled, the fireman suddenly dropped with a slug through his spleen. The baffled would-be robbers disappeared in the darkness.

The train pulled into Delano with the dying Radcliff. For a little while Haswell was a hero, and then, ironically enough, he was arrested for the murder of the fireman. However, it was proved in court by a ballistics expert that a bullet fired from the express-coach and down through the grating could not have inflicted the fatal wound; it had come from the gun of one of the bandits.

Sheriffs Borgwaldt of Bakersfield and Kay of Visalia trailed the men toward the Coast Range. The men who had robbed the previous trains had headed for the Sierra; these had gone in the opposite direction. Were these the same men? And why did they fail this time, while their success had been so easy the other two times?

The suggestion was offered by many observers that new men were at work at Alila. The Southern Pacific agent at Fresno disagreed. He told a Fresno newspaper reporter:[8]

"I don't think the fact of their having been excited and frightened is a good argument in favor of the supposition that the robbers are new at the business. They evidently expected to have things all their own way, and the resistance of the messenger took them by surprise. Then they had reason to believe that the fusillade which followed would be heard at the station, which was only a short distance away. So they did not wish to run the risk of being captured by persisting in the undertaking."

It seems impossible that John Sontag could have been involved in the Alila hold-up. He had gone to Fresno to look for work shortly after the Modesto fire, and there is much evidence to show that he was in bed with pneumonia at that time. The argument that Evans knew about the gold shipments to the Bank of California would be invalid now, as he had severed his connections with the bank. However, he could have taken time off from his nursing duties to go south to rob the train and then come back to Fresno. It was physically possible, but why wait until he was seventy-five miles south of Fresno before he tried and failed? Police officers and detectives thought they knew the guilty parties, and those suspected persons were neither Evans nor Sontag.

This was the hold-up which led to the accusation of the Daltons, and may have been indirectly responsible for their subsequent lawless careers. After each preceding robbery scores of men had been arrested, much to their annoyance, and later released, much to their relief. Both arrest and release proved highly amusing to the general public which laughed without caring who saw it. The ineffectual attempts of the officers to locate the culprits resulted in a great deal of adverse criticism, and they writhed under the jibes directed their way. The detectives employed by the Southern Pacific and Wells, Fargo & Co. were asked in effect:

"What are we paying you for?"

Goaded by the corporations, the poor officers tried desperately to pin the guilt on someone, and their apparently unjust treatment of the Daltons is easily explained.

The two sheriffs, Borgwaldt and Kay, had trailed the bandits to Huron, a lawless community, where the antelopes, Basques, and sheep obliterated their tracks.

Scratching his head for a clue, one officer remembered that an unsavory report emanating out of Oklahoma pointed in the direction of the Daltons. So Will Smith, railway detective, decided that their movements might be worth investigating.

After coming to California the Dalton boys had remained quietly with Sam Oldham at Kingsburg for several weeks. Then they decided to visit their brother William at Paso Robles, and a friend named William McElhanie went along. Brother Will's ranch was their headquarters at the time of the Alila robbery. Will Smith believed they could have ridden from Paso Robles to Alila, stopped the train, and then scurried back over the hills to avoid detection. He asked Sheriff O'Neil to accompany him to Will's ranch. The latter, fore-warned of their coming, advised Bob and McElhanie to keep out of sight as he feared that reports from antagonistic officers in Oklahoma had already prejudiced the case against them, or else he believed they were guilty. At any rate, he hid them in the attic and blandly entertained the officers all night. The two fugitives fretted and fumed in their cramped quarters, but the next morning Smith and O'Neil departed none the wiser. Bob then decided to decamp and mounting his horse, he followed the rim of hills to Tehachapi, crossed the Mojave desert, and finally reached Oklahoma.

Grattan was arrested in Fresno by Will Smith, but was released when several of his friends testified that he had been playing cards with them in the Grand Hotel at Fresno at the exact time of the hold-up at Alila. Grattan shrugged, laughed good-humoredly over the affair, and went to San Francisco. After some cogitation Smith decided that Grattan's alibi was too glib and that his friends had been too willing to testify to anything, so he went to San Francisco, and re-arrested him. Smith took Grattan to Visalia, where he was brought to trial for the Alila hold-up and found guilty by the jury.

If the jury was correct in its findings that Grattan and Bob Dalton had stopped the train at Alila, then what happens to later charges that Chris Evans and John Sontag were guilty of the same offence? Only two men had been involved! Since the court records of Tulare county still show that the Daltons were guilty, and this decision has never been reversed, then Evans and Sontag must have been innocent. However, Emmett Dalton, a reputable citizen of California during his later years, always insisted that his brothers had not been involved in this attempted robbery. Either the jury was wrong, and must bear the onus of having ruined two fine young men; or it was right, and then it was a cruel thing to blame Evans and Sontag in later years for a crime for which other men had already been tried and convicted. That the Daltons escaped and thus avoided paying the penalty imposed by law has no bearing on the question of guilt. Apparently someone had to suffer, and when the two men originally found guilty got away, someone else had to pay.

A fourth hold-up took place in the evening of September 3, 1891, two miles south of Ceres. Grattan was in the Visalia jail at that time waiting for his trial to begin. Bob was in Oklahoma. Again two unknown men were the attackers. The Southern Pacific passenger train, No. 19, the same which had been robbed near Goshen, left Modesto (known to-day for its "water, wealth, contentment, health" slogan) at 8:15 on scheduled time. It stopped at Ceres, five miles to the south, in order to let a passenger get off. While the locomotive was still gaining momentum after its stop at Ceres, two men slid down from the tender and forced the engineer, Neff, to stop it. Neff, and the fireman, Lewis, were marched to the express coach. Reed, the express messenger, and his assistant, Charles, were on the alert, and when the bandits fired broadsides down the side of the train to discourage investigation, Reed turned off the lights. The two men then picked up their guns and waited for the outlaws in the darkened coach. The latter were clever, and forced the fireman to enter with a lighted candle. When he was ordered to light the lamps, Reed, apparently placing a higher valuation on the gold than on the fireman's life, threatened him with painful and instantaneous death if he complied. Lewis was in a dilemma, but finally decided that his posterior was less vulnerable than his anterior and backed out in spite of the oaths and threats of the bandits. While he was still moving slowly in reverse, an outlaw threw a bomb over Lewis' shoulder, which rolled into the coach but failed to explode. In the meantime, two railroad detectives on the train, Harris and Lawson, entered the affray with sufficient enthusiasm to thwart the robbers. Len Harris, during the fracas, received a bullet in his neck, and when the train reached Merced he was taken to a hospital. He recovered. A posse trailed the bandits to Newman where they eluded further pursuit.

Three tramps had been riding on the brake-beams. They testified that one of the bandits was tall and lean; the other short and fat. This description caused men of this conformation much annoyance during the next few days. The following facetious editorial was penned by the editor of the Modesto *Herald*:[9]

"Constable Parker and his deputy, Spiers (from Ceres), arrested a dozen men in Modesto on Friday morning because they were short or tall—one of the robbers being large and the other small. Only the middleweights of Modesto escaped these lynx-eyed officers of our neighboring town.

"They arrested a barber here and as the fellow clearly proved an alibi, Spiers was in favor of turning him loose, but Parker pointed out that the barber was a small man, as was one of the robbers. As the barber couldn't explain this away, Spiers concluded it was suspicious and he had the fellow crawl into their buggy and go with them to the scene of the robbery. Arriving on the ground, the barber declared that he had never been there before, and as, as Spiers pointedly remarked, he couldn't have stopped the train without having been there, and as he didn't appear to be so very short after all, Parker reluctantly turned him loose, with the admonition that he guessed he wasn't guilty, but not to go doing it again.

"The barber walked back the five miles through the heat to Modesto, and was mad enough when he got here to waylay the first train that came along."

Shortly after the irate barber had been released, Sheriff Eugene Kay received word at Visalia that two men had just arrived at Maggie Rucker's ranch, south of Traver. Judging by the condition of their horses, they had come fast and far.

Maggie Rucker merits a word in passing. She was a woman picturesque in appearance, uncommon in personality, and pungent in speech. In her ability to hunt, ride,[10] and shoot she was similar to "Wild Bill" Hickok's great and good friend, Calamity Jane of Deadwood. Like the latter, she had a soft spot in her heart for those in trouble and never failed to help them. They might be outlaws, but if they were down-trodden and under-privileged, they would always find Maggie Rucker's door open. She owned and personally operated a dairy farm at Cross Creek, a place which had been originally established as a stage-station on the old Butterfield transcontinental line. It was located four and a half miles south of Traver and another two miles down the stream to the west of the Southern Pacific railway. Maggie Rucker delivered milk and other dairy products to the residents and restaurants of the flourishing town of Traver. A neighbor, D. C. Hayward, residing five miles southwest of Traver, had induced J. G. Cohoe, an experienced butter and cheese maker from New York state to install a creamery at his ranch in 1888. This was the first venture of this nature in the San Joaquin and proved successful. To this plant went the surplus milk from the Rucker dairy. Besides her Cross Creek dairy farm, Maggie owned grazing lands in the high mountain country.

Her nephew, Eugene Curtis, stated that during certain seasons of each year she hunted bob-cats, deer, cougars, bears, and coyotes with reckless abandon and unvarying success. In her handling of a pack-train of mules, whether it involved throwing a diamond hitch or hurling verbal brickbats, she was superb. When Will Dalton and Riley Dean were in trouble they went to her Cross Creek farm; later Chris Evans and John Sontag were to seek sanctuary at her ranch near Camp Badger; and when Grat Dalton was in distress he sought surcease from his woes at her valley home. Emmett Dalton told the author:[11]

"I never had any acquaintance with Maggie Rucker of Kingsburg, but I was informed by my brother Grat, that it was at her place that he stopped for two or three days after he tore down the Visalia jail."

The report that two possible criminals were at the Maggie Rucker ranch called for an investigation. Sheriff Kay and his deputy, George Witty, went there in a hurry. In response to a knock, Will Dalton came to the door. He seemed surprised to see the officers, and when he learned their errand he showed neither trepidation nor guilt, and quietly surrendered.

The other man, Riley Dean, ran out through another door and crawled under the back porch. He had a long record as a trouble maker. Andreas Pico, who had received *Los Moquelamos*,[12] a Mexican land grant of eleven square leagues in 1846, had been annoyed by an endless procession of squatters, and the most pestiferous of these had been Dean. This tract of land included within its boundaries the site of present Lodi.

Later Dean had settled in Tulare county, and had become notorious in connection with his sporting saloon, which was said to have been the social center for the cock-fighting, dog-fighting, and bare-knuckle fraternity. The officers believed that Will Dalton was in bad company.

From his vantage point under the porch Dean dominated all approaches with his Winchester. Dalton doubtless saved the lives of the two officers. He warned them that Dean was not bluffing, but would shoot to kill. He was wanted on some petty misdemeanor charge in Hanford, and hated John Hall, the constable at that place. Dalton told the sheriff:

"If you will trust me to go back of the house alone, I'll try to convince Dean that Hall is not here. Then he may come out."

Kay let Dalton go, and the latter succeeded in bringing Dean out without any trouble. The two men were taken to the Visalia jail. Will's brother, Grattan, was there at that time. In response to a telegram five men arrived on the evening train from Modesto. They were Sheriff Purvis of Stanislaus County; Hume and Thacker, representing Wells, Fargo; and Smith and Lawson, railway detectives. Dalton and Dean were taken to Modesto to stand trial for the Ceres robbery. Will Dalton made a good impression on the officers. He talked and acted like a gentleman, and neither whined nor showed any animosity. Even the detectives became convinced of his innocence and feared that again they had made a mistake. It must have been galling for them to have Will Dalton's innocence finally established by one of their own group, a detective named Devine, who had met Dalton at Maggie Rucker's home, south of Traver, on the same night as the train was stopped at Ceres. Since the two places were a hundred and twenty miles apart, obviously Dalton was not guilty. In his opening statement to the court District Attorney Fulkerth told the judge that the railroad detectives were refusing to swear to their original stories, and he asked that the case against Dalton and Dean be dismissed. It was.

No one suspected John Sontag at this time. One of the three tramps, already referred to, was named J. L. Race. He had stated that the tall robber was a blonde. This did not fit Sontag, who was very dark. Both Dalton and Sontag were tall men, and so Will Dalton had been the temporary victim. He was interviewed by a reporter from the Fresno *Expositor*:[13]

"Had I been guilty, and knowing that train robbery is a capital offence in California, and if I had had courage enough to stop a train or shoot a detective, do you for a moment believe I would have hesitated to kill both Sheriff Kay and Deputy Witty? But knowing I had committed no wrong, I allowed my arrest."

Dalton left the Modesto court-house a free man and was promptly re-arrested at the door for the Alila hold-up. He was taken to Visalia, tried, and acquitted by the jury. He walked out of the Visalia court-house a free man and was promptly re-arrested at the door for a robbery in San Luis Obispo. He was taken there, tried, and acquitted by the jury. One can hardly blame Dalton for saying somewhat lugubriously:[14]

"The truth is I am like Paddy Miles' boy—no matter what goes wrong or what depredation is committed, Bill Dalton is always charged with same."

But the consecutive arrests which he suffered perhaps saved him from worse troubles. He was in the Modesto jail when Grattan broke out at Visalia, and this fortuitous circumstance made it impossible for any prosecuting attorney to tell him:

"You have made yourself an accessory after the fact, and compounded a felony!"

Will was in the San Luis Obispo jail awaiting trial when all of his brothers, excepting Emmett, were killed in Kansas in an attempted bank robbery. He had planned to visit his relatives in Oklahoma and, considering his disgruntled state of mind, might easily have been induced to join his brothers in that fatal venture at Coffeyville.

It was shortly after the Ceres hold-up, a few miles south of Modesto, that Chris Evans and his family left the latter city and returned to Visalia. Later it was asserted that it must have been more than a coincidence that a train robbery so near Modesto made it possible for him to return to Visalia and live quietly there without other visible means of support until the next summer when he went to his mine at Sampson's Flat. The flaw in this argument was that no money had been taken from the express coach near Ceres. Whoever the bandits were, they had failed on that particular occasion. The memory of the public is often short-lived!

A cottonfield negro was an inmate of the Visalia jail while Grattan was there. The latter, who combined an air of arrogance with Southern courtesy, had impressed the former so favorably that he gladly promised upon his release to return with a file and a hacksaw. The result was that Grattan not only released himself but the two other prisoners; W. B. Smith, accused of robbing a freight car at Tulare, and John Beck, charged with horse stealing. The three men walked along the streets looking for a good team of horses. A fleet span of grays, belonging to George Mc-Kinley, who was attending a special committee meeting at the Methodist Church, was taken. Dalton was a good judge of livestock, and behind these fast trotters the three fugitives raced toward Goshen and the Southern Pacific mainline. The time of the escape was fixed between seven and eight o'clock in the evening because McKinley was in his church during that time. Grattan left the other two men to their own devices at Goshen, and walked north to Maggie Rucker's ranch along Cross Creek. The other men took the southbound train out of Goshen and disappeared in the direction of Los Angeles. The next forenoon the McKinley team and buggy were found in Tulare. Who drove them there is uncertain. Some old-timers have said that a friend of Dalton took them to that place to throw officers off the scent; a more likely story is that some unknown person in need of transportation simply appropriated them. The gray horses, all unknown to their owner, were doing heroic taxicab service that night. It was not until after the sheriff's deputies had located the McKinley team the next day that they also learned to their chagrin that their new jail was empty.

After remaining with Maggie Rucker a few days, Grattan went to visit a friend named Joseph Middleton in Squaw Valley. The latter took Grat to a place of safety in a mountain midway between Squaw Valley and Mill Creek. The latter stream empties into Kings River about two and a half miles above Piedra. Dalton's camp on this mountain, located eight miles southeast of Piedra, was thenceforth to be known as Dalton's hideout, and is sometimes referred to as Dalton Mountain. Middleton soon rode to Reedley and notified officers there that Grattan was hiding near his home. Whether or not this was the right thing to do, the reader must settle for himself. Dalton, as all successful outlaws must be, was suspicious, and kept a close watch on all approaches to his mountain domicile. A stray greyhound, perhaps an outlaw in his own right, had attached himself to Grattan with doggish devotion, and, when the proper moment arrived, was to "sound off" in time to warn his human friend and benefactor. The posse hired livery rigs at Reedley and, to allay suspicion on Dalton's part, did not go to Middleton's ranch, but spent the night at the Jud Elwood place, located along Mill Creek, about eight miles upstream from Piedra, and not far from the present Pierson Dude Ranch, which has entertained guests from every state in the Union, as well as from fourteen foreign nations.

In the morning the deputies cautiously approached Dalton's camp. The latter's crossbred hound opened the festivities with staccato barks of anger, and Grattan, thus alerted, quickly supplemented his lurcher's threats with warning shots. The officers respected the man behind the gun, and hastily left for Reedley by way of the Elwood ranch. Grattan, now in no particular hurry, strolled at a leisurely gait to the latter place. Elwood, not a member of the posse and then busily engaged in plowing, was ordered to unhitch one of his horses, remove the harness with the exception of the bridle, and then Dalton mounted the resentful beast and rode it a few miles toward the north. How far he went is uncertain, but the plow-horse returned of its own volition to its home corral that evening. Dalton secured a more suitable steed somewhere else and rode it to Merced.[15]

Two things were to distinguish Elwood's later career. He was a member of the posse which captured John Sontag the morning following the fight at Stone Corral. He was also to be associated with the group which actually discovered the Kern River oil-fields. Jud operated a hotel at Bakersfield at the time, and his brother Roe (James Monroe) owned a woodyard at the same place. An old Irishman told them that he greased his wagon with the oil which bubbled up through the water in the river. At first his auditors all laughed at his preposterous yarn, but finally Roe induced his father, Jonathan, to come to Bakersfield, and, aided by the other two brothers, Judson and Burton, the four men conducted a laboratory experiment. Cans were fixed along the edge of the river where bubbles were constantly appearing, and the impounded substance proved inflammable. Then the Elwoods, assisted by John Marlar and George Wiseman, dug a well about twenty feet from the river-bank, using picks and shovels, and soon were able to scoop up buckets of oil. This was the first oil-well in the Bakersfield region and was brought in on May 2, 1899.

Grattan Dalton visited with a friend, Judge Gray, at Merced for a short time. The latter gave him a fine saddle horse, which Dalton rode south along the Sierra to Tehachapi, across the Mojave Desert, and thence to Oklahoma. The rapidly shifting course of events had made outlaws of the Daltons, and when they re-assembled at their mother's home the scene was one of extreme pathos. It was a rainy and dismal evening when they rode up; she was preparing supper and the older brothers ate with their rifles across their knees while twelve-year-old brother Sam watched the road for possible pursuers. The mother's emotions may well be imagined:[16]

"She was standing in the door as we mounted and wheeled away. I had never seen her weep before. Perhaps it was the rain washing against her face as she lifted her hand toward us while the youngsters clustered about her. Mother of outlaws, extending a hand of final blessing toward her renegade sons. Looking for the last time, through lightning-riven rain, upon the living face of Bob.

"I felt unutterably cruel and despicable as our horses splashed through the muddy road. I saw her next from the cot where I lay fighting for life in a bullet-riddled body."

The fifth hold-up, and the third one involving Train No. 17, came on the night of August 3, 1892, at Collis.

This station, named in honor of Collis P. Huntington, was later re-named in honor of two realtors who sub-divided the land in the region and brought in colonists. The first syllables in the names of W. G. Kerchhoff and Jacob Mansar were united to form Kerman.

At the command of two masked men who crawled down from the tender, Engineer Al Phipps stopped his train. He and the fireman, Will Lewis, were marched to the express coach and, to their amaze-ment, offered cigars. They lit them. Then Lewis was told to light the short fuse attached to a dynamite bomb. He asked:

"How shall I do that? I know nothing about bombs."

The bandit leader snarled:

"What do you think I gave you that cigar for?"

The fireman gingerly touched the fuse with his light-ed cigar and jumped back to avoid destruction. The expressman, George D. Roberts, had been busy at his desk, and had unlaced his shoes for greater comfort. When the first bomb exploded it blew the shoes off his feet, but otherwise did no damage. He thought this was odd. But his thankfulness was short-lived. The next bomb hurled him against the wall and dislocated his shoulder.

The two outlaws then entered the coach and de-manded the keys. Roberts refused. He was pistol-whipped, and the keys taken from his pocket. Three bags of silver and one of gold were taken. The loot was reported to be $50,000. These bags, weighing nearly 200 pounds, were loaded on the fireman, a brakeman, and the half-crippled messenger and carried by them to the waiting buggy some hundred yards away.

A threshing crew was camped about 200 yards away from the scene of the hold-up. The two owners of the threshing machine, J. W. Kennedy and John Arnold, had just returned to camp and were planning to retire when they heard the explosion. It was then near midnight. Taking their rifles they cautiously approached the train. However, they had no opportunity to shoot as the clever bandits always managed to be shielded by one of the railway men. A bomb had been detonated in such a way that it broke one of the piston rods; this, however, did not prevent the locomotive from limping into Fresno. That night there was much excitement in the county seat!

A search of the ground near the hold-up revealed that a team had started rapidly toward the west, but the trail was soon lost. Some half-wits accused the Daltons, but they were now busily engaged in train robberies in the Middle West. Emmett Dalton, after he had become a respectable citizen of Hollywood, told the author that neither he nor his brothers ever held up trains in California, but that infuriated by baseless charges of such conduct and constantly pursued by officers, they decided to become guilty as charged after they had returned home.

The robbery at Collis took place in August; on October 4th of the same year the Dalton boys, after a thrilling career as bad-men of the Middle West, were wiped out at Coffeyville, Kansas. Within ten minutes after they had attempted to hold up two banks simultaneously eight men had been killed, including Bob and Grattan Dalton, and several had been wounded. The lone survivor of the brothers was Emmett. He received a bullet through his upper right arm, another in the back hip which emerged in the groin, and twelve buckshot in the back from a shotgun while stooping to help his brother. He survived, was sentenced to life imprisonment, and pardoned, because of his youth, in 1907, after having served fourteen and a half years. He married Julia Johnson, his boyhood sweetheart, who had waited for him, and became a highly successful building contractor at Hollywood. Still later he went into real estate. His verdict concerning the life of an outlaw is the mature judgment of an expert, and worth quoting:[17]

"It was not because we changed from train robbery to bank robbery that brought about the gang's destruction. There is no such thing as a successful outlaw. The end of all violators of the law has been the same right through history. It is impossible for the few to pit their brains against the world for any length of time. This is being demonstrated daily in the lives of the big city racketeers.

"If a lot of ward heelers were thrown into jail, the backbone of racketeering would be broken, for racketeering is simply a combination of money and politics. I have made more money in a single real-estate deal, than out of all the robberies of the Dalton Gang."

Since the Daltons were eliminated by geography, other suspects must be investigated. Shortly before the Collis robbery Evans had come home from Sampson's Flat due to a foot injury. He limped around with a carpet slipper on his cut foot. The trainmen admitted that neither of the two robbers limped. But they resembled the two who had stopped the train near Ceres; one was tall, the other was short. A Visalia paper reported the antagonism Evans had shown during the trial of Grattan Dalton. Detectives operating in the community also knew about the animosity often expressed toward the Southern Pacific by John and George Sontag. Both Chris and George were short; John was tall. These men were placed under surveillance, especially the two Sontags.

George Sontag had been convicted on a charge of forgery in Nebraska, and had served two years in the penitentiary of the goldenrod state. He had been around. He was also inclined to get drunk frequently. The bartenders employed by Si Lovern, the Palace Hotel, and the Exchange Hotel, knew him well. When he was in his cups he was prone to babble. Regardless of the innocence or guilt of Chris Evans and John Sontag, it was the vicious verbosity of George which was to lead them into dire distress. And at times George could be irritatingly laconic. When the police interrogated him about the hold-ups and suggested that he could tell them the truth if he would only talk, he grinned and said "If!"

CHAPTER 8

HERE COMES THE LAW

EARLY in the morning of August 2, 1892, John
Sontag appeared at the Frank I. Bequette stable
in Visalia and hired a fast trotting team. He said that
he was going to Sampson's Flat to bring back his
brother George and Chris Evans. But were they in
the mountains? James M. Leslie,[1] in later years a
prominent leader in civic and business affairs and a
president of Sun-Maid, a raisin co-operative, was to
testify in court that Evans had spent the night of August 2nd with him at the Pease ranch, south of Selma.
Chris, according to Leslie, did not leave this place
until 10 o'clock the next morning. Furthermore,
Evans freely admitted the truth of Leslie's testimony,
and stated under oath that he had gone from the Pease
ranch to Fresno, where he had consulted his lawyer
with respect to certain legal matters which had arisen
in connection with his mine. In the meantime, where
had Sontag gone?

John Armstrong, a Fresno liveryman, was to assert
later on the witness stand that Sontag had "parked"
the Bequette team in his stables about 3 o'clock in the
afternoon of August 2nd. It had remained there the
rest of that day and all of August 3rd. After having
carefully fed and watered the horses, Sontag took

them out about 7:45 in the evening, and drove slowly toward the west side of Fresno. Shortly before midnight the Southern Pacific passenger train was robbed at Collis. The next forenoon, August 4th, John Sontag returned the horses to the Bequette livery stables. They showed signs of hard driving. Had they been to the mountains, or had they been to Collis? It is all very confusing, and the plot begins to thicken.

During the following afternoon, August 5th, the Evans family was preparing for its annual trip to the Redwood Ranch. John Sontag came over to the Evans home from his quarters at Grandmother Byrd's house, and began to clean the two shot-guns. He loaded them with birdshot, and placed them carefully in a closet in the front bedroom so they would be out of the way of the small children. Molly's Ballard rifle was also cleaned, but left unloaded. This is important in view of what happened later.

George Sontag was staying at the Palace Hotel in Visalia. Eva Evans was busy with her household tasks, and was therefore not particularly glad to see George when he came to the house for a visit. She had no time for entertaining just then. In the meantime John had returned to his own room in Mrs. Byrd's house. George chided Eva, who was an excellent rifle shot, because she did not know how to shoot a revolver. He argued plausibly enough that a rifle was too cumbersome to be carried around for self-protection. To please him, she accompanied him into the backyard and fired his old Army Colt at a target for a while. When there were only two bullets left, she returned to the house, and laid the gun on the bureau in her bedroom just inside the back door.[2]

John had returned to the Evans home while Eva and George were back of the house shooting at a target. Later the two brothers went down to the main part of Visalia. When George began to drink heavily John left him in disgust, but lingered in town for some time. Finally he was told that his younger brother was doing a lot of babbling and John collared him and took him to the Evans home. George was in a slap-happy state and insisted on engaging in boastful talk-talk, which amused the small Evans children but enraged John. Smith, a detective for the Southern Pacific, and Witty, a local police officer, arrived and took George to the sheriff's office for questioning. He was not placed under arrest at the time.

After John and George had gone down town earlier in the afternoon, Eva had busied herself for a time at the sewing machine completing her new sun-bonnet. Then she had suddenly remembered that her mother had asked her to pick some figs. So she left her sewing, and went back of the house where the big tree was located. While she was engaged in fig-picking, John and George had returned, and shortly thereafter Smith and Witty had arrived and taken George with them. John had then gone into the front bedroom where the guns were stored. Eva was unaware of what had happened, and did not know that John was in the house.

The day was warm and all the doors and windows were wide open. The front and back doors in the

Evans house were in direct line, and when Eva entered through the back door with her basket of figs she could see through the house to the front door. She was startled at the sight of two big men standing there, and hurried to the door to meet them. She knew that one of them was George Witty, a local deputy sheriff, and was to learn later that the other was Will Smith, a railway detective. The latter, a large and forceful individual, asked:

"Where's John Sontag?"

"I don't know."

Smith had seen John enter the house and perhaps assumed that Eva was trying to shield him. So he snarled:

"You're a damned little liar!"

This was Eva Evans' testimony made in court under oath. Smith, also under oath, stated unctuously that he had said:

"Little girl, I think you are mistaken."

Perry Byrd told Scott Gillum later that George Witty had applied a lewd epithet to Eva that afternoon which was far more insulting than the profane remark attributed to Smith.[3]

Eva turned and ran out the back door to get her father. He had been feeding the livestock in the barn and was on his way to the house when he saw two men stop the sheriff's team in front of his house. Thinking that his family was busy in the orchard, he was hurrying to the house when Eva met him in tears and told him what the men had called her. Evans entered the back door and paused long enough to pick up the revolver lying on Eva's bureau. He placed it in his back pocket and went into the front room where the two officers were standing.

"Gentlemen, what do you want?"

Smith answered:

"We want John Sontag."

Evans replied:

"He is not here. He went down town."

Smith lost his temper and roared:

"That's a God-damned lie. He is right here in this house."

Leroy Smith, a Dinuba attorney, and at that time a schoolmate[4] of Eva Evans, told the author that young George Witty was a desk deputy; that is, he confined himself largely to paper work in the office, and had had little or no experience in shooting. When Will Smith asked for a deputy to accompany him to the Evans home, Witty was the one given what appeared at the moment as a mere routine assignment. It is too bad for all concerned that Sheriff Eugene Kay did not send himself there that day. Then much misery might have been avoided. Probably by temperament and certainly by experience Witty was in the wrong room when Smith began to roar profanely at Chris Evans. In a crisis a nervous man is always much more dangerous than one who is cool and calculating.

As a result of Smith's rage, the atmosphere was instantly surcharged with tension and Witty pulled out his gun. Why he did so no man knows, but one guess is as good as another and it may be that he planned to forestall trouble, but he was probably nervous and he squeezed the trigger. The bullet whizzed past Eva's head and out through the open back-door. Since it cut through the atmosphere and disappeared into space, it was impossible later for Chris to prove that the deputy had commenced hostilities by firing his revolver within the Evans home. The father felt fortunate that the bullet had missed his daughter, but said later that it would have been helpful to his defense if it had lodged in the wall or furniture from where it might have been recovered, identified, and offered as Exhibit A.

The sudden explosion in the front-room was followed by the equally sudden appearance of Sontag, who slapped the portieres aside which separated the two rooms. He had a shot-gun in each hand, and snarled:

"Here, Chris, take one."

"No, I don't need it. I have something better."

Everything happened quickly. Witty, smitten with buck-fever, had unintentionally fired his gun; Sontag, muttering "What the Hell?," had jumped into the front-room like an avenging angel; Evans now reached for his revolver, and the two officers turned and ran. Smith did not run down the path toward the gate, but cut diagonally across the front-yard through a tomato patch, and tried to crash through the picket fence which surrounded the Evans property. This fence was not built out of the fragile lathes so common at a later period, but of redwood stakes of stove-wood thickness and similar to those now in use in providing a trellis for Thompson Seedless vines. This sturdy fence, built by Evans to protect his garden and home orchard, was a necessity due to the numerous cattle which then strayed in the Visalia area. When Smith, with his head thrust between two stakes like a dairy cow locked in a stanchion, tried to worry his way to freedom, he found this enclosure stronger than he had anticipated.

Sontag, who had run out on the porch, saw Smith with his head down, his posterior up, and his knees pumping furiously, resembling nothing so much as a sprinter on a treadmill because, although he was making the dirt fly, he was getting exactly nowhere. His big shoes, unable to gain traction, reminded John of the spinning drivers of an overloaded locomotive trying to start a freight train on a rainy morning. The sight made him laugh, but this mood quickly changed to anger. Any thought, however remotely related to the Southern Pacific, always did this to him, and Smith's connection with that corporation added fuel to his fury. Sontag steadied his shotgun against a porch support and fired a double-barreled load of bird-shot at the inviting target. Smith received the blast where it would do the most good. The hot lead in his pants gave the detective added momentum, and he went through that fence like a bat out of Memphis, and headed for town with more speed than comfort, his flat feet spraying out gravel behind him, and shouting as he ran, according to Eva Evans' ballad: "O, take me to a doctor, for I know I'm going to die!"

At the same time Witty had high-tailed it down the path, but before he had gone fifteen feet Evans' first shot drilled him through the shoulder. The deputy spun half-way around, dropped his gun, but managed to keep running. Evans pursued him, but was hampered by his sore foot, still encased in a loose carpet slipper. He fired once more and then found that his gun was empty. Witty managed to cross the street and collapsed on a neighbor's woodpile. Evans limped back to the house and, in spite of his aversion to profanity, told the astonished Eva:

"I got that son-of-a-bitch!"

She had never seen her father's eyes blaze in anger before. It frightened her.

In the meantime John had untied the sheriff's team, and as soon as Evans could climb into the wagon they drove away. Why did they leave with the sheriff's team? And why did they leave at all? Evans and Sontag became outlaws at that moment. Later a newspaper was to print the following comment:[5]

"They (Evans and Sontag) were never able to explain away to their neighbors' satisfaction their resistance and flight. For there was in Tulare county and in Fresno county a large party who did not let their sympathy run away with a conviction that if Sontag and Evans were innocent they should have stayed to prove it. They were first of all for law and order. And they had a civic sense that demanded that the train robbers, whoever they might be, should be brought to justice."

During all this excitement, Mrs. Evans and her other children were placidly picking nectarines in the orchard back of the house. They heard the shots, but

did not connect them with their own home. They
also saw the sheriff's team as it was driven down the
road, but did not recognize the men as Evans and
Sontag. But they were not to remain long in ignorance.

A neighbor came running into the orchard and in
great excitement announced that there was a dead
man on her woodpile. Other neighbors appeared and
began asking questions all at once.

"What was the shooting about?"

"Why?"

"Where did the men go?"

"Was it true that George and John Sontag were
bandits?"

Then the officers came, and there were more questions, some of them brutal. Molly and Eva were told
bluntly:

"The Sontags are train robbers. George is an ex-
jailbird. John and he have been robbing trains. You
know how John hates the Southern Pacific. We have
George in jail now, and he has confessed."

George had not confessed, but the women could not
know that. And then more questions, and more
threats, until Molly became hysterical.

It was then that Grandmother Byrd's Tennessee
mountain anger came to a boil, and she took her
daughter away. When time for supper drew near the
excitement gave way to hunger, and people began
to drift away. At last even the officers left. Witty
had been taken to the hospital, and Smith had had the

pellets of birdshot removed from his beam. If Molly's Ballard rifle had been loaded Sontag would have used it and then Smith would have been "obliterated into oblivion."

Eva was too busy to become hysterical. She washed, fed, and put her brothers and sisters to bed. When Molly finally returned the two women lay down on the bed in the front bedroom and talked quietly. Suddenly they heard a step on the porch and a voice whispered "Molly." The door was softly opening and Chris and John were standing there. Why had they come back?

The explanation offered by Evans seems ridiculous now. The members of the Home Guards, a military unit affiliated with the National Guard, were leaving on the train that evening for Santa Cruz for their annual bivouac. When they left they planned to take George Sontag, then in the Visalia jail, with them as far as Fresno, where he would be left to stand trial for the Collis train robbery. Since Collis was located in Fresno county it was necessary for him to be tried there. Chris and John planned to hide near the railway station and by a sudden sally rescue George and take him to the mountains for safety. It seems like a crack-brained idea now, and Molly and Eva thought so then. But Evans was firm. He said that George would be framed and that nothing could save him, once he got into the clutches of the lawyers employed by the Southern Pacific railroad corporation. Molly was asked to go to Grandmother Byrd's house and get some extra clothing for John. Eva was to get meat from the smokehouse back of the barn and feed the horses. Later they would load the wagon with supplies. The men then disappeared into the night in the direction of the railway station.

When Eva entered the smokehouse she had a premonition that she was not alone. However, in the Stygian darkness she could not see a thing. She learned later that several men were hiding in the smokehouse, and that other men were behind the barn, and one lay in the ditch in front of the barn. Deputy Sheriff Dan Overall, whose son Orval later became a famous athlete at the University of California and a star baseball pitcher with the Chicago Cubs, had rounded up a posse by making the following offer:[6]

"Come and help us get Evans and Sontag. I'll make you a deputy, and give you ten dollars and an oyster supper."

While Molly and Eva waited for their men, they stood whispering on the back porch where they were concealed by a large jasmine vine. Eva told her mother what her father had said after he had shot Witty. Molly answered:[7]

"Your father is crazy; there is no other way to account for what has happened."

The night was bright and the landscape lay drenched in moonlight. And down the road, apparently oblivious to the fact that they were easy targets for lurking deputies, stalked Evans and Sontag, with their rifles slung across their shoulders. George had not been brought to the station, and so their hare-

brained plan to rescue him had come to naught. Now
the men were hungry. They ate their supper in the
kitchen without any light save that provided by the
moon. Supplies were carried out to the barn and
placed in the wagon. Sheriff Kay's horses were hitched
to it, and the team backed out. Suddenly Eva saw a
man raise himself out of the ditch, and she warned
John by pulling his sleeve and pointing. The stranger
hailed them:

"Who's there?"

John answered:

"What do you want?"

The man in the ditch then fired into the team and
both horses went down screaming. The two men and
the two women shielded themselves behind the dying
horses, and both Evans and Sontag returned the fire.
The result of this second gun battle on that 5th day
of August, 1892, was two dead horses and one dead
man. Oscar Beaver, the only man to go over the top
that night, had tried to earn Overall's "ten dollars and
an oyster supper." He had failed. Later Evans was
to refer to him as a "poor drunken fool," but whether
or not he deserved that comment, Beaver had died
trying. None of the other would-be deputies or oyster
eaters could say as much.[8]

Both Evans and Sontag were lame. Evans' injury
has already been alluded to several times. Sontag had
broken his ankle some weeks before this while trying
to police an unruly horse. Now the two partially

crippled men, without horses, food, or extra clothing, limped rapidly away into the great void.

What is the explanation of all the fury unleashed this day? Omitting for the nonce the question of their innocence or guilt with respect to railroad robberies, a psychoanalyst might offer this explanation. Evans, by nature gracious and sympathetic, grieved over the unfortunate John Sontag. He had opened his door to the lonely wanderer when he was weary of heart and plans had been made that John should abide within the Evans family forever. To his subconcious mind the Southern Pacific railway symbolized the evil forces which were destroying the rights of free men. Smith and Witty were instruments of that corporate control. Once John and George came into the grip of that octopus, they would be forever stilled. In proposing to keep them free Evans could not know that he would release only fever and fret and tumult!

CHAPTER 9

APACHE AND POSSE

"I 'VE got twenty-seven notches on my gun, and I'm going into the mountains tomorrow and Evans and Sontag will make twenty-nine."

The man who said this was a United States Deputy Marshal named Vernon C. Wilson, known to his acquaintances as "Vic." This statement sounded boastful to those who heard it, and Eva Evans, to whom it was addressed, thought it was a trifle rude.

Wells, Fargo and the Southern Pacific had posted a proclamation which read in part as follows:

"Whereas said Wells, Fargo & Company and said Southern Pacific have heretofore offered large rewards for the arrest and conviction of any of the parties engaged in the above named robberies;

"Now, therefore, the said rewards are hereby withdrawn and in lieu thereof the said companies do hereby jointly offer a reward of $10,000 for the arrest and delivery to the sheriff of Fresno or Tulare Counties of said John Sontag and said Chris Evans, or $5,000 for the arrest and delivery to either of said sheriffs of either John Sontag or Chris Evans; the said rewards to be payable upon delivery."

The official announcement described Evans as forty-five years of age, five feet, eight inches tall, and weighing one hundred and sixty pounds. Sontag was said to be thirty-three years old; five feet, eleven; and weighing a hundred and sixty-five. They had last been seen on Sunday, September 4th, at the home of Supervisor Sam Ellis, in Stokes Valley near Boyd's Grade. They had left there about 7 P.M., driving a big, Roman-nosed chestnut horse hitched to a cart. The proclamation was signed by A. N. Towne, general manager of the Southern Pacific, and E. M. Cooper, manager of Wells, Fargo & Company, and dated September 6, 1892.

After the fight at Young's cabin, the words "arrest and delivery" were deleted and the words "dead or alive" were inserted.

In those days $10,000 would buy one of the best ranches in the county and men, most of whom had no personal animus against Evans or Sontag, were anxious to become man-hunters. Since the railway bandits had tampered with express coaches carrying the mails it became a federal matter, and a United States Deputy Marshal was assigned to the case. Wilson brought with him from Arizona two famed Apache Indian trackers, Pelon and Jericho.

Will Smith, who had been in command up to this time, was very jealous of Wilson, but his mismanagement of the case had made him "lose face." He had no success in raising a posse and finally had to join the one led by Wilson. A Fresno paper stated that "no one would volunteer to go under his leadership,[1] as the people have lost all confidence in his methods." The same opinion was expressed in the Visalia papers:[2]

"The county clerk seems to think that Smith and

Witty went to the house of Evans a week ago today, merely to get Sontag's trunk, and not to make any arrest. Others think that the detective had not at that time, sufficient evidence to arrest Evans or John Sontag for complicity in the robbery. But if Smith wanted nothing but the trunk he was hardly justified in peering around into other rooms, on being admitted within the house."

Another Visalia resident had this to say about Smith:[3]

"H. N. Denny, of this city, who went to Evans' house to get a trunk, and who was near by when the shooting of yesterday occurred, thinks Detective Smith is a coward. He jumped into the express wagon and asked Mr. Denny to drive him into town. Denny explained to him how he could head the robbers off, but Smith would listen to nothing of the kind, and told Denny to drive on to town, leaving Witty to himself, wounded."

The worst thing that anyone ever said about Chris Evans was that he had a fiery temper. He was gentle and kind until some one began to push him around; then he did not like it. A reporter of the period summarized the situation as follows:[4]

"Up to this time, Chris Evans had been considered one of our most upright and honorable men. He always worked hard and dealt fairly with everybody. Smith is credited with being an over-anxious amateur detective. He has undertaken to land men on all sorts of charges before, but has always failed dismally.

"Of course, in this last case, Smith has about ruined it all. The way he went after the suspected men was ridiculous. There is no doubt that if a man had gone quietly to Chris Evans and said that he had a warrant for him, Chris would have gone along, and all of this trouble would have been avoided."

There resided at Visalia at that time a Mr. McKeown. For many years he had been the janitor in the local grammar school. He was very popular[5] with the school children and highly respected by all. When trouble descended upon the Evans family he felt very sympathetic toward the children in that family and tried to shield them from persecution. Thoughtlessness is the privilege of youth, and many unkind and cruel remarks were made about the outlaws, Evans and Sontag. The other school children were only echoing what they heard their parents say at home. The small boys in the Evans family often came home from school bearing the scars of battles fought for the family honor. When McKeown heard that a marshal and Indian trailers were in Visalia, he felt it incumbent upon himself to warn Eva. Since McKeown was inoffensive and getting along in years, he could go and come without attracting undue attention. As soon as Eva was informed of the presence of these professional man-hunters, she went down town to do a little sleuthing. She was especially desirous of knowing how public opinion was re-acting toward the marshal, the Indians, and her father and fiance. It was when she unexpectedly encountered Wilson that he made the remark quoted at the beginning of this chapter.

The bloodthirsty boast infuriated her and she went home and wrote a letter to her father. The contact man at that time beween Evans and his family was Clarke Moore. The latter, admittedly a friend and partisan of Evans, refrained from going directly to the Evans home. That would never do. Had Moore been seen leaving the Evans home he would have been trailed and the location of the fugitives quickly discovered. So he employed a trusted but relatively unknown messenger, a sort of second go-between. Moore's errand boy was at the Evans home when Eva, seething with anger, returned from town. The letter which she sent by this messenger to Moore, who delivered it in person to Evans, contained a description of Wilson and his two Indians, and closed with the following paragraph:[6]

"I'll be much obliged if you will kill him, and when you do here is a note to pin on him: 'Send on some more killers with notches on their guns.' Signed Eva Evans."

Shortly after this note had been delivered Clarke Moore was arrested because of his outspoken defence of Evans. He stood trial the next spring for "aiding and abetting a criminal before and after the act of murder." He was acquitted.

This trial took place during March, 1893. One of the chief witnesses was Pelon, the Apache, who was described as follows:[7]

"Pelon, the Apache trailer, was the first witness called in the Clarke Moore trial yesterday. Pelon is a

copper-colored, sinewy, straight man, dressed in brog-
ans, overalls, and blue coat and brass buttons. Around
his neck he wears a string of beads, and his coarse,
straight black hair, like a horse's mane, hangs down in
three or four plaits between his shoulder blades. He
is an ugly customer, with a cool, cat-like mouth, and
with black eyes that burn like fiery coals."

Before Wilson could kill Evans and Sontag, he
would have to find them. Where were they? What
had happened to them during the six weeks which
had elapsed since that fateful night of August 5th?

Evans told his family later that John and he had
walked all night. The oak forest, of which the present
Mooney Grove is but a fragment, at that time extended
from Waukeena,[8] near Corcoran, in the west, to the
fantastic buffalo wallows lying northeast of Visalia,
near Yettem. At sunrise they reached the latter area,
which looks as if it had been geologically cooked at
some prehistoric date, and suddenly cooled. Looking
back, after they were clear of the forest, they could
see a spiral of dust ascending heavenward. It meant
pursuit was coming close. The buffalo-wallow country
was sparsely settled, but luck was with them. They
saw a cabin in the distance, near the present site of
Yettem. This they managed to reach while the posse
was still some miles away. They told the astonished
and frightened settler that they wanted to borrow his
house for a little while. It did not make sense to him,
but the time for argument was short, and he and his
family were sent scuttling to the barn and told to
keep still or else! They did.

Evans then left the door slightly ajar, and sat down in a rocking chair. He was tired. His chair was placed beside the wall in such a way that anyone entering the door would see him, but would not reveal his presence to persons on the outside. When the posse arrived, the men remained mounted while the leader, Supervisor Sam Ellis, dismounted and walked to the door alone. When no one answered his knock, Ellis walked in without invitation. Evans, resting comfortably in the rocking chair, held his Winchester across his lap in such a way that the barrel was pointing directly at the supervisor's belly. The mouth of the rifle, held by the unflinching man in the chair, must have looked as big as a cannon. Ellis had only a split second in which to determine his future, both as to action and life. Evans said later:

"Sam staggered, and I thought for a moment he would fall. But he was game, and rallied. Turning to his men in a matter of fact way, he yelled: 'Nobody here, boys!' Then they all rode away and the family in the barn came back and served breakfast. I felt sorry for the settler and his family for the fright we had given them, but we were told that life was so lonely and monotonous that they were glad for a little excitement. Now they would have something to talk about for a long time to come."

Evans had counted the posse; it numbered fifty. In it were men whom he had considered good friends and neighbors. It was disillusioning. But the desire for excitement and reward had proved enticing, and in some cases, was to prove fatal. Evans particularly resented the presence of Sam Ellis with the posse. The latter had been Molly's first beau, and had remained a friend of the family throughout the years. Chris made a mental note that he would have a heart-to-heart talk with Sam at some future date.

After eating and resting in the lonely settler's cabin, the men proceeded toward the foothills. John's ankle became worse with every mile, and before they reached Blue Mountain he was ready to collapse. Evans had to help him reach their destination. Years before, when Evans had courted Molly, they had discovered a cave; it would serve a useful purpose now. The entrance to it was hidden by wild currant bushes; no one would ever find it except by accident. The inside of the cave was roomy, with a high ceiling and a dry floor. Best of all, it contained a never-failing spring of cold, clear water. Evans buried Sontag's leg up to the knee in the wet sand, and there it remained during the next four days. By that time the pain had been allayed and the swelling reduced so that he could walk.

Four days of enforced fasting made any kind of food acceptable, and when they reached the Rutherford ranch, nine miles away, an excellent breakfast of bacon, eggs, fried potatoes, coffee, and hot biscuits tasted like the mythological and heavenly nectar and ambrosia. Evans had always refused to let his children eat hot biscuits prior to this time; he had believed them to be unhealthful. After his experience this particular morning he repented, and told his youngsters the next time he saw them that he could no longer deny them such delightful food.

For a week the members of the Evans family heard nothing from Chris or John. The agony of their suspense may be imagined. Then, one night, they came home. Evans wanted to know how things were going. Molly and Eva told him. Everything was hay-wire.

Two days after the trouble began, officers came to the house and asked all sorts of personal questions. Where did the family get its money for household expenses, now that S. Sweet & Co. had withdrawn its credit at the store? The answer: The Byrd family was supporting Molly and her children. Where was all the money taken from the Southern Pacific and Wells Fargo? The officers wanted to know. Perhaps the Evans family wanted to know, too. Molly could have used some of it!

Mrs. Chris Evans had been presented with a new parlor set by her husband when they resided at Modesto. It consisted of three pieces; a sofa and two chairs, upholstered in brocaded mohair of dark blue and gold. They were very beautiful, and the first new furniture that Molly had ever had. It was also to be her last. The officers, looking for hidden wealth, slit these open with their sharp knives and ruined them completely. Next they turned their knives and attention to the mattresses, and gutted them. These officers were really sharp, in more ways than one. It seems cruel and unnecessary now; it seemed so then to Molly and Eva. They protested without avail. The little children, observing the vandalism, cried in sheer terror, but when have the cries of little children ever availed against bullies? The next day, Sheriff Eugene Kay, who was always a gentleman, came and apologized. He even left some money in partial payment, but the damage had been done, and Molly was destined never again to possess nice furniture.

But the nights were even worse than the days! Regular officers, no matter how rude and officious they might be, were better than the bums who infested the premises at night trying to intercept Evans and Sontag, and attempting to spy on the family. Loungers and riff-raff from the Visalia saloons earned easy money by serving as special deputies. They lay in the grass in the orchard, and sneaked behind the barn. Eva, who liked to go walking at night, often stumbled over these guardians of the law. It was infuriating. It troubled her father, but there was little that he could do about it just then.

Chris and John remained only a few minutes on their first visit. In the meantime things went from bad to worse. S. Sweet & Co. served the first notice of foreclosure; this was made final in November. In the meantime the peeping Toms kept on peering, ogling, and crawling. Eva Evans described conditions as follows:[9]

"One night, just a few days after Dad had gone away, it was so hot I couldn't sleep. I got up and went out on the back porch. It was so lovely under the stars that I decided to walk for awhile. I had on just slippers and a nightgown. The steps from the back porch were only about two feet from the house, and led down past my bedroom windows. As I started down the steps, a man began crawling out backwards from this narrow space between the steps and the house. By the time he got to his feet, I had reached the bottom of the steps; so I just kept on walking slowly towards him in my long white nightgown, with my pale yellow hair all over my shoulders. He seemed afraid to turn, and I backed him for about forty feet before he turned and ran like a scared coyote.

"After this, I started looking for men, and I found them—lying down in the vineyard, behind the shed, under the trees—all over the place.

"How could I endure it if I could not walk alone in the dark? If I could only see my father, and tell him how I had been robbed even of this, I felt sure he would do something about it.

"One night I was suddenly awakened by the sound of Dad's voice, almost a whisper, but that wonderfully penetrating voice of his was audible from the next room, where he was talking to Mother. I jumped out of bed and in a moment was in his arms. He assured me that everything was all right, that no one was going to kill him, and that now he would tell me what caused the trouble. But first I told him about the men all over the place at night."

On their first visit home, the two men remained only a short time. A few days later they returned late in the evening and stayed until dawn. Christopher Evans made an explanation that night to his family which, in fairness to him and his record, is worth quoting:[10]

"Do you remember what I told you in the few minutes we had to talk when we were here last? That John had said, 'It's the S. P. after me!' You know what that means, don't you? If they mark a man and go after him, he's doomed. They own the courts and the judges. It's less trouble to convict an innocent man than it is to hunt down the guilty one.

"Do you recall that several years ago a box of gold watches and rings was found on the steps of the South Methodist Church? Some robber wag's idea of a joke. Maybe he was behind in his dues to the church, and ironically paid with something he did not dare use. Those watches and rings were traced to the Goshen train robbery, and one of the local officers told me that ever since then there has been a detective in Visalia, looking for other clues, hoping to pin this crime on a Visalia citizen.

"You know by the papers what George did the morning of the day the trouble started. He went down town and got drunk, went from one saloon to another, bragging about what he knew about the Collis hold-up. He told contradictory stories that were carried to the sheriff's office, and he was arrested. John was told of this before he returned home that day.

"Do you recall that it was reported, after every one of the several train robberies in the San Joaquin Valley, a tall and a short man committed the crime?

Everyone knows what the railroad people did to John, and how he hates them. If George was guilty, here was the short man. Then his brother John must be the tall one; so they came after John.

"When I came into the house that day, I only thought of what they had said to you. Then I recognized Witty as a local officer, but I didn't know who the other fellow was. They turned to flee the instant after Witty fired, because just then John stepped into the room with both shot-guns. When Witty pulled his gun, I believe he meant to cover me and search the house for John. That shot was a clear case of 'buck ague'—he was so nervous that he shot without meaning to. The fight was on; I knew I could not stop John, and without even waiting to see if you had been shot, I pulled that revolver, and, as they ran, gave my attention to Witty, the man who might have killed you.

"I don't blame John for not giving himself into their hands. With only one lung, and his heart in the shape it is, prison would be death in a short time. I wouldn't let them take him; he has suffered enough at their hands. You know what happened after that; now there is no turning back!

"I have never robbed a train. If I had, you would not be penniless now. But I've killed one man, and wounded another. Regret or remorse would be useless.

"Molly, I know it is going to be terrible for you and the babies. It's been so bad ever since we returned from Modesto. There's no money, and now the credit's gone. You are not to worry about John and me. We have lots of good friends in the mountains; we can hunt. You know I don't much care what I eat, so it keeps my body going. I can't protect you from cruel tongues, but I'll be watching over you; never fear. I'll never be far away. Bill Downing has offered to come out to the house, on his weekly trips with a load of lumber. He often came to see us, anyway, so his visits will not attract attention. You can save the newspapers and give them to him; also have a letter ready with anything I need to know. We'll keep out of sight, and try not to kill anyone else.

"We would not have returned Beaver's fire if we had not thought it was the end of everything. We thought we were completely surrounded. I was the most surprised man in the world when no gun answered our shots at Beaver. I'm sorry he's dead. Poor fool; poor drunken fool. Sober, he probably could not have been induced to go out alone to challenge whoever was in the barn.

"We are going now. Daylight must find us in the foothills. I'll do something to frighten away the prowlers. I'm sure they are not the Sheriff's men; just bums, hoping to pick up some information to sell."

Shortly after this second visit Evans sent word that he wanted a horse and cart, as John's ankle was still weak. Eva bought a Petaluma cart and hitched Jim, a big-footed, leather-skinned, Roman-nosed, sorrel horse to it, and sent horse and cart by special messenger to a designated place. Thereafter the men rode into Visalia frequently and Molly and Eva heard the big horse going by from time to time during the long and lonesome nights. Evans was keeping watch over his little flock.

On one of his periodic visits to his home, Evans told his wife that Sam Ellis had not learned his lesson. When Evans and Sontag were hiding in the cave on Blue Mountain they had seen several man-hunters go by with Sam in the lead. So Chris said: "I think I'll visit Ellis tomorrow."

The next day was a Sunday, September 4, 1892. Mr. and Mrs. Ellis came home from church with two dinner guests, Scott Gillum and Johnny Keener,[11] young men who were at that time bachelors. When the hosts went into the kitchen they found Evans and Sontag there. Just what was said at this conference is not certain, but Ellis never again joined a posse. The hungry dinner guests, left alone in the front room for a long time, must have been somewhat mystified. The hosts were embarrassed, no doubt, but could not leave the kitchen to do any explaining. Finally the table was set and the Ellis family with their invited and uninvited guests sat down. Evans took the seat at the head of the table with his guns stacked in the corner directly behind him. Sontag sat around the corner of the table to Evans' right. The chicken dinner was excellent, but the spice of good fellowship was lacking. Gillum told the author that during the meal Evans said:[12]

"Sam, if it were not for your wife, I'd kill you today. But I knew her when she was a little girl, and

I dangled her on my knee then. I don't want to make her a widow, but if you ever hunt me again you will die."

William Elam, a widower, whose wife had been a sister of Mrs. Ellis, arrived about 5 P.M. with a small herd of cattle. Sontag was sitting in the backyard with a Winchester across his knees. Elam was introduced to him. Gillum and Keener were still present, as Evans would not trust them to leave. Mrs. Ellis, who was pregnant at the time, had been upset by the visit and threats of the outlaws, and had gone to bed with nervous prostration. Elam could see Evans through the open door of the bedroom, sitting in a rocking chair and talking soothingly to her. The outlaws left about 7 P.M.

Molly was frantic with fear each time the men came home for a visit. The bums in the orchard might give the alarm, and the deputies might show up with belching guns. Death was just around the corner. One day Mrs. Richard J. Place, a neighbor, walked over to the Evans home and was met at the door by little four-year-old Johnny who made the startling announcement: "My daddy is in the bedroom." Mrs. Place told no one, but others were presumably less reticent. That evening Molly and Eva accompanied their men to the barn. When the big, wide rolling door was pushed back, it sounded like the rumble of distant thunder. Leroy Smith,[13] a schoolmate of Eva Evans and a near neighbor, heard it and inquisitively went to the open window of his upstairs bedroom. It was a balmy night in September. Big Jim was backed out, and Sontag rode in the cart while Evans walked behind, holding the reins, and watching for trouble. It came!

After they had reached the main road, they had proceeded about five hundred feet and were directly opposite the Owens barn, set back from the road about two hundred feet, when a sudden fusillade rang out. Big Jim, stung by buckshot, plunged and hurled Evans off his feet. Volleys were fired from two other directions; the outlaws were caught in a three way crossfire. Evans managed to enter his cart, and they sped away. Young Smith leaned out of his window and listened to the rapid drumming of the big horse's hoofs until it droned away into nothingness. He did not know it then, but later his father was to acquire this steed and Leroy would drive it to Yosemite on his annual vacation in the summer of 1894. He re-named the horse "Sontag" and told the author that under the thick hide of the horse's thigh he could feel five buckshot, souvenirs of the gun-battle in which the sheriff testified[14] that sixty rounds had been fired. After this battle Evans gave Big Jim and the cart to some friends in the mountains who had befriended him. The horse, with his blazed face and four white stocking feet, was a dead give-away. It was safer for the men to walk.

The women and children left behind each time the outlaws had to flee lived in an agony of suspense until they could learn for sure that no one had been seriously hurt. The wear and tear of this continued nerve strain was cumulative, and eventually evidences of impending prostration and general debility would appear.

The number of men deputized at one time or another to hunt Evans and Sontag finally reached the amazing total of more than 3,000. The woods were so full of man-hunters at times that at least eleven deputies were seriously wounded by other officers. Men who went deer hunting in the mountains during those days were in danger of being shot by over-zealous posses. A few such scrapes led otherwise righteous citizens to lose all respect for the representatives of law and order and to express sympathy for the fugitives trying to escape from the clutches of such fumbling minions of authority. On one occasion two clerks, Clarence Foin and Henry Minor, employed by the B. T. Scott grocery store of Fresno, were captured on their way to Yosemite to spend their annual vacation. Unfortunately for these two young men, they were riding in a cart drawn by a chestnut horse. According to the reports current at that time, Evans and Sontag were travelling along mountain roads with a similar horse and cart. So the poor boys were surrounded by a belligerent posse and held in custody for hours by some of its members while others rushed to Fresno to collect the reward. When the angry, agitated, and disheveled clerks were finally released, it may be assumed that they hoped that Evans and Sontag would thenceforth fight with resolution and shoot straight and often.

Many such incidents, in addition to the antagonism then generally felt toward the railway monopoly, indicates why Will Smith could say truthfully:

"Chris Evans has numerous friends in the County (Tulare), and men have been heard to say on the streets of Visalia today that they admired his nerve and hoped he would escape all his pursuers. The Railroad and Wells, Fargo are as heartily detested by these men as Evans is admired. One thing is evident from what has occurred, and that is that the whole southern San Joaquin Valley contains a large number of sympathizers. The community is not to be counted on to help the officers or to convict the bandits under any circumstances."

In the meantime Vernon C. Wilson and his two Apache scouts, augmented by a posse of ten, were pressing hard on the trail of Evans and Sontag. On one visit to Visalia a friend came to the Evans home and warned the two outlaws that their return to the hills was blocked. Chris and John fooled the posse, and headed due west across the plains. At Traver they stopped to feed their horses at Harrison Peacock's livery-stable. The stable-hand was asleep on his cot in the tack-room and, in a rather semi-comatose condition, he accepted fifty cents for the barley. The next morning he was astounded to read the following note which had been left on an up-turned water-bucket beside his resting place:[15]

"We are sorry to have disturbed you at this time of night, but owing to the urgency of our business, and the necessity of our progress, we cannot help it. Signed: Evans and Sontag."

While the two outlaws were feeding their horses at Traver, their pursuers had made camp for the night six miles east of that place in the direction of Visalia. The two Apaches led the posse the next morning along the trail left by Evans and Sontag. This eventually took them to Dunlap and thence to Sampson's Flat where Evans had a gold claim.

It is not fair to say that all of the men who joined the various posses were actuated by mercenary motives. While some were tempted by the blood money, others were all unknowingly followers of St. Andrew. The latter was noted for his spirit of self-abnegation, and was content to bask in the reflected glory of men greater than himself. He liked to stand close to his big brother, St. Peter. Such men, on a much lower scale, resembled Paul Revere, the little man who felt flattered when asked to run errands for the "big boys" during the American Revolution. The reader has known no doubt men of retarded development, physically mature but mentally adolescent, whose greatest conception of sublunary felicity is the privilege of calling a supervisor, a sheriff, or even a Congressman by his first name. The author knew a pompous individual who often boasted that "me and the sheriff is pals" in a tone which clearly indicated that this sacred relationship was helping Heaven's high cause. Such men existed in the days of Evans and Sontag. They led dull and drab lives, suffered from inferiority complexes, and craved attention. So they strutted behind the officers like little boys, and when the outlaws shot too close for comfort they, like little boys, ran home. They never seriously threatened Evans and Sontag, although they had a certain nuisance value.

A third class of men who joined the posses were those truly interested in maintaining law and order. One of these was typified by William Elam, who was selected by Vernon C. Wilson because of his size, intelligence, and courage. Elam admired Wilson and told the author that the marshal was a remarkably handsome man, beautifully proportioned, well-educated, and devoid of all fear. But Elam did not approve of Wilson's methods. The former was personally acquainted with both Evans and Sontag, and knew that they travelled only at night. Yet Wilson insisted on following the trail in the daytime, when the outlaws remained in hiding. Elam predicted that this would lead to disaster, as it did, and when he advised caution, another officer snorted:

"Yes, caution is needed, far more than advice!"

Elam proposed that various members of the posse be stationed during the night along the trails at strategic points. Sooner or later Evans and Sontag would pass that way and could then be liquidated without any harm coming to the posse. But Wilson thought he knew best. Shortly thereafter Elam and some other members of the posse resigned. No money was forthcoming, and the men could not afford to pay their own expenses. Neither Wilson nor Burke were at fault, and were not blamed. The agencies employing the posse were negligent.[16]

When George Washington, familar with the enemy and the terrain, told General Braddock how to fight the French and Indians, he was snubbed and his plan rejected. Wilson decided to ignore the advice of the men who knew Evans and Sontag, and shortly thereafter met Braddock's tragic fate.

The posse which Wilson led into the hills consisted of thirteen men, an unlucky number as later events proved. Three men were interviewed during the next few days in the mountains. Ed Mainwaring, a young Englishman, was told by Wilson that Evans and Sontag would be shot on sight; they would be given no chance to surrender. Mainwaring reported this to Evans. Clarke Moore, a personal friend of Evans, was intercepted at the Young cabin, and Wilson told him profanely:

"I am not going to kill you to-day, but I hope that when I find Evans you are with him, so that I can kill you both."[17]

John Coffee, also a friend of Evans and a native mountaineer, corroborated this threat. He testified later that the marshal had told him that he intended to shoot Evans first and ask questions later, and that he hoped to get Moore at the same time.

These statements were read into the court record later as evidence of the fact that it was no use for the outlaws to surrender; if they met the posse the only possible escape was to shoot; there was no alternative.

Moore also swore later that Warren Hill, representing certain interests, had offered him large sums of money, finally raising the bid to $50,000, if he would betray Evans and Sontag. The residents of the Sierra Nevada, most of them of Tennessee birth or descent, could not be bought. Generations of fighting revenue officers in their old mountain homes had bred in them a clannishness and a distrust of government men which stood Evans and Sontag in good stead now. They were used to feuds. And, then, Evans was a miner at Sampson's Flat and the owner of the Redwood Ranch; he was one of them. They felt that he belonged.

Evans and Sontag had disappeared in the vastness of the Sierra Nevada on August 5th, and the climate at that time is equalled only by the beauty of the mountain scenery. But by the middle of September the nights begin to get uncomfortably cold. Yet the men did not dare to build a fire as the hills were full of man-hunters. One morning, after having spent the night in a cold camp, they decided to visit Jim Young, who owned a cabin which he occupied only part time. However, he kept food and bedding there, and had told the outlaws it was at their disposal if and when they needed it. Young was present when they arrived and made them comfortable, but they looked askance at the presence of a big, husky nineteen-year-old boy named Sam B. Williams, destined in later years to be prominent as a rancher, civic leader, church deacon, and deputy sheriff of Fresno county. Noticing that Evans and Sontag were dubious about the stranger in their midst, Young assured them that Williams was to be trusted. The latter had just come out from Tennessee and Young, on one of his periodic visits to Fresno, had met the handsome young Southerner who was anxious to visit the Big Trees, especially the already famous General Grant. Since Williams was well recommended by mutual friends, Young had invited Sam to stop at his cabin on his way to the Sequoias. Most of Evans' friends in the mountains were from Tennessee; when he learned that Williams belonged to the same group and place, he lost all distrust of the young man. Williams shared a bed with Evans in the loft of Young's cabin for two nights and during that time the older man, finding a sympathetic listener, unburdened himself to a remarkable degree. According to Williams, Evans warned him that a life of crime did not pay, but that he had been ruined by the Southern Pacific and had tried to redress the balance by helping himself to some of the company's unjust earnings.

For two days the men loitered in the center of a sylvan wonderland. During the second day Evans went to his mine at Sampson's Flat accompanied by Jim Young, Clarke Moore, John Sontag, and Sam Williams. They returned to Young's cabin and slept peacefully there that night, all but Sontag who always took his blankets and disappeared in the night, presumably to serve as a look-out.

Jim Young's cabin stood in a small clearing. Directly in front of the door, about sixty yards away, some big pine trees had been felled and left lying. They formed a natural rampart. The cabin was small, twelve by fourteen feet, had one door, and one small window, the latter measuring two by two and one half feet. A ladder inside the cabin led to the loft. The only egress was through the door.

Young's nearest neighbor was a mountain home-steader, a young Englishman named Ed. Mainwaring. The latter stored some of his tools and other equipment in the larger Young's cabin, located about a half a mile from the Mainwaring shack. When the diminutive size of the former is considered, it may be assumed that Mainwaring's domicile was so small that he had to back out to turn around. The latter spent his time hunting, fishing, and caring for his little apple orchard. Although a native of "the tight little isle," he shared the point of view of the mountain people with respect to Evans and Sontag. In his old age he recalled what happened that hectic day:[18]

"On the morning of September 13, 1892, I was out in my orchard as usual. I saw Jim Young coming through the trees, and when he came up to me he said there were two men in his cabin who wanted some breakfast. He asked me if I would help them, since he was going down for supplies.

"Thinking nothing of it, I walked over to Young's cabin. Inside were Sontag and Evans. I greeted Evans casually. He asked me if I would mind helping him get some breakfast. Naturally, I said sure. You don't ask questions under those conditions.

"Meanwhile, Sontag, a great big fellow, was stand-ing at the window with a shotgun."

Mainwaring stated that he answered their questions

and told them what he knew of plans relating to their intended destruction. During the conversation Sontag, who had left his post by the window, busied himself frying ham and eggs and cooking coffee; Mainwaring peeled and sliced potatoes and fixed a batch of biscuits. Sam Williams set the table and served as general flunky. The young men were preparing an excellent breakfast, but no one was ever to eat it.

Evans, ever on the alert, glanced alternately at a newspaper of recent date and the trail.

Some miles away the posse had stopped at the Barton ranch, and Wilson profanely asked the housewife:[19]

"Have you seen *Christ* Evans?"

The mountain woman, like all other residents of the hills, was friendly to Evans and Sontag. She was nettled by the sneering question, and replied with asperity:

"Yes, I have, and when you see him, you will see Hell!"

There was more truth than profanity in her prophecy.

The Apaches lived up to their fame as excellent trackers. Casting about for a clue, they located the camp occupied by Evans and Sontag some nights before. Evans had discarded a pair of faded red suspenders, which Pelon spied and appropriated. From this camp it was easy to trail the two men to Young's cabin.

At the latter place everything was quiet and peaceful. The appetizing odor of a delicious breakfast pervaded the atmosphere. Mountain birds were singing in the trees. In the immediate vicinity could be heard the call of the mountain quail, and from a great distance came the faint drum-like roll of the pine grouse cock. But trouble was approaching in the form of a posse of thirteen, which included Vernon C. Wilson; Warren Hill of Fresno and Alfred Witty of Visalia, both deputy-sheriffs; Will Smith and the handsome half-breed, "Bad-Man" Frank Burke, detectives; and Pelon and Cameño Dulce, the Apache scouts. The latter had replaced Jericho, who had returned to Arizona.

Suddenly Evans saw several men clambering over the log barricade in front of the cabin. Behind them were other men on horseback. Evans snapped:

"John, we are trapped! Here comes the posse."

Evans liked Mainwaring and did not want him to get hurt or involved; neither did he want him to reveal the presence of John and himself. So he sternly told the young Englishman to take a bucket and stroll down toward the spring two hundred yards away. This would serve a double purpose; it would take Mainwaring out of harm's way, and it would lull the posse into thinking Mainwaring was alone in the cabin and merely going about his household duties. It worked. Evans admonished the restive young man further:

"If you turn your head to warn the posse, or start to run to show them we are here, I'll drill you right between the shoulder blades."

The nervous young man, trying to reconcile his instructions with the fear of impending doom, executed a fantastic cake-walk to the spring, and the approaching posse, seeing nothing amiss and sniffing breakfast from afar, assumed the cabin to be unoccupied.

Sam Williams, who had gone outside to dump some garbage, entered at this pregnant moment and Evans hissed:

"Get out, Sam, there is going to be a lot of Hell raised here in a few moments."

Williams had come West for excitement and adventure, and this seemed to be it. So he countered by saying:

"Well, I'd like to see a little Hell; it might as well come now as later."

Evans was in no mood for trifling and made the youngster scram. Sam went outside without attracting undue attention and crouched behind some bushes growing on an elevation directly in back of the cabin where he was to have a ringside seat overlooking the battle of Young's cabin, now about to begin.

The two men inside the cabin waited impassively. Suddenly John blurted out:

"Good God, Chris, one of these men is Andy McGinnis!"

Why did the presence of Andrew McGinnis with the posse arouse undue excitement? Because the latter was supposedly one of Evans' best friends. After the fire at Modesto, Evans had assigned to Andrew McGinnis the task[20] of collecting various and sundry bills owed to the livery-stable by persons in and around Modesto. Evans had permitted McGinnis to keep most of the money. Later Andy had removed to San Francisco. Perhaps the $10,000 offered for Evans and Sontag, dead or alive, had seemed enticing to the bill-collector. There seems to be no other explanation for his presence with the posse. He had gone from San Francisco to Fresno, but had failed to hire a mountain guide. Finally he had decided to join Hill's posse.

Evans had no time just then to indulge in idle speculations concerning the presence of McGinnis with the attacking force. To John's astounded ejaculation, he snorted:

"Yes, it is. And the other man is the one Eva wrote about. I'll get the marshal from this window; you go to the door and when I fire, you yank it open and take McGinnis."

When Wilson, followed by Andy, was only ten feet from the door and thinking only of breakfast, Evans drove his gun barrel through the window pane, and Wilson received, instead of ham and eggs, a double-barreled load of buckshot in his belly. A split second later Sontag hurled open the door, and blasted away at McGinnis, who went down in a heap. The Apaches jumped behind a flat rock, about sixty yards away, and Frank Burke, who had turned aside to investigate a melon patch, took a head-long dive behind a prone pine log. The Indians remained quiet for some minutes, but Burke immediately tried to snipe at the two outlaws now in front of Young's cabin. Witty, a brother of the man shot by Chris at Visalia, was wounded by Evans. The latter also fired at Warren Hill, but missed him and killed his horse. Hill mounted one of the spare horses, and led the mad retreat of the posse, which blazed a new trail out of the mountains never before travelled by mortal man. Some miles away Hill cut across the backyard of a mountain rancher's home, and knocked down a broom left standing beside a bush. The young daughter of the house ran out, picked up the broom, and shouted sarcastically:

"Hey, come back here. You dropped your gun."

While ten of the posse were executing a strategic retreat, Evans and Sontag kept a close watch on the rock hiding the two Indians, and the log protecting Burke. The Apaches, lying face down behind their flat rock, occasionally raised their rifles over their heads and fired without looking. Their aim, like their hopes, was high and most of their bullets passed over the roof of the cabin and landed among the bushes where Sam Williams was hiding. In later years Williams could be facetious about his experiences that day, but at the time it did not appear so funny; he was in a hot spot. Burke was proving a doughty antagonist and shooting too close for comfort. Therefore Evans kept clipping away at Burke's log, but the detective was too old a hand at this game to expose himself needlessly.

Suddenly McGinnis regained consciousness, and tried to sit up. Evans went over to his former friend and McGinnis said:

"Don't kill me, Chris, I'm hard hit. I'm out of it."

"I ought to kill you, you dirty dog, but if your life is worth anything to you, keep it."

Just then Burke, seeing Evans' attention distracted by McGinnis, fired hurriedly and the bullet went through Sontag's arm. Evans quickly drove Burke back to cover, and turned to help John. A blinding explosion suddenly caused the world to turn black for Evans. A bullet had clipped his skull, tearing off the edge of his eye-brow. Chris staggered for a moment, but regained his equilibrium sufficiently to turn around, and saw McGinnis raising himself on an elbow, trying to fire again. Evans' rifle roared, and McGinnis was out of this world.

Leaving Burke and the two Indians back of their barricades, Evans assisted John into the woods toward safety. Williams followed them[21] to a secluded spot where they were screened by trees. He had come to the mountains on a saddle horse followed by a pack-mule; the latter had cost him ten dollars. This hybrid beast carried an assorted supply of groceries, utensils, and medicines. Included in this pack was a big bottle of peroxide which was then considered a valuable anti-septic. Williams sharpened a stick, used it to probe the wound, and poured peroxide into it which foamed and fizzed. Then he donated his silk handkerchief and Evans and he inserted it through the wound and made a tourniquet. This crude first-aid treatment of the period had to suffice.

Evans then picked up the two rifles and the two shotguns and, with the feverish and wounded man following him, led the way over twelve miles of rough mountain trails to the Downing ranch. Here they sought a haven of rest. It was not denied. The mountaineers never failed them. Jane Downing fed them, and put John to bed where she nursed him for ten days. At the end of that time, he was well enough to fight or flee as the case might be.

After Evans and Sontag had disappeared down the trail, Sam Williams decided he was no longer needed at Young's cabin. The two dead men lying in front of the door, deserted even by their friends, were beyond all earthly help; the posse was in full retreat miles away; and Sam had come to the mountains to see the Big Trees. The excitement was over, so he saddled his horse, packed his mule, and set out for the area later known as Grant's Park. The majesty of the Sequoia gigantea exceeded his wildest dreams, but he was grieved to see that the lumber firm of Smith & Moore was then engaged in destroying these ancient and beautiful redwoods. Today many huge stumps remain as mute testimony of the vandalism of that period, and serve as favorite platforms for tourists who like to be photographed on the remains of these forest giants. Fortunately lovers of nature were able to shout "Woodsman, spare that tree" emphatically enough so that some were to be saved as an inspiration for future generations.

Since no one reported the presence of Williams at the battle of Young's cabin, and because he himself made no comment at the time, Sam was never interrogated or asked to testify in court. Evans, after his release from Folsom, was to verify Williams' statements of what had happened that day.

After the outlaws had departed and things had

quieted down, Mainwaring approached the cabin from the spring where he had been lying, and said he "yelled until the remaining members of the posse, including the two Indian trackers, came out of the brush. They were pretty badly shaken up, so we got ready to take the dead men back to Visalia. I placed their bodies over their horses, threw the diamond hitch over them, and we started for Visalia."[22]

Before they left Young's cabin, Mainwaring smelled scorched food. He went into the cabin and threw the completely ruined breakfast into the stove.

While all the foregoing happenings were engrossing the attention of courageous men at Young's cabin, the fleeing posse had reached the stage-station on Mill Creek. The men bolted for Bill Traywick's saloon and began to gulp whiskey to soothe their jangled nerves. Morrell quoted one deputy, a former Texas ranger, as follows:[23]

"Them there fellers are sho some fighters. I ben in this heah business of runnin' down border cattle rustlers and outlaws and thot I'd been in some fighting, but this heah scrap today sho has got my goat. And them railroad detective fellers told us we would have a picnic, and that your outlaws were cowards and yellow and wouldn't fight. Somebody's put a big joke on me sho, and that leader of your outlaws he's some shucks. He's twenty Davy Crockett's rolled into one. I never see'd such shootin' in my life. I say, mister barkeep, gimme one more jolt of your grog, and it's me for the Mexican border."

Shortly after the fight at Young's cabin, Evans was

reading the newspaper at the Downing home. He always tried to keep up with current events, especially as they pertained to him. In this paper he learned about the fate of the Dalton brothers.

A few minutes before nine o'clock in the morning of October 5, 1892, five men on blooded horses rode slowly into Coffeyville, Kansas. They passed some negro workers who, with picks and shovels, were tearing up a portion of Union Street. On the sidewalk were little children on their way to school. Bob Dalton had planned to use the hitching rack beside the Opera House, but due to the street repair work under way, this had been taken down. So he had to re-arrange his plans in this respect. He also had to select another street for a quick get-away, as the horses would be liable to stumble over the debris scattered up and down Union Street. When the bandits slowed down to take stock of the situation, one of the negro workmen, leaning on a shovel, said:[24]

"Them cowboys has got plenty weapons."

To which another replied:

"Yah, they been down in the Territory. Lots of folks been down there shooting wild turkeys."

Bob sat his horse quietly while he cogitated. Then he soliloquized:

"We lay our plans carefully. Everything forseeable is taken care of. Then these monkeys have to tear up Union Street just when we need it most. It's a mell of a hess."

Having thus relieved himself concerning the uncooperative attitude of the denizens of Coffeyville,

Bob suddenly wheeled his horse, and the others followed him into the alley back of a blacksmith shop where there was another hitching rack. The five men dismounted and marched on foot to their rendezvous with fate. Bob and Emmett walked in front; Grattan, Powers, and Broadwell behind. When they reached the Condon Bank, the last three men walked in and ordered the four men present in the bank to hold up their hands. Charley Gump, a drayman, was sitting on his wagon directly in front of his bank. He saw the stick-up through the window, jumped off his dray, and yelled: "The Daltons are here."

Bob and Emmett had not yet reached the First National Bank. When Bob heard Gump's warning shout, he fired to check the alarm and hit Gump in the hand. But Charley kept on running and shouting. In the meantime, Powers and Broadwell had raked up $1,500 from the counters in the Condon Bank, and Grat had ordered Charles Ball, the cashier, to open the doors to the vault. The latter had a sickly body, but there was nothing wrong with his nerves; he told Grat coolly:

"It's a time lock. It doesn't open until 9:45."

It was then 9:42, and Grattan hesitated. This was to prove fatal. He decided to wait three minutes. During this time the posse was to form which destroyed the Dalton gang. Ball was bluffing; he wanted to save the $18,000 in the vault. He did, too. If Grat had only known it, the door was unlocked and all he needed to do was to open it. No doubt of it, Ball was the hero that day.

Over at the First National Bank, Emmett and Bob were having better luck. Seven men, including one deputy-sheriff, were present when they entered. The cashier emptied the contents of his vault into a canvas sack thoughtfully provided by Bob. By that time the bullets were raining in the general direction of the front door of the bank, so the two brothers went out the back way and reached their horses without too much trouble. They waited and fretted a few minutes because the other three men did not appear. When the shooting began to assume undue proportions, they rushed to the rescue. When it was over, four bandits had been killed: Grat and Bob Dalton, Bill Powers, and Dick Broadwell, and four citizens of Coffeyville: Lucius Baldwin, a hardware clerk; Charles Connelly, the city marshal; and two business partners, George Cubine and Charles Brown, who operated a store specializing in fancy foot-wear much in demand by cowboys. They were former friends of the Daltons, and had sold them the expensive, high-heeled boots they were wearing that day. Four men had been wounded: Thomas Ayres, cashier of the First National; T. A. Reynolds, a clerk; Charles Gump, the drayman; and Emmett Dalton.

According to a popular legend, Chris Evans' brother Tom was with the Daltons that day. It was said that he was the unknown man killed at Coffeyville. This is nonsense. Every man killed in that fight was identified. Emmett Dalton, almost fatally wounded, and later a fine citizen of California, can surely be considered an authority in the matter. His testimony should settle that question once and for all:[25]

"The Dalton gang comprised the following men: Bob, Grat, and Emmett Dalton, George Newcomb, Charley Bryant, Bill Powers, Charley Pierce, Dick Broadwell, William McElhanie, and Bill Doolin. These ten men are absolutely the only ones ever connected in any way with our lawless enterprises."

Many commentators found the entire Evans and Sontag affair amusing. One of them wrote at this time:[26]

"There is a rumor that Evans and Sontag have crossed the continent and are somewhere in Europe. It may be that they have decided to spend the winter in Italy. It would be easy for them to escape any time they wanted to. There is nothing to hinder them."

News of the two big battles at Young's cabin and Coffeyville, fought within three weeks of each other, soon spread far and wide throughout the nation. They made the headlines. In the first battle, the bandits won; in the second, they lost. The hastily formed posse at Coffeyville had performed magnificently against five notorious outlaws; the posse members who had ingloriously run away from Young's cabin had a hard time explaining their conduct. The fact remained that two cornered men had whipped thirteen.

A few days after the fight, Eva Evans went shopping in Visalia. She met Pelon and Cameño Dulce, the Indian trackers, on the sidewalk. They took no apparent notice of her, although one may be sure that they were not unaware of her presence. What attracted her attention and aroused her amusement were the faded and discarded suspenders of her father, not worn over the shoulders as is customary, but draped down over the fat buttocks of Pelon. He of the red galluses told McKeown later in the day:

"Injuns go home. Evans and Strong heap brave men. No fight um!"

What he had to say about the other members of the posse was less complimentary.

One old plainsman, an expert with both rifle and Colt, refused to join any of the posses, and was frankly scornful of most of the man-hunters. He bluntly put it in this way:

"I ain't got a bit of use for no part of Chris Evans. He shoots too entirely much where he is aiming at!"

The next time Eva saw her father she asked him accusingly why he had not pinned her note to Wilson's breast. He answered:[27]

"There were several reasons why I did not do so. I did not know how badly John was hurt; one of them (Burke) was still sniping at me from behind a log; and last, but not least, I did not want the whole world to know what a blood-thirsty little devil you are."

But when he said it he smiled fondly at his daughter, and she knew that he was not displeased with her.

CHAPTER 10

TANGLED TESTIMONIES

WHILE Chris Evans and John Sontag were moving in and out among the beautiful hills like characters out of a story-book, George Sontag was having a bad time. It was his reckless talk during the early morning hours of August 4th which at last had cast suspicion on the two Sontags and Evans. George, after considerable imbibing the next day, was in that woozy condition known in modern speech as "tight." He was sprawled out in a chair at the Evans home, and the small children were feeding him grapes. Many different stories have been told how and when George Contant, alias Sontag, was apprehended by the officers. George Witty's testimony during the trial should settle the matter. W. D. Tupper, the district attorney, cross-examined the deputy:[1]

"Anybody go down to the house with you?"

"Yes, sir."

"Who?"

"Will Smith."

"Where was he when you went into the (Evans') house?"

"He stayed out in the buggy."

"You and he went in the buggy, did you?"

"Yes, sir."

"Anybody come back from the house with you?"

"Mr. Sontag."

"You mean the defendant in this case?" George's indictment referred to him as Contant, his true name.

"Yes, sir."

"Did you have any conversation with this defendant at that time?"

"I told him that I understood that he was on the train that was held up at Collis. I told him we would like to interview him down at the sheriff's office."

"Well, what did he say?"

"Well, he stood there for a moment, and then he said, 'All right, I will go.'"

"Did he say anything else besides that?"

"No, I think that is about all he said, I don't remember."

"He went with you and Mr. Smith to the sheriff's office, did he?"

"He and I walked out to the buggy and got into the buggy with Mr. Smith, and went down, yes, sir."

John Sontag was present when the two officers called for George, but did nothing by word or look to dissuade George from leaving the house in the custody of Witty.

Thereafter George had nothing but trouble. Later during the same afternoon, Smith and Witty returned to the Evans home and asked for John Sontag and were shot. In the evening Oscar Beaver was killed. George's statements to the officers that afternoon and evening were incoherent due to his drinking. He was held in jail that night. When he faced the officers for questioning the next day, it may be assumed that the actions the previous day of his brother and friend had not helped his case. It was a hectic day for George. He was interviewed several times and those present at various sessions were: Sheriffs Kay of Visalia and Cunningham of Stockton; William E. Dickey, John Thacker, and James B. Hume, detectives; and T. A. Elliott and A. H. Murray, court reporters. At the conclusion of the last meeting, Sheriff Cunningham told George:[2]

"Of course, we ask you this, for we suspicion you of this train robbery, to be plain with you. Of course, any person might be mistaken, and we thought we would ask you this, to state the case. So, we will have to take you to Fresno on a charge of train robbery. Of course, these things are unpleasant, but when these things occur, the officers of the law must make an effort to protect people and property. We will try and see that you are used like a gentleman."

To which George replied magnanimously:[3]

"If you find me guilty of train robbery, you hang me up."

George was placed in durance vile at Visalia. During the night of August 12th he did the hardest work of his life. With a file and chisel he tried to cut his way out of jail, but the time was too short for the stint of work he had assigned himself. Morning found George exhausted on his cot and a gaping hole in the ceiling. The officers decided they had better take him to Fresno. Besides, George was a comparative stranger in Visalia and had very few friends there. Talk of lynching him was heard among the riff-raff, and the officers were worried.

Therefore, at the request of the Tulare county officials, two Fresno officers, Sheriff John M. Hensley and Constable Ed. Vogelsang, went to Visalia on August[4] 17th, and took George to Fresno. A mob was waiting for George at the Fresno depot, and he was taken off the train at the edge of town, smuggled through some box-cars on a siding, and whisked off to jail while the deputies who had met the party rode beside him with drawn guns. His bail was fixed at $20,000.

George was brought to trial shortly before the fight at Young's cabin. A touch of comedy enlivened his first day in court. One of George's attorneys asked for a continuance on the grounds that Chris Evans and John Sontag, material witnesses for the defense,[5] could not be found and subpoenaed. Laughter and loud applause! Motion overruled.

It was a long and interesting trial. The transcript of *The People of the State of California vs. George C. Contant, Robbery,* consisted of 798 double-spaced typewritten pages of long foolscap. Forty-two witnesses were called, nine for George and the others for The People. Judge S. A. Holmes presided, and the district attorney, W. D. Tupper, was assisted by Reel B. Terry. The attorneys for the defense were the two law firms; Sayle & Coldwell and Goucher, Jacobs & Jones. One wonders where George secured the money to engage five first-class lawyers.

Reel B. Terry opened the case for the prosecution. He was a nephew of the famous Judge David S. Terry, at one time a member of the California State Supreme Court. The latter had been a stormy petrel in California politics. He narrowly escaped hanging at the hands of the Vigilantes at San Francisco, he killed United States Senator David C. Broderick in a duel, and later threatened to shoot Justice Stephen Field, a member of the United States Supreme Court, at his earliest opportunity. One day Terry and his wife entered a railway restaurant at Lathrop and discovered that Field was seated at an adjacent table. When Terry approached the jurist in a truculent manner and slapped his face, he was shot and killed by Field's bodyguard, David S. Neagle. There were he-men in California in those days. The younger Terry was as brilliant, merciless, and dramatic as his famous uncle. In handling a jury he was as skillful as two lawyers of more recent years; the historic Earl Rogers and the fictitious Perry Mason, both of Los Angeles.

The following is an attempt to summarize in a few pages all that was brought forth on that occasion. Any reader who objects to this review is welcome to study the 798-page transcript and write his own condensation. Here goes:

George was an interior decorator, paper-hanger, and house painter. Adolf Hitler's early vocation comes to mind. In Minnesota the cold winters prevented him from working full time, and his pocket-book suffered. John wrote him a letter offering him work in the mine at Sampson's Flat. George arrived in California in December, 1891. He suffered from eye-trouble, went to San Francisco for treatment, heard that his wife had given birth to a son, and returned to Minnesota. The next summer he received another invitation from John to work for Chris and him, and again George came to California. At Lathrop he sent a letter to Visalia informing John that he would stop off at Fresno. A day after his arrival John appeared there with a team and buggy and took George's trunk to Visalia and stored it in Evans' barn. It was arranged for George to take the train to Reedley, where he could make connections with the star-route mail-carrier and ride with him to Dunlap.

George loitered in Fresno, did some drinking, and finally decided to visit a girl-friend at Visalia. He followed his biological urge, went to Visalia, met the girl, guzzled considerably, and by train-time he was inebriated. While waiting at the railway junction at Goshen, he and a casual acquaintance had a few toasts. George admitted that when he boarded the train for Fresno there had been too many "bottoms up," and he was drunk. He fell asleep, and remained oblivious to his surroundings while the train sped through Fresno. He was in a slightly comatose condition when the brakeman shook him and put him off the train at Mendota. He spent the next day fishing in the San Joaquin River with two trainmen, who later identified him as the man who was held in the Fresno jail.

He took the next train back to Fresno and arrived there at midnight. George learned the next morning that the mail-carrier from Reedley did not make the trip to Dunlap more than twice a week. George disliked the idea of wasting time in the sleepy little village of Reedley, so he idled away his time in Fresno, mostly in the company of the Visalia girl, who had become a resident of Fresno for the time being. Coldwell asked George about her:

"Did you tell her where you were going?"[6]

"Yes, sir."

"What did you tell her?"

"I told her I was going up to the mountains, that there was some mining property up there, that I wanted to look at, and I told her that I expected to be back in a short time, and I says, 'Do you intend to stay here?' She says, 'Well, I do.' 'Well,' I says, 'If you are here, if I come down, where will I meet you?' 'Well,' she says, 'You can find me in the park most any night'."

This witness, who gave her name as Mrs. Ida Ross, was cross-examined by Tupper:[7]

"Where do you live, anyway?"

"Where do I live?"

"Yes, sir." (to a lady!)

"Well, I did live in Fresno, my folks live in Visalia."

"Well, didn't you live at Sequoia Mills?"

"Well, I was up there a little while."

"How long?"

"Well, I was up there about two weeks."

"What was your business up there?"

"Well, I was working."

"For whom?"

No answer!

"Well, that is all."

On July 23, 1892, George took the train to Reedley, and from there he rode with James Dick, the mail carrier, the twenty-eight miles to Dunlap. He stayed with John Howell that night, and the next day Chris Evans came down from the mine to meet him. The two men walked back the eight miles to Sampson's Flat where George stayed until August 1st.

James Young testified[8] that on that date Chris Evans, George Sontag, an unnamed young boy, and he set out for Visalia. A black mare, owned by Clarke Moore and used in work connected with the mine, needed to be re-shod. Some legal complications had also arisen over the mine ownership, and Evans found it necessary to go to Fresno. James Young and the boy rode their own horses; Chris and George took turns riding the black mare. One man would ride a few miles, dismount, tie the horse, and set out on foot. At Dickey's store, ten miles north of Visalia and eight miles east of Traver, Evans left the other men and set out on foot for the Davis ranch, two and a half miles northeast of Traver.

Before the men parted Chris warned George not to tell Molly he was in the valley.[9] George rode the black mare to the home of Mrs. Byrd, where his brother rented a room. George and John slept together that night. John seemed astonished when George told him Chris was in the neighborhood. He said:

"I have rented a team from Frank I. Bequette. Tomorrow I was going up there to get you."[10]

The next morning he went after the team and told George he would find Evans; he thought he knew where the latter had gone. He also told George to remain in Visalia until Chris and he returned. George promised. He rode with John into the main part of Visalia, and got off about five blocks from the railroad station. John drove off toward the Sierra Nevada. George was lonesome, and took the train for Fresno in hopes of finding his girl-friend. He met John on the street, and the older brother asked angrily:

"Kid, what the hell are you doing here?"[11]

George promised to return to Visalia on the evening train, and went to the depot and bought a ticket. Then he made the rounds of several saloons, and missed his train. He waited for the midnight flyer which was three hours late. It had been robbed and partially crippled at Collis. During the excitement George mingled with the crowd and learned what had happened. On the train he talked to L. H. Glazier, a brakeman, whose home was at Bakersfield. The latter had picked up several souvenirs from the damaged express coach, and gave George a screw with a broken head.

On this particular morning the passenger train, due to the little difficulty at Collis, arrived at Goshen three hours behind schedule. At this junction George transferred to the little "milk train" which connected the county seat with the Southern Pacific mainline, and when he finally arrived at Visalia it was five o'clock in the morning. The various inns and taverns in the town sent hacks to the station to pick up passengers, and in one of these George rode to the Palace Hotel where he rented a room. George told the hack driver,

Edward Bradley,[12] that the train from San Francisco
had been robbed, that he had been a passenger on it,
and gave a detailed account of what had happened.
He showed his souvenir and said he had personally
picked it up at Collis.

The main entrance to the Palace Hotel was by way
of the barroom, which was open twenty-four hours
a day. George had been up all night, and was sleepy
and ready for bed, but decided that first he would have
an early morning night-cap, if there is such a thing.
Louis Ness,[13] the bartender at the Palace Hotel, was
regaled with the same story George had previously
related to Bradley.

At one time George had rented a room at the home
of S. B. Noel, a carpenter. George liked to sleep late
in the morning, and the Noel children insisted on
playing marbles in front of his bedroom door. For
two reasons this was very annoying to George. First,
he was unable to sleep. Second, since he was forced
to lie awake, he kept brooding over the fact that the
rolling marbles reminded him of the erratic dice which
had refused to respond to his profane blandishments
in the saloon game during the early hours of the same
morning. So George had transferred his sleeping
quarters to the Palace Hotel, where there were no
obstreperous children. Although George disliked the
Noel youngsters, he had remained on good terms with
their father and therefore greeted Mr. Noel cordially
when the latter, up bright and early and ready for
work, stepped into the bar for his morning "pick-up."

George described for his former landlord his alleged experiences as a passenger on the train which had been robbed during the night.[14]

The detectives heard about the boastful yarns George was spinning, and quickly established the fact that George had not been a passenger from San Francisco. However, they believed he might have helped rob the train, and could then have possibly, during the excitement, boarded it and ridden into Fresno as a passenger. He could then have gotten off there and mingled with the highly agitated crowd without attracting undue attention. Since he had bought a ticket for Visalia earlier in the day, it would have been easy for him to again board the train and approach Glazier, whom he had met while fishing at Mendota. All this should have provided George with a fine alibi, but when he was finally brought to trial it was at this point that he was to make a poor impression on the jury. He was to tell the court three stories. He had taken the train at San Francisco; he had taken the train at Fresno; he was finally to say that he had done neither.

Now let us go back to Chris Evans and follow his peregrinations after he had reached the valley floor and subsequent to his separation from George. The first night Chris had spent at the Davis ranch, about two and a half miles northeast of Traver. Where he had gone the next day no one knows, but that evening he had appeared at the Pease ranch, then operated by James M. Leslie. Evans had slept there that night. Coldwell, during the trial of George Sontag, was to cross-examine Leslie about this particular visit:[15]

"Did Chris Evans transact any business with you at your house?"

"He did."

"What was it?"

"He spoke about some stretchers, fifth-chains, that he had there; said he might call and take them away, but if he didn't he would let me know, and asked me if I would be so kind as to take them up to the depot (Selma), and ship them to Visalia."

Evans left the Pease ranch the next morning about 10 o'clock, and went to see his lawyer, N. C. Coldwell, about his mining claim in the mountains. Thereafter no one saw him who could identify him until he appeared at his home in Visalia about 8 o'clock the next morning.

Soon after the trial had commenced it became apparent that Chris Evans and John Sontag were being tried *in absentia*. This led Coldwell for the defence to protest:[16]

"If the court pleases, this is not a hearing of any case against John Sontag and Chris Evans. Virtually all the so-called evidence has been against those two men, and not against my client. Nothing has been offered to show George Contant had any connection whatever with this robbery."

Coldwell was overruled. The first witness called was Alfred Phipps, the engineer of the train robbed at Collis. His testimony was the most important of all the witnesses arrayed against George if quantity is an index. In the transcript 167 pages were collected from him. He was asked to identify George as the short man in his cab that night. Coldwell and Tupper wrangled for some time and finally Phipps was permitted to go on:

"You asked me if I identify that man. I say no, gentlemen, but I say that those clothes and that man's appearance, more particularly that hat, compares with the description of the man that stood on my engine that night."[17]

Phipps, during his testimony, went off on a tangent into an interesting discussion of the relative merits of Carbon Hill vs. English coal. He was stopped. He had seen George when he went fishing near Mendota, and the man he was shown in jail was the same person. But he refused to swear that the man in the cab was George. He further stated that the short man at the robbery spoke with an Irish-Canadian accent. This led Coldwell to ask:[18]

"Do you know Christopher Evans?"

"No, sir."

"Never saw him at all?"

"Never saw him that I know of."

"Did you ever hear that Chris Evans was a Canadian, of Irish descent?"

"Only what I have heard about his life in the papers since this train robbery occurred."

The second witness was Charles E. Babb, a brakeman, who was dead-heading down the line[19] from Mendota to Fresno. He was riding in the cab at the time of the hold-up. Roberts, the express messenger, distinctly 4-F as a result of the explosion, was nevertheless drafted with Lewis, the fireman, and Babb, to carry the money-bags to the waiting buggy. They did not see the horses which were tied behind the Rolinda schoolhouse. Babb told Eva Evans during the trial that the short man did not speak with an Irish accent and did not have a beard. She felt that this eliminated her father, but it could have been George.

John P. Jackson, a sub-treasurer of the United States at San Francisco, presented a receipt showing that Wells, Fargo had accepted $500 in silver coins destined for the Bank of Arizona at Prescott. This bag had been stolen and not recovered.[20]

The express messenger, George D. Roberts, a prominent citizen of Los Angeles and at that time a member of its Board of Education, was the fourth witness for the prosecution. He was asked to tell what happened at Collis.[21]

"I think the two doors went off almost together, what we call the front door and the back door on the side of the car, and then the third one came inside, right at my foot, right inside, and blew me and the stool and everything else right up in the air, blew the whole side of the car out."

After considerable cross-examining, he continued:

"They waited a few minutes, and then commenced throwing more bombs in, put the fireman up in front of this hole through the door, pushed the fireman up in front of him, and threw the bombs over his shoulder in that manner; take him back and throw another, and kept talking out there."

He told the court that the language used by the robbers was foul and filthy; it nauseated him. He re-

fused to quote it verbatim, and was visibly embarrassed when the court ruled that, regardless of the
presence of ladies, he would be required to do just that.
It was pretty bad.

Roberts stated that his experiences that night had
led to evil physical results:[22]

"The effects was that my bowels were paralyzed and
that I was subject to have them—everything taken
from me with an instrument for about 25 to 6 days afterwards. I am still suffering from the effects of it, and
from nervous prostration."

Edward Pollitz, a San Francisco broker, testified
that his firm had sent through Wells, Fargo a shipment of 1,700 pieces of South American coins destined for the Fourth National Bank of New York
City, from whence they were to be shipped to South
America. This money was packed in two bags, which
had been dug up in Chris Evans' backyard, and which
Pollitz identified in court. The value of the 1,700
coins was $1,020 in United States money.[23]

William Hickey, a detective, told the court that he
went to the Evans home with an order to search for
George Contant's trunk. He found it in the barn,[24]
and between it and the wall he discovered a piece
of cloth, which he presented as one of the exhibits.
This material matched exactly that of the mask which
Hickey and Sheriff Hensley had picked up near the
scene of the robbery. The trunk was taken to the
sheriff's office and opened in the presence of John
Thacker, another detective. From it were taken the
coat, trousers, and hat which were identified by Phipps

as those worn by the short man at the hold-up. The
value of Hickey's exhibits was weakened by the fact
that no neutral observers had been present when they
were discovered.

Molly and Eva Evans were placed on the stand by
Coldwell and cross-examined by Tupper. They denied absolutely any knowledge of the contents of
George's trunk.[25] They also denied emphatically that
they had at any time either seen or owned any cloth
similar to that produced as an exhibit by Hickey.

The quality of the horses involved during the hold-
up came up for consideration. In the last analysis the
entire case of the prosecution rested on the speed and
bottom of the Bequette team Could it have travelled
as fast and far as Tupper and Terry contended that
it had? Terry, in his opening speech for the prosecution, stated:[26]

"Upon Tuesday morning, in accordance with and
pursuant to agreement, which he made with Mr. Bequette for the hiring of this team and horses, Mr. John
Sontag went to the stable of Bequette and got a team,
and a large buggy, large enough to carry three people.
We will show that that was more than an ordinary
team; it was an extraordinarily good team; I will show
you by the owner of it that he has frequently driven
it 13 miles an hour. I will show you that it was a very
good team. That Mr. John Sontag, after getting that
team upon the morning of Tuesday the 2nd of August,
at the stable of Bequette, rode around to Christopher
Evans's house, and there got into the buggy Mr.
George Contant. I will show you that about three

o'clock in the afternoon of the 2nd day of August, Mr. John Sontag put that team up in this town, at the stable of Armstrong Bros. I will show you, gentlemen of the jury, that upon the evening of the 2nd of August, Mr. John Sontag registered at a lodging house. I will show you that by the testimony of a man who knew him and who saw him put his signature upon that book."

The lawyers for the prosecution presented the following synopsis of John Sontag's meanderings:

He drove the Bequette horses from Visalia to Fresno on August 2nd. The weather is very hot during that time in the San Joaquin and the horses, even by the most direct route of that period, would have covered fifty miles. Sontag placed them in John Armstrong's stable about 3 o'clock in the afternoon. They were curried, fed, and watered, and remained quietly in the stable the rest of that day and all of August 3rd. In the evening Sontag asked Armstrong to grease his buggy and to give the horses an extra good feed of grain as he had a long drive to make that night. He took the team out at 7:45 and drove away toward the west side of Fresno. It was the contention of the prosecution that he drove to Collis by way of the Rolinda schoolhouse, and back to Fresno, and thence to Visalia by a round-about way, since he approached it from a road to the east. Hence the team had travelled ninety miles between 8 o'clock in the evening of August 3rd and 8 o'clock in the morning of August 4th. Could horses, even the best, have gone that far in twelve hours? The lawyers badgered each other about it. Finally the owner of the horses, Frank I. Bequette, was called, Tupper for the People, cross-examining:[27]

"Well, what did he (John Sontag) say?"

"He said he wanted a good stout buggy and spoke for a certain team I had, a bay team."

"Well, what character of team is that for endurance and hard driving?"

"Good horses, good team."

"How fast can those horses be driven to the mile, or by the hour, hitched to the kind of buggy that they were hitched to?"

"Well, I have driven them ten miles an hour myself."

"Did you state the color of the horses that you let them have, that he drove away with on Tuesday morning?"

"They were bays."

"Bay team; about what sized horses?"

"About 1050."

Coldwell cross-examined:[28]

"Well, now, if those horses had any special superiority over other horses in your stable, what was it?"

"Well, they were a little better travellers."

"Speedier?"

"Yes, sir."

"Anything else?"

"Well, I think a little more endurance."

During the time the merits of the horses were under discussion the following colloquy took place:[29]

Terry: "I think the question should be amended also. Men that were in fear somebody was after them."

Coldwell: "That would have some effect upon the man, but hardly on the horses."

Terry: "I think it would, if the fellow could wield the whip pretty well."

It was established by several witnesses and admitted by George that he had arrived at Visalia at 5 o'clock in the morning of August 4th. After a few drinks in the Palace Hotel bar he had gone to Grandmother Byrd's house. He had lain on John Sontag's bed and slept for about an hour. Then he had gone to the adjacent home of Chris Evans. While he was eating breakfast with Molly Evans and her family, they saw Evans and Sontag approaching from the east. It was then about eight o'clock.

Molly Evans was questioned in court about the time of arrival, the condition of the horses,[30] and the contents of the buggy. She related that she went to the barn to greet the men, but denied that she saw any bags in the buggy. She admitted that the horses were tied to the barn, without food or water, from eight until eleven. This seemed an unusual treatment to accord a team which had travelled as far as the prosecution stated.

After breakfast, Evans went to his woodpile and busied himself splitting kindling. John loafed for a while, and then walked down town and had a shave and a bath. Edward Bradley, the hack-driver, said he saw John Sontag in front of Slocum's saloon at 9 A.M. About 11 o'clock John returned and took the horses back to Bequette's stable.

One of the men who had a tough time in court

was Clarke Moore,[31] known as one of Chris Evans' best friends. It was he who had guided Henry Bigelow to the John Coffee home in the mountains where Evans and Sontag had been interviewed. Then Bigelow had taken Moore to San Francisco and paid all the expenses of the trip. Tupper was suspicious of the whole thing:

"Now, state to this jury why Mr. Bigelow paid you money and paid all the expenses of your trip a week to San Francisco; why did he do that?"

"I don't know any reason only while he was up there (in the mountains) I bore his expenses."

"His expenses where?"

"Around through the neighborhood there, where they would accept anything."

"Well, now, let us find out how much expense of his you bore. Who did you pay any money to for him?"

"Mr. William Garton."

"How much?"

"Well, whatever lodging and meals were."

"What was it about?"

"I presume it was a dollar or a dollar and a half."

"Well, who else did you pay any money to for Mr. Bigelow?"

"No one else that I can think of."

"Then you bore his expenses of a dollar or a dollar and a half, and in return he gave you a week's blowout in San Francisco, did he?"

"Yes, sir."

"And you don't understand why he did that?"

"He never explained it to me."

"Well, what is your idea about it?"

"Well, my idea was, that some people thought his report (of meeting Evans and Sontag) wasn't true."

"Uh-uh. Some people thought his report wasn't true, and your presence in San Francisco would verify it, would it?"

"Well, I suppose so, yes."

"Didn't he take you down there to the *Examiner* office to let his employers know that he was telling the truth?"

"I don't know that he did or not."

"Didn't you go to the *Examiner* office with him?"

"I was there a dozen times with him."

"And didn't you go to the *Examiner* office and tell gentlemen that he did see Chris Evans and John Sontag?"

"They asked me in regard to it, and I said yes."

The cross-examination went on and on. Moore stoutly denied that he had been paid for his verification of the Bigelow story, either by the latter or by members of the editorial staff of the *Examiner*. But he did admit that he had had a fine vacation at the expense of Henry Bigelow.

James B. Hume, detective, was the officer in charge of the investigation[32] which led to the finding of the money sacks in Evans' yard. His assistants were John Thacker, Will Smith, and Frank Burke, all detectives. At the time he went to Visalia, Chris Evans and John Sontag were fugitives in the mountains, Molly and

Eva Evans were attending the trial at Fresno, and George was in jail. Coldwell asked Hume:

"Then why was it that at the very time when your presence in the case would be required, you left the town where the Court was being held, and while the Grand Jury was in session, and going to an adjoining county to make this search?"

"Because I had ample time to do it at that time, and I went for the purpose of restoring it for the value of it, for the purpose of restoring it to its owner too, the further reason of using it as testimony, if successful."

"You had waited twenty-seven days."

"Well, it is immaterial."

"Now then, was there any more reason for hurry or expedition upon or after the 29th of August, than there was before?"

"Well, there was a good deal of commotion in Visalia, and all men that were available for my purpose, were busy, and I didn't care to commence the search until I was ready to make it thorough; I didn't want to exhibit my opinion of its being there, and make a partial search, and go off for somebody else to avail themselves of my opinion of the matter, and continue the search, or any parties interested, and remove it during any interval that I might be at it. I was prepared to go there. Wilson and Burke were there, they were honorable men, and we went down there and arranged with them that night to search the next morning, make a search of the premises thoroughly."

The detectives went to the Evans home on August 30th equipped with a pick, shovel, and a long slender iron rod which was poked into the ground wherever it appeared to have been disturbed recently. In a short while they found the money bags. Since no neutral observers were present, many persons scoffed at their discovery, and the supporters of Evans said the money had been planted there.

George Contant (Sontag) was the last witness called during the trial. His testimony filled 117 pages in the transcript. He stated that his father, Jacob Contant, had died while George was still an infant. He had used his stepfather's name until he had learned that his true name was Contant. This explained why he and John used different surnames. He was asked to describe his brother,[33] then a fugitive in the hills. George testified that John was taller than he, but weighed less. George, only five feet, eight inches tall, weighed a hundred and ninety, and said about his brother:

"Yes; he is not quite as heavy-set as I am, but he is a pretty powerful man."

John, he thought, weighed a hundred and eighty pounds. He was asked why the older brother limped. The usual explanation has always been that his ankle had been injured while he was a brakeman. This was not true. His lung had been pierced at that time. His more recent injury had been sustained when a bale of hay fell out of a buckboard and broke his ankle. Thus George tried to set the record straight.

Any one who reads the transcript carefully, as this

author tried to do, will come to the conclusion that either George told the truth or else he had memorized his recitation thoroughly. He admitted nothing, and usually had an apt answer to all interrogations. But the circumstantial evidence was against him, and his morals were shown to be rather elemental. The jury found him guilty, and he was sentenced to Folsom for the rest of his natural life.

Life and excitement seemed about over for the young man. But George was resourceful. Life was not over yet, and the excitement was just beginning.

CHAPTER 11

THE BATTLE OF THE PEBBLE

WHEN two men are isolated for long periods of time from others of their kind, they are apt to get on one another's nerves. Admiral Richard Byrd knew this to be true. Therefore, when he wanted to take observations in the vicinity of the South Pole he permitted no one to stay with him; he lived alone for several months.

Evans and Sontag, good friends and loyal companions, found the winter of 1892-1893 a trying one socially. They suffered neither from the mountain cold nor from any lack of food; it was the endless monotony. Venison was plentiful in those days; fish could be had by merely chopping a hole in the ice and dropping a hook and line into the water; flour and coffee were abundant. Their various hideouts were warm; fuel lay in piles all about them, waiting to be burned. They derived much comfort from the presence of a tremendous feline, a hybrid between a bobcat and a house cat, which never failed to snarl in ample time as a warning that strangers were near. Remarkable tales are told about this monstrosity. But even this abnormal pussy could not atone entirely for the lack of other human associates. Evans and Sontag became bored with their existence, and little things began to exasperate them.

It was then that Evans, the senior member of the firm, conceived an idea which at least had the merit of ingenuity. He began to unfold a plan[1] to John, so fantastic at first glance that it seemed a burlesque on rationality, but one which appealed to Sontag and took his mind off trivial annoyances. It was no less than an audacious scheme to get George out of Folsom! And, believe it or not, it came within a pebble of succeeding.

At the time little was said about Evans' share in George's attempted jail-break, and his defenders hushed up the matter. But the evidence now available tends to show that the breath-taking idea was Evans' "baby."

Chris, who never hesitated to take superhuman risks when they were warranted, knew that it would be impossible to storm Folsom from the outside. To do this an army led by "Blood and Guts" George Patton, supported by a fleet of tanks, would have been necessary. But Evans, although he had never heard of the term, planned to use a "fifth column."

Evans and Sontag, expert mountaineers, could travel freely through the mountains during the winter months wthout fear of detection. They went down to Sampson's Flat and interviewed a miner. The latter may have had a low intelligence quotient, but he knew enough to carry out orders from superior mentalities. They sold him the idea of going to Folsom bearing a message to George. When the latter learned about the grandiose plan, he was delighted. Folsom was a dull and stupid place in the estimation of George, and he was willing to cooperate in the contemplated campaign. In order to insure the miner's loyalty and silence, George assured him that as soon as his liberty had been secured, he would rob a train and give the miner half of the proceeds. The poor dupe was overjoyed.

In order to further their plans, Evans and Sontag made eight trips to Visalia . One of these involved staying in Visalia during the Christmas holidays. It must have been a gala occasion for the little Evans children. One wonders how they managed to keep still and reveal nothing. Their suppressed excitement must have been great. Evans' oldest child was Eva, aged sixteen, and the youngest was a mere babe in arms. It must puzzle the reader, as it does the chronicler, how two outlaws, with a $10,000 reward, dead or alive, hanging over their heads, could spend two weeks there and remained undetected. Either the people of the community liked the hunted men, feared them, or were just stupid.

The chief person in this drama, next to the outlaws, was Eva Evans. She was both intelligent and beautiful. She possessed much of her father's physical courage, integrity, and intelligence. The mother, Molly, was also endowed with these qualities, but the responsibility of caring for her large family had worn her nerves to a frazzle. Then, too, in her position as a mother, she had a perspective of the problem facing them not vouchsafed to the others. This made her lie awake at nights wondering what the end would be. The over-all picture was not reassuring. Molly's brother, Perry Byrd, resented the position into which she had been thrust, and said in a fit of anger: "Hanging is too good for Chris; he should be burned at the stake!" All this family squabbling made Molly nervous and unhappy. Finally, to make both ends meet, she had to take in washing. She had no time for attacks on Folsom; her battle was with poverty.

Hence it was to Eva that the two outlaws turned for assistance. Being strong mentally and attractive physically, she was able to bend people to her will and make them do her bidding. Bart Patterson[2] of Dinuba told the author that in those years Eva Evans wore her light-colored hair in ringlets cascading down over her shoulders. She was a small girl and years later, when Mary Pickford was known as America's sweetheart, Patterson said the pictures of her reminded him of Eva Evans. Louis Fowzer, a professional photographer, told her once: "You are so small, yet you are so round. You have the loveliest arms I've ever seen on a young girl." There were no beauty contests in those days; had there been, no doubt she would have been crowned Miss Visalia and Miss California.

Eva listened to her father's plans and agreed to do whatever she could to further his ideas. His confidence in her was never misplaced. Her part in the scheme was not known until many years later, when the statute of limitations gave her immunity. Not that she feared the consequences, but she was shrewd.

One hot afternoon in June a stranger appeared at the back door of the Byrd home in Visalia. He asked for food. This was just after the fight at Stone Corral. John Sontag was lying in a dying condition in the

Fresno jail; Chris Evans was seriously ill at the same place. Grandmother Byrd went to the door, and the man told her his name was Johnson. Mrs. Byrd, by this time suspicious of all strangers, called her granddaughter.

"Eva, here is a young man who says he is hungry. It is funny he does not go out and get a job, instead of begging from poor people. You can talk to him."[3]

The man was dressed in one of those cheap suits which the State of California then presented to all of its discharged convicts. He was a typical blonde, with blue eyes, fair skin, and yellow hair. His poor clothes and rather disheveled appearance could not hide the grace of his delicately built body. He told Eva:[4]

"I'm Johnson. I've come to see Mrs. Bolivar and the baby."

This sounded like insane gibberish to Mrs. Byrd, but it clicked with Eva. She knew instantly that this unknown person was familiar with a code name known only to her father, John and George Sontag, and herself. Who in the world was this fair young man?

Some time after John Sontag had become a resident at the Evans home, Eva had over-heard him apply the name "Bolivar" to her father. She asked John:

"Who in the wide world was Bolivar?"

"He was a grand fellow who never hesitated to fight for his friends," replied John. That was all he would say. From her father she learned a little bit more about this historic character. Evans told her:

"Simon Bolivar was a great South American liberator, who fought valiantly for human freedom against oppression. He became the hero of the common people in South America."

"Then why does John call you 'Bolivar'?"

"Oh," answered her father with a laugh, "That is just one of his romantic notions."

One day John addressed Chris in this fashion in the presence of George. The latter, like Eva, wanted to know the significance of the appellation, but John was non-committal. However, thereafter George at least knew the name, for some reason, had a special significance when applied to Chris Evans. This knowledge was to bear fruit, both bitter and sweet, a little later.

After George had been sent to Folsom, Eva had occasion to write to him. She tried to establish a code which could be used if necessary, and she thought of the name "Bolivar." She trusted that he would have enough native acumen to grasp her meaning; he did. She sent him a letter one day in which she included the apparently innocuous statement:

"Mrs. Bolivar came to see us a few days ago. She brought the baby and stayed over night. She certainly has a nice baby."

George wrote a clever, guarded, and cryptic reply. Eva then knew that she had a method, fool-proof in its very simplicity, which would enable her to convey messages to George which would get by the unsuspecting penitentiary censors. Late in May, George wrote to Eva that a friend named Mr. Johnson would call on her at some future date, and any favors she could show him would be appreciated. Now, at the end of an unusually hot June day, a man stood at her door, asking for food, saying his name was Johnson, and asking for Mrs. Bolivar and the baby. It was all very exciting.

Eva hastily assembled some food on a large platter, and took it out into the backyard, where Johnson and she could have privacy. When Johnson thanked her he revealed that he was of foreign birth; he spoke in broken and guttural English with a German accent. He did not explain the reason for his presence at this time; Grandmother Byrd caused him to lose his aplomb. He looked over his shoulder in a furtive manner, and said suddenly:

"I better not talk to you now already yet; dat old voman, she yust give me a dirty look."

Eva laughed. She knew that her grandmother suspected that the ex-convict was a detective. To Mrs. Byrd the two terms were a distinction without a difference. However, realizing that Johnson was on the verge of being panic-stricken, Eva comforted him by saying that he should come again that night at eight o'clock.

That evening, out under the big pear tree, Johnson outlined the plan which George had made pursuant to the message sent to him by Chris and John. Johnson had just been released from Folsom, where he had served a sentence for trying to rob the Yosemite stage-coach. There he had become well acquainted with George Sontag. Johnson, which was not his true name, was the younger son of a German baron, and possessed a charming personality and was very intelligent in some respects. However, there was something lacking in his make-up. He was either mentally deficient or mildly insane in certain vital aspects. Eva Evans, who liked him very much, believed that he was totally indifferent to the sanctity of human life and willing to kill any person at her suggestion with the same nonchalance a normal man would have shown in destroying a chicken-killing skunk or rat. If it would be unfair to call Johnson crazy, it would not be unjust to say that certain parts had been left out when he had been assembled.

In those days it was customary to present all men, when they left the penitentiary, with five dollars. This bill Johnson still had in his possession. He had "panhandled" and "hitch-hiked" all the way from Folsom to Visalia. The "shacks" on the train had recognized him for what he was by his prison clothes, and had thrown him off the trains three times. On the way to Visalia he had heard about the fight at Stone Corral. Now he wanted guns. Eva demurred. She did not want any more killings, and she did not know where to get any artillery. Johnson assured her that there would be no need of shooting anyone:[5]

"Dees men in da plot, dey all vork in da kvarry, breaking stones up, undt guards mit rifles, dey vatch dem all da time. Der iss no vall undt dey haf only a short vay to go up da hill var da country iss rough mit lots of trees undt brush.

"George vishes you vould help me git guns undt den he vants me to sneak into da kvarry at night undt

I vill hide dem in von spot; den I vill leaf shalk marks
on da tank-house, undt George vill den know dey are
dere. Den dey vill vait for a shance to capture da Captain off hiss guard. Diss Dalton vill do. He iss big
shtrong man; he can hold him.

"Dey vill climb da hill den, making da guard go
aheadt, undt vill not let him go till dey reech da
voods.

"George feels bad in prison undt iss villing to dake
any risk to git oudt. He vill be sorry dat he cannot
meet his broder now, but he still has good reeson to
vant to git oudt. I tell George I vould help him, so I
tought I vould come here vunce."

Si Lovern, the owner of the saloon in Visalia where
the man-hunters, supposedly chasing Evans and Sontag, spent most of their time hanging over his pool-
tables and bar, was a friend of Chris Evans. No doubt
the liquid refreshments which he dispensed to the
special deputies slowed down the pursuit by serving
as a depressive soporific. One day he told Eva:

"You remember them bums that hung around my
place, that was supposed to be huntin' your Paw?
Well, they pawned their guns for one last drink and lit
out of town."

Here was a solution of the problem facing Eva and
Johnson. The latter was told about these guns. Would
it not be ironic justice if the guns used by the blood-
hunters looking for Evans and Sontag, could be taken
to Folsom and used to rescue George? Well, that is
exactly what happened. It took Johnson several days
to "case the joint", but eventually he brought several

rifles and revolvers to Eva. She helped him wrap them into a quilt and blanket. Eva contributed one weapon. It was the revolver that Witty had dropped in the front yard of the Evans home that day that Chris had shot him through the shoulder. It held five cartridges; the sixth had been fired in the Evans front-room and had whizzed past Eva's head. The empty shell was still in the chamber. Reader, remember this.

Johnson, with a blanket-roll on his back, then set out for Sacramento. He looked like a typical bindle-stiff of the period. He carried out his part of the program perfectly. It may seem incredible now, but Johnson delivered his guns at the proper time and place without any difficulty. George secured them.

The pay-off came at 3:30 o'clock in the afternoon of June 27, 1893. Some convicts, among them George Sontag, were outside the walls of Folsom "making little ones out of big ones." The man in charge of them was Lieutenant Frank Briare. Suddenly Dalton pulled a revolver out of his pocket, and poked it into the neck of Briare. The latter dropped his rifle, and a convict picked it up. "Smiling Frank" Williams, a lifer, produced a revolver out of thin air, and George Sontag proved to be an even better magician; he plucked a rifle out of the atmosphere. Four prisoners were now armed; they had two revolvers and two rifles. It had happened quicker than it has been told here.

Dalton promptly told Briare to march up the hill. Several of the convicts, aware of the impending jail-break, picked up guns which Johnson had cached behind some rocks, and promptly joined the procession.

They jumped into a line directly in front of the lieutenant, and felt perfectly safe. They were. The only
man exposed to the potential fire of the guards on
the wall was the man directly *behind* Briare. But the
officers did not dare to shoot him, because in so doing
they would also kill the lieutenant. Neither could they
shoot the other convicts, who were shielded by the
lone and helpless Briare. The armed guards on the
high, gray walls of Folsom could only pray for a miracle. While they were gnashing their teeth in im-
potent rage, it came!

No one now knows who performed the miracle.
It narrows down to two men: Briare or Dalton. One
or the other stepped on a loose pebble and fell. The
other fell with him. Both rolled down the steep incline. Their going left the other convicts out in front
without a shield. For an infinitesmal part of a moment they were petrified, but the unfriendly greeting of
bullets just honing for a home and lodging made them
dive behind the loose rocks in the quarry. Dalton was
shot at the end of his roll, but managed to crawl behind
a protecting rock. Briare, though bruised, was not seriously injured. But he had had some bad moments. All
this had taken less than a minute. Now all was mad
excitement.

All of the other convicts at work in the quarry, unaware of impending events, had been too dazed by the
amazing developments to do anything but stare. They
were now thankful that they had committed no overt
acts. Years of being ordered about by guards had made
them docile, and they were herded into a corner. The
men near the top of the hill were under heavy fire.

The loose stones proved to be a poor barricade. Bullets richoched, chipping splinters off the rocks; the latter were more dangerous than the hot lead.

"Smiling Frank" Williams, a small man loved by all who knew him, raised himself to shoot, and Death stopped and called his name. His entire chest was torn away. When the officers finally picked him up, they found a pistol in his hand. One shot had been fired. But the papers were wrong when they stated that Williams had fired once. He had not! The revolver in his hand had belonged to George Witty. It had been Eva Evans' contribution to the arsenal. And the empty shell was all that was left of the historic shot fired in the home of Chris Evans on August 5, 1892. Later, much later, Witty was to be faced with arrest for embezzlement, and when he shot himself he did it with another weapon.

Ben Wilson fell with a splinter of rock through his side; Thomas Schill, a rather inactive participant, decided to give himself up and was seriously wounded for his pains; Joseph Duffy stood up to fire and fell screaming behind a rock; three men now remained shooting at the officers. They were Dalton, Abbott, and Sontag.

Dalton raised himself painfully to fire his last shot. His gameness was equalled only by his great size and strength. Johnson had told Eva Evans at Visalia:

"Dey vill vait for a shance to capture da captain off da guard. Diss Dalton vill do. He iss big, shtrong fellow; he can hold him."

Dalton had done all that any man could have done. He had captured the officer and had held him. Victory had been only a few feet away when an insignificant little pebble had turned the tables, or rather the ankles, at the crucial moment. Dalton must have found it maddening. He had gloried in his strength, but pride goeth before a fall. Robert Fitzsimmons had said shortly before this: "The bigger they are the harder they fall." The reader may be reminded of the pebble used by little David in felling the gigantic Goliath. As Dalton tried shakily to align his sights, a bullet tore through his brain. His sentence had been life; it was now death.

George Sontag was also game to the core. Whatever his faults, let no man say otherwise. He received a shot through his leg, another mushroomed through his shoulder, and he then collapsed. This left Abbott. He tied his shirt to his rifle barrel and waved it in token of surrender. The fight had lasted over an hour. The firing ceased. The guards behind the Gatling guns had won. The battle of the pebble was over.

Warden Aull, Captain Murphy, and several other guards, now moved cautiously up the incline and disarmed Abbott and Sontag. The casualties were: Dead, Williams, Wilson, and Dalton; severely wounded, Schill, Duffy, Abbott and Sontag. None of the officers had been injured.

If a loose pebble had not tripped some one, the attempted jail-break would have been a success. This close Evans came to success in his plan to rescue George. But in one sense he had succeeded. He had been able to divert John Sontag's mind during the long, monotonous months in the hills.

CHAPTER 12

THE FOURTH ESTATE

ONE of the greatest orators in the British House
of Commons was Edmund Burke, representing
an Irish constituency. In those days European society
was divided into three estates: The lords temporal,
the lords spiritual, and the common people. One day
the eloquent "dun Irishman," as Charles James Fox
called him, pointed dramatically to the newspaper reporters in the gallery, and said:

"And there sit the members of the fourth estate,
more powerful than all of the other three estates combined."

He thus paid tribute to the power of the press, and
the members of the newspaper profession have cherished the name he applied to them until the present
time.

Evans and Sontag were not unmindful of the value
of a friendly press. They were therefore willing at
all times to grant interviews to enterprising reporters.
The fourth estate had been christened at the time of
the battle of Bunker Hill; its power had increased
tremendously during the one hundred and seventeen
years which led up to the vicious little scrap at Young's
cabin.

The newspaper which gave the most favorable copy

to Evans and Sontag was the San Francisco *Examiner*. Two factors entered into its policy.

First, the political antagonism between George Hearst and the "Big Four" who owned the Southern Pacific. George P. West stated it thus:[1]

"George Hearst left his father's Missouri farm to join the gold rush and spent the fifties as a miner in the foothills of the Sierras, a tall, bold adventurer with the strong aquiline nose of the Southern mountaineer. He was of the Southern faction by birth and temperament, and when, loaded with millions, he married a genteel girl of Virginia-Missouri stock and built a mansion in San Francisco, he had little in common with the men from Yankeeland who lorded it over the State as owners of the new railroad."

George Hearst, a Democrat, and Leland Stanford, a Republican, were at different times elected to seats in the United States Senate. There was no love lost between them.

Second, the son, William Randolph, acquired the *Examiner* and continued his father's old contest. As a young man he was a liberal in politics, and fought in defence of the wage slaves, as he called them, and against all forms of corporate control. He felt a genuine kinship with the weak and heavy laden. Whenever he heard rumors that a member of the submerged tenth was suffering undue persecution, he would send a reporter to ferret out the facts. Annie Laurie, one of his favorite columnists, was sent to the Emergency Hospital disguised as a fainting street girl in order to expose its lecheries and cruelties.

At that time a rival newspaper, the San Francisco *News-Letter*, edited by James Watkins, was publishing a daily column, *The Town Crier*, conducted by Ambrose Bierce. This man, who had attained to the rank of major in the Union Army during the Civil War, mixed equal parts of irony, satire, wit, and venom in his writings. In 1886 a serious train wreck occurred at Oakland, and a few days later the railway officials posted the following notice:[2]

"Hereafter, when trains moving in an opposite direction are approaching each other on separate tracks, conductors and engineers will be required to bring their respective trains to a dead halt before the point of meeting, and be very careful not to proceed until each train has passed the other."

The inquisitive Mr. Bierce pounced upon this morsel and printed it in *The Town Crier*, with a demand for an explanation. None being forthcoming, or even possible, he exercised his vitriolic pen on the intelligence quotients of the morons responsible for such senseless tripe. The result of this attack on stupid railway officials was a visit from William Randolph Hearst. In his old age Bierce was to write some fugitive sketches of the tall young man who had appeared suddenly at his small lodgings at Oakland and had mentioned the San Francisco *Examiner*. This was early in 1887. Asked Ambrose Bierce:[3]

"Were you sent here by Mr. Hearst?"

Here is how Bierce explained his impressions as he recalled them years later:

"That unearthly child lifted its blue eyes and cooed

'I am Mr. Hearst', in a voice like the fragrance of violets made audible, and backed a little away. Twenty years of what his newspapers called 'wage slavery' ensued, and although I had many a fight with his editors for my rights to my self-respect, I cannot say that I ever found Mr. Hearst's chain a very heavy burden."

Ambrose Bierce was turned loose on all malefactors of great wealth, with emphasis on the directors of the Southern Pacific. Collis P. Huntington, a successful lobbyist at Washington against all bills directed toward the curbing of the railroad corporations, finally met his master. The railroad was sponsoring the Funding Bill which would have delayed its settlement with the Federal Treasury for ninety-nine years. Bierce, sent to the national capital by Hearst, whipped Huntington at every turn. The former proved to the latter that the pen is more powerful than the pocketbook. Huntington learned the hard way how true was the statement made by Abraham Lincoln in 1864, when his friends wanted him to chastise the New York *Tribune*. Its editor, Horace Greeley, was often guilty of printing garbled versions of the great war president's official statements. When the latter's supporters urged him to correct these misstatements of facts, he replied:[4]

"No man, whether he be private citizen or President of the United States, can successfully carry on a controversy with a great newspaper, and escape destruction, unless he owns a newspaper equally great, and with a circulation in the same neighborhood."

The man who could defeat Huntington indicated the calibre of the man who was to enter the lists in favor of Evans and Sontag. Ambrose Bierce and Chris Evans were embroiled in a contest with the same autocratic power; only their weapons of attack were different. They were to be allies, but Bierce was to prove this time that the pen is more deadly than the pistol.

In his method of attack Bierce used his pen at times as a bludgeon; at other times as a hypodermic needle filled with venom. In style he ranged the entire gamut from impertinence to invective. It was during these years that he wrote his short stories on which is based his fame in the literary world. They were either weird stories dealing with the Civil War, or stories of horror, among the latter being *Black Beetles in Amber; The Monk and the Hangman's Daughter;* and *Cobwebs from an Empty Skull.*

Enlisted with Bierce and Evans for the duration of the war were the crack reporters of the *Examiner,* the star columnists, and the owner himself. It began to look like a crusade. When Bierce went to the *Examiner,* he named his new column *Prattle*: *A Transient Record of Individual Opinion.* One day, without Eva Evans' connivance or knowledge, he printed in his column some lilting lines set to a cowboy's lament which she had written as a satire on Will Smith and George Witty. Thus her version of the beginnings of the trouble was conveyed to thousands of devout followers of Bierce. Her composition, a sample of which is given below, was written to be sung rather than read:[5]

"Come all you bold detectives, a story I'll relate
Of how poor Smith and Witty, they almost met
their fate.
They started out one August day when it was hot
and dry;
And, O, it was so very sad, but I'll tell the truth to
you,
Poor Witty, he was wounded, and 'Smithy'—how
he flew!
And in his haste to get away, he went right through
the fence,
With Sontag right behind him—and John's not
seen him since.
He ran down to a neighbor, and unto him did cry:
'Oh, take me to a doctor, for I know I'm going to
die!' "

After he had read about the fight at Young's cabin,
Bierce was moved to write:

"If there were brave men before Agamemnon
There is certainly none behind Chris Evans."

During the turmoil of the Evans and Sontag activities, Bierce was in poor health and lived quietly
at Sunol, not far from the famous frog farm which
supplied edible frogs' legs to the fancy restaurants.
Here Eva Evans visited him and expressed the appreciation of the family for his many kind words. On
July 9, 1893, he wrote as follows in "Prattle":[6]

"John Sontag, you are dead, as I suppose—
Though some will have it you are still alive.

They hold that death is not of life the close,
  And souls on bullet wounds and buckshot thrive.
  I can't believe it, howsoe'er I strive,
But think you are as dead as good Queen Anne—
  Though why that lady's chosen as the type
Of deadness, Goodness knows. A deader man
  Is old Methuselah. But let us wipe
The tears that spring for both and get a-going:
John Sontag, you are dead, Rapelje crowing!

Now truly, lad, I find it very hard
  To be right sorry; though I feel I ought,
For you had courage—*teste* Marshal Gard,
  With others of the various gangs that fought
  You and Chris Evans; and still others thought
The same—particularly one called Dan,
  Who, Eva says, 'stampeded like a cow';
By which she is supposed to mean he ran
  With a more lively sense of why than how.
Now let's get on; in death unmourned you're
    sleeping.
But Huntington's alive. For *that* there's weeping!"

The fate of Ambrose Bierce was long a mystery. He seemed to tire of life and those who knew him and his problems did not blame him. When the Mexican liberals were fighting Huerta, the cruel murderer of that charming little reformer, Madero, Bierce suddenly appeared at El Paso and told other newspaper correspondents that he planned to enter Mexico and help Pancho Villa. He thought that his military experience might be useful. One day he disappeared south of the border, and was never heard from again.

One of the American correspondents attached to Villa's staff was George F. Weeks, a former member of the editorial staff of the San Francisco *Chronicle* and later the publisher of the Bakersfield *Californian*, and a great admirer of Bierce. He made an effort to solve the mystery of his friend's total eclipse. After the Armistice, which ended World War I, Weeks was engaged in the publication of a magazine in Mexico City. His assistant, Don Edmundo Melero, educated in the schools of Philadelphia, had been a staff officer for one of Pancho Villa's corps commanders. He had often been at Villa's headquarters on official business, and remembered seeing Weeks there together with the other newspaper correspondents. One day Weeks asked him about Bierce.[7]

"*Ambrose Bierce!* Did I know him? I rather think I did! Why, we were good friends—the best of friends! We used to talk together by the hour. He could speak no Spanish, and I was the only one there who spoke any English, and so we became fast friends. He was never weary of asking me questions about Mexico and the revolution, and I was never tired of giving him information and talking with him on all sorts of subjects. I never met a man whom I liked better."

Asked about Bierce's fate, he replied:

"No, I never knew what became of him. Not long after that I left the army and went elsewhere. But he was there when I left."

Some days later Melero met a staff sergeant who

had served with Tomas Urbina, one of Villa's best generals. After Villa had fallen out with the Constitutionalists, he ordered Urbina to attack a body of them camped near Icamole, a small place located about halfway between Saltillo and Monterrey. The staff sergeant related that on the way thither a long pack train of mules carrying ammunition to the Constitutionalists was captured. The cavalry squadron guarding the ammunition train escaped, but the Mexican muleteer and an elderly American gentleman were captured. Neither had made any apparent attempt to flee. The Mexican pleaded piteously for his life. He said he was no soldier, merely an employee in charge of the livestock. The American, who could speak no Spanish, said nothing, even in English. When General Urbina ordered them both shot, the mule-skinner went to pieces. The old gentleman, a veteran of the Union Army and familiar with the "red badge of courage," still said nothing. He merely looked, with a mixture of contempt and pity, at the craven wretch groveling on the ground.

The sergeant went on to describe Bierce perfectly; his martial bearing, sardonic look, snow white hair, and long, flowing mustaches. Later he identified him from several photographs. He further stated that at the time of the execution, when several sharp orders were barked at the two condemned men, the Mexican mule-driver kneeled and extended his arms beseechingly toward the firing squad. Bierce, neither understanding the orders nor what was required by Mexican army regulations on this particular occasion, stood at ease. As a former United States Army officer, he knew that orders must be obeyed. Therefore he glanced inquiringly first at his companion and then at the officer commanding the firing squad. In response to a second sharply spoken command, he knelt silently and calmly extended his arms. Perhaps Ambrose Bierce thought this was the etiquette required on this particular occasion.

General Urbina, who had ordered his execution, as well as the other Mexican officers and soldiers, were all impressed by the lordly air of disdain with which the white haired American regarded the entire proceedings. He had remained in character to the last; it was all "Prattle" to him!

One of the most brilliant newspaper reporters on the Pacific Coast during the gay, old nineties was Henry D. Bigelow of the San Francisco *Examiner*. He was given the exciting assignment of interviewing, if possible, Evans and Sontag in their mountain hideout. This could not be done without the connivance of the Evans family. So Bigelow appeared in Visalia one day when the hunt for the two outlaws was at its height. He won the confidence of Molly and Eva. The result was a scoop which appeared in the *Examiner* for October 7, 1892. It is too long to be quoted in its entirety, but parts of it follow:[8]

"It is impossible at the present moment to describe the means which I took last Tuesday to interview Chris Evans and John Sontag, for I have given my word that certain incidents shall remain secret for the time being. Suffice it to say that they were of the most difficult description and only found after the arduous labor of several weeks.

"I am permitted however to state that the personal interview which I had with the two men took place at a point north of Kings River, and in the neighborhood of the town of Centerville, and that it was dictated to me in substance at different times during the stay I made with them there at one of their several camps.

"The rendezvous had been designated as a small house standing in a tiny gulch that overlooks the great Fresno plain, and I reached it after a descent which lasted from the morning dawn until noon. It had been stipulated in the agreement that I should carry no weapon save a pencil, and that no one should accompany me. Let it be explained just here that the answer to the request which I made to them for an interview was ten days in reaching me.

"Finding the house with some difficulty, I knocked at the narrow white door. It was opened by an elderly man, tall, gaunt, and grizzly.

"At hearing my name repeated twice, he admitted me cautiously, at the same time scanning the plain anxiously. His house consisted of five rooms, including the kitchen, and to the right was a door at which he knocked lightly. A key was turned on the other side, and after a moment or two he threw open the door. I entered alone, and before me, seated on a square double-bed, were two men.

"The man to the left had a pointed red beard, with a long soft mustache of the same color. His face was bronzed with exposure; the eyes, which I caught first, were Irish;—that is, the strange half gray and half Spanish tinge which you find so often in the County Kerry, with pupils large and honest; his hair thick, soft and light brown color.

"The man to the right had long, thick black locks, soft because they had been uncut for weeks; black human eyes veiled in long dark lashes; a tight, curly beard, with curling mustaches. The proclamation for John Sontag's arrest states that he is 'rather good-looking'. It is not enough; he is *very* good-looking.

" 'So you came after all', said Evans, taking my hand.

" 'And why not?' I replied, greeting Sontag at the same time.

" 'Oh, we thought you'd back out'.

" 'I assure you, Mr. Evans, that I feel safer in your company than in that of any other man I know.'

"At which we all three laughed, and they let me sit on the edge of the bed between them, and first of all they asked me for the news. Indeed, they were hungry for it, and for the companionship of man, too. In telling them the events of a fortnight I had time to observe our surroundings.

"Against the wall at the right leaned a Winchester rifle and a shot-gun; opposite and next to Sontag was another Winchester of newer make than its fellow. Both men were well-dressed, and their shoes were almost brand new. John was dissatisfied with his, however; he had bought them only a few days before in some Modesto store, and the dealer had given him a No. 9 brogan instead of a No. 8. In consequence he was compelled to wear three socks on each foot to prevent blistering. I tried to remedy the fault by exchanging footgear with him, and presently we were on what might be called a footing of neutrality."

During the days Bigelow spent with the two outlaws he secured answers to questions which were then printed in the *Examiner*; these all tended to build up a public opinion sympathetic with the two fugitives. Bigelow himself came away completely convinced of the innocence of the two men, and said so. The city-bred man was also exhilarated by the exciting life led by outlaws.

"The interview with Evans was not had altogether in the cabin I have described. Some of it occurred up in the mountains, where I suppose the detectives' posse will enjoy a merry chase some day. During the time I spent with them I was initiated into that custom of watchfulness which is observed by the fugitive who has a price of $10,000 put upon his head—alive or dead. While the two ate a third would keep watch with a shotgun resting in his lap. This was compulsory as far as I was concerned."

Bigelow's story of the outlaws made good reading and aroused tremendous interest in them. In fact, Bigelow's own sister, Constance, became so enamoured of their cause, that she insisted on being taken to the scene of their activities. After the battle of Young's cabin, she met Ed. Mainwaring and in due time they were married. Mainwaring, typically British in the best sense of that term, became a government forest

ranger. His exciting experiences with Evans and Sontag were, in later years, to intrigue his eight children,
all of whom, according to their mother, adored Ed.
Mainwaring.[9]

One of Mainwaring's sons, Dan, resembled his
uncle, Henry Bigelow, in literary skill. While still a
student at Fresno State College, he wrote a novel,
One Against the Earth, with its setting in the San
Joaquin, which was a best-seller. His short story, *Fruit
Tramp,* emphasizing local color, possesses enough
merit to make it required reading in many English
courses on the college level. And readers who enjoy
detective stories are familiar with his "whodunits,"
all written under the pseudonym of Geoffrey Homes.
Among the best known of the latter are *Finders,
Keepers; Forty Whacks; The Man Who Murdered
Goliath;* and *Then There Were Three.*

After the battle at Young's cabin, Bigelow again
visited Visalia. He had heard rumors that the Southern
Pacific directors were bringing pressure to bear on
Governor Markham to call out the militia. He suggested that Eva Evans accompany him to Sacramento.
The legislature was then in session and he thought
it might be advisable for her to appear both before
it and the governor.

"When they see what you are like, they must understand that Chris Evans[10] is not just a bandit. You must
tell the Governor that many men of the local Home
Guard in Visalia are friends and even relatives of Chris
Evans; it would not do to call out the militia."

The visit to Sacramento was made, but Eva found

it unnecessary to interview any one. Bigelow made a preliminary call on the governor and received assurances from Markham that no such action was contemplated. Eva, much relieved, then accompanied Bigelow to San Francisco where she met the lovely Mrs. Bigelow, their two adorable children, and Bigelow's beautiful sister, Connie, already referred to.

On this visit an amusing incident occurred which showed the emphasis all reporters place on "the story," besides shedding some light on the character of Henry Bigelow. The latter took Eva to dinner one night preparatory to taking her to a show at the Tivoli. During the meal a very beautiful woman entered with her escort. She was the leading actress in the play *Trip to Chinatown*, then being shown in San Francisco. Shortly thereafter two other women, flashily dressed, entered and took another table. One of the latter pulled a revolver from her purse and held it under the table in such a manner that Eva and Bigelow could not help but notice it.

The former asked breathlessly:[11]

"Whom is she going to shoot?"

"That very good-looking young Irishman, who just came in with that very beautiful woman some minutes ago."

"Stop her!" begged Eva.

"I should say not. Just think what a lovely story it will make for me. I'll have another scoop."

But Eva became so indignant and stormed at Bigelow so furiously that he finally went to the manager and explained the situation. The woman with the gun fancied that she was being jilted in favor of the New York actress and didn't like it. Naturally a killing in the high-class cafe would be bad publicity and the manager took steps to have "the pistol packing mama" ejected. But Bigelow resented having his story spoiled. Perhaps he was only "kidding" Eva when he said:[12]

"She would not have shot him until he was going past her table on his way out. Maybe she would not have hit him, and even if she had, it might not have been fatal. But think what a sweet story it would have made, and I would have had a scoop on it. That fellow is one of my best friends."

Bigelow escorted her to the Tivoli and left her there as he had to report to the *Examiner* where he worked the night shift. He had arranged for another escort to take her home after the show. When this man slipped into the seat beside her, she was still upset about the near-tragedy at the dinner. Observing her distraught condition, the man managed by his sympathetic attitude and adroit questioning to draw the entire story from her. During the intermission, when the lights went on, Eva was astounded to see beside her the same man who had been so nearly shot that night. She was at first embarrassed, then angry, but he laughed and said:[13]

"I was just trying to get a line on my friend—my best friend—Henry Derby Bigelow, who would let me get shot so he could 'scoop' the story. I might have known it! Look how he sold Queen Lil down the river! You want to look out—he'll feed you to the presses some day."

But Henry Bigelow never fed any member of the Evans family to the presses. His sympathy for them was genuine, and he always treated them with gentleness and kindness.

Henry Bigelow and Orrin Black were sent to Fresno to represent the *Examiner* during the trial of George Sontag. Black had been a court reporter in San Francisco and had seen something of the seamy side of life. Henry Bigelow, practical joker and humorist, had been amused by the colorful dialect of some of the mountain folk he had met. Many of them were originally from the hills of Tennessee and a decided contrast to the people Bigelow and Black met in the San Francisco cafe society of that period. One day Bigelow told Eva Evans:[14]

"You know, I don't believe Black has ever heard a good woman swear. Let's take him out to see Aunt Sue this afternoon."

They did, and after the proper introductions had been made, they got Aunt Sue to tell them how Warren Hill's posse had mistreated her garden. With a sly grin, Bigelow asked:

"What was it you said to your daughter when you left home to come down to the trial?"

The little old lady in gray, very earnest and a bit incensed, replied:

"I said to Emmeline, says I, 'Emmeline, while I'm gone, if any of these Gawddamned sonofabitches that air a-lookin' for Chris come a-fixin' around this place, just you take down yer Paw's shotgun and blow 'em plumb ter Hell'!' "

The look on Orrin Black's face amply repaid Bigelow for his little jest. Aunt Sue had a soft, drawling voice and did not mean to appear tough; she was merely expressing as best she knew how her emotional reactions when injustice threatened her home and possessions.

Suddenly, one day in 1896, Bigelow died from a hemorrhage. Some one, perhaps Orrin Black, wrote his obituary for the *Examiner*. A part of it follows:[15]

"There was never a stranger character than this gifted lad. As a writer he was possessed of a rare grace and a remarkable versatility. His masterly work in finding and interviewing Evans and Sontag for the *Examiner* in their bandit retreat far up in the Sierras, while numbers of peace officers were unable to accomplish the feat, is justly creditable to his record as one of the most brilliant achievements in newspaper history. In sharp contrast to that were the tact and delicacy with which he interviewed an unhappy wife who abandoned her wealthy husband to live in poverty and obscurity with a woodchopper. . .

"It was impossible for him to take life seriously. In his eyes it was an opportunity for diversion. A characteristic incident of his newspaper career was his going to Honolulu at the time of King Kalakaua's death and inducing the widowed Queen to observe the European queenly custom of posing beside the bier of her lord. His description of that tableau was

one of the finest and most heartless bits of humor ever
written; but 'Petey' could never return to the islands
after that. No conception of reverence was possible to
him. In that picture of the bereaved woman standing
beside the wreck of all her happiness and greatness,
he saw only a grotesque caricature, and yet it was his
own fertility of invention that conceived and brought
about the situation. In the furtherance of whatever
purpose he might have in hand, he was without pity
or mercy, but the strangest part of it all was that no
malice tinctured his conduct.

"Anger was impossible with him, and jest and
laughter sat ready on his tongue. He was the embodi-
ment of irresponsibility. There was no permanent
place for him in the hard, grinding, groaning, serious,
suffering world, and so nature employed the most con-
venient means for correcting the error of his advent.

"He goes hence with the kindly thoughts of innumerable persons who loved him for the sweetness and
winsomeness of his character and the indomitable
gayness of heart that brought more radiance than pain.
'The mountains will be the place for me', he said when
the end was at hand, and all but he himself knew that
he was dying. May he find rest there at last."

Even after his death the memory of his buoyant
and dynamic personality lingered on in the hearts of
his friends. One day Eva Evans overheard Orrin Black
singing to himself in the press room of the *Examiner*.
The music was from *The Mikado* by Gilbert and
Sullivan, then the rage in San Francisco. The tune
was from that portion of the musical comedy entitled

"Tit-Willow," but the words were his own. Incidentally Bigelow's intimate friends always called him "Petey."[16]

On a tree by a river a little tom-tit
Sang "Bigelow, Pete Bigelow, Pete Bigelow!"
And I said to him, "Dickey-bird, why do you sit
Singing 'Bigelow, Pete Bigelow, Pete Bigelow' "?

"Is it weakness of intellect, birdie?" I cried,
"Or a rather tough worm in your little inside?"
With a shake of his poor little head, he replied,
"Oh, Bigelow, Pete Bigelow, Pete Bigelow!"

What about the young man who had almost furnished a "scoop" for Henry Bigelow because of the hate of a woman scorned? He, too, became a champion of the Evans family. A graduate of Dublin University, Edward Morphy had arrived in San Francisco by way of New York at an auspicious moment. When he applied at the *Examiner* for work, Senator George Hearst's funeral was in progress. The star reporter, whose duty it was to write its story, had succumbed to grief and fire-water, and was unable to function. Morphy, still dusty from his train ride across the continent, sat down and dashed off an account that combined all the elements demanded by the occasion. It was he, later editor of *The Argonaut*,[17] who was sent out one day to find enough material to fill seven parallel columns about characters of the city. The last column had him stumped until he invented "The Last of the McGintys." It was a tragic story and Phoebe Apperson Hearst cried when she read it. She sent five twenty-dollar gold pieces to her son's newspaper office with orders to give it to the under-privileged McGintys and a request that their pictures appear in the next edition. Morphy and his colleagues on the paper were dismayed, but after spending some of the money for liquid refreshments, they toured Telegraph Hill until they found two ragamuffins who looked the parts and saved the day.

Orrin Black's wife was one of the greatest columnists of the period. She was a forerunner of Dorothy Dix, Eleanor Roosevelt, and Dorothy Thompson. Her pen-name was variously Mrs. Orrin Black, Winifred Black, Winifred Sweet, Mrs. Bonfils, and Annie Laurie. She was to befriend the Evans family, especially Eva, on many occasions.

One of the most remarkable men who came to the support of Chris Evans[18] was a poet who wrote excellent prose, a prose writer whose verse ranged from the ridiculous to the sublime, a man who had been at different times a cook, horse thief, squaw man, pony express rider, white renegade, Indian fighter, teacher, editor, attorney, judge, politician, world traveller, outlaw (Judge Lynch almost hanged him in northern California), and a conservationist. He was the original leader in the movement for reforestation. He was a self-made man, and like others of that ilk he worshipped his creator. He was an extrovert, who refused to be ignored, and forced the world to recognize him. This versatile person was Joaquin Miller.

He was a Hoosier, born near Hiner, Indiana, in 1841. The doctor who was present at his birth was also named Hiner, and the baby was christened Cincinnatus Hiner. Whether the doctor or the village or both were responsible for the name Hiner is uncertain. In later years Miller often said that his second name was Heine and that his namesake was Heine, the great German poet. That made it sound much better. When he was trying to win recognition as an author Ina Coolbrith of Oakland, famous as a librarian and a friend to struggling young writers, told him that he would never be able to overcome the handicap of a moniker like Cincinnatus Hiner. So he took her advice and changed his name to Joaquin in honor of Murieta, the outlaw whom he admired.

When Joaquin Miller arrived in Visalia to interview Evans and Sontag he was an internationally known figure. No author at the present time holds the spotlight as Miller did then. He was a figure out of a story book. His red flannel shirt, high topped boots, buckskin blouse, wide brimmed hat, and long white beard were famous not only in the United States, but in Europe, especially in England, where he had been a social and literary lion. He had both shocked and pleased the British. When he placed a wreath of hay on Lord Byron's grave, it offended the Vicar of Wakefield. When he was entertained by the Barretts of Wimpole Street and met Robert Browning, who had just returned from a vacation spent in Italy's sunny clime, he punned: "Robert, you're browning!" The British very well expected clever things like that from wild westerners, don't you know? He fulfilled the average Englishman's concept of what an American

from the wild and woolly west should be. Only two
other men were ever to approach him in personal
popularity with the British; Buffalo Bill Cody, an
Indian scout and showman; and John L. Sullivan, a
superman in the prize ring.

A sketch of his career will indicate why this romantic literary figure was a valuable addition to the
forces supporting Evans. He had come west in a
covered wagon with his parents when he was eleven.
After two years in Oregon he ran away to northern
California and worked in a mine near Redding in
Shasta county. Swinging a pick and wielding a shovel
proved too strenuous for the thirteen year old boy and
he became a cook's helper. He was wounded while
helping the miners repel the Indian attack in the
Battle of the Castle Crags. Later he left the mining
camp and joined the Shasta Indians and married the
daughter of the chief. By her he sired a son and a
daughter. His mother said boastfully years later: "My
son Hiner had begat his man and killed his man before
he was sixteen."[19]

The four or five years Miller spent in northern
California in his youth are rather legendary. He
claimed that he rode the pony express for a time, that
he made two trips to Mexico for horses, and that he
served with William Walker, the gray-eyed man of
destiny, in Nicaragua. His so-called eye-witness account of the Walker expedition is the best book thus
far written about it. However, no historian now be-
lieves that Miller was there. In his *Songs of the Sierras*
he included his justly famous poem "William Walker

of Nicaragua." He was with the Indians at the time of the Pit River massacre and narrowly escaped death. In 1859 he was accused of stealing a horse and was lodged in the Yreka jail. He broke out shortly before he was to be hanged. By this time he was frightened and went back to his parents and settled down. His Indian wife had been killed accidentally and he took his two half-breed children home to his mother. His little son soon died of the measles, and in time the daughter rejoined her mother's tribe. Years later she developed tuberculosis and Miller sent her to a hospital in San Francisco where she died. Juanita, as she was named, was buried at *The Hights*, Miller's home at Oakland. Another and more famous daughter, also named Juanita, was a product of his marriage to Abbie Leland.

Miller became a college student and matriculated at Columbia College, now the University of Oregon. He read the Bible, Shakespeare, and law. He was admitted to the bar by George S. Williams, later President Grant's attorney-general.

In 1862 the gold mines in the Salmon River district in the Nez Perce country were being developed. Miller and a friend named Isaac Mossman organized a pony express company which operated between Walla Walla, Washington, and Millersburg, Idaho. It was a wild country and a turbulent time, and every ride was an adventure in itself. Miller rode part of the route himself. He was an expert rifleman and could shoot a revolver accurately with either hand; he was Hopa-

long Cassidy in real life. The Miller & Mossman line
followed the old route of Lewis and Clark. The firm
made huge profits carrying mail and gold-dust.

But Miller could never stay put very long. Soon he
heard another call; he wanted to become a writer. So
the express company came to an end. The earnings of
the two partners were put into two roughly equal
stacks of gold-dust, and Miller said:

"Ike, take either of these piles you like, and I'll take
the other."[20]

This was done. The two men, in this typically frontier fashion, terminated their business association, and
separated as friends. Miller went home to his parents,
paid off the mortgage on his father's land, and bought
a newspaper at Eugene, Oregon. His editorials proved
too friendly to the Confederacy to suit the Federal
Government, and eventually his plant was shut down.

One of Miller's favorite contributors, during his
brief editorial career, had sent in poems which she had
signed "Minnie Myrtle." Miller rode down to Fort
Orford to meet Minnie Myrtle Dyer, and liked her
even better than her poetry. He courted her three days
before he married her. They celebrated their honeymoon by riding horseback through the Oregon wilder-
ness. Later he wrote:

"Toward evening of the first day out we came upon
a great band of elk. I drew my revolver, and with
wild delight we dashed among the frightened beasts."

They lost the trail and spent the first night together
on a hillside, tired, hungry, and cold. The closing

of his paper by government orders ruined him financially, and he worked hard at various tasks to support his family:

"I practiced law, mined, fought the Indians, and indeed was the busiest man in trying all means to get on."[21]

Finally he decided to become a cattleman in eastern Oregon. He drove a herd of cattle over the mountains to the plains beyond. With him rode his wife, and slung in a willow basket from her saddle horn, was their first born child. There were to be three children from this marriage, two sons and a daughter. The latter, named Maud, was destined to become a famous actress.

The appearance of the world-famous Joaquin Miller in Visalia in May, 1893, created a sensation there. His account of his visit with the Evans family in Visalia and his interview with Chris under the magnificent General Grant tree in the mountains was given a full-page spread of six columns in the *Examiner* for Sunday, June 4, 1893. It included drawings of Miller, Evans, the bole of the General Grant, and empty shells picked up at the cabin where Black had been shot. The article was entitled "The Bard and the Bandit."

In the light of subsequent happenings it seems that Miller was sincerely captivated by the Evans family, both young and old. He was to remain their friend and benefactor for the rest of his life. He went to Visalia hostile to the brigands, as he called them. His conversion was not only swift, but sure. In fact, his report was so favorable to the outlaws, that the *Exam-*

iner felt constrained to print the following caution on the same page:[22]

"It is hardly necessary to say that the *Examiner* disclaims any share in the sentiments expressed by Mr. Miller."

The following are samples from his account:

"I approached Mrs. Evans, their mother, through her brothers, men of high character, who have helped build up the beautiful city they live in and who hold places of trust—responsible, quiet, thoughtful, hard-toiling, truthful men.

"I found three generations in one little old house, the seven towheaded babies ranging from the cradle to the altar, the pale mother of the seven and the mother's mother.

"Bullet holes all around here—tops of palings shot off, barns pierced, boards riddled, and all this shooting going on over the heads of the bare-footed, towheaded babies, the pale little mother and the poor, silent old grandmother. I wonder that they are not all crazy, instead of being only sick and sad.

"And how did the battles begin? Well, the oldest child is sixteen, pretty, refined, educated to a high degree for a laboring man's daughter. To say that two men loved her would be quite enough. Bear in mind that what I am about to say did not come from her lips or from those of any of her family, still I think it true that a detective and one of the alleged brigands both loved her. Her father, the detective, and the alleged brigand found employment on the railroad. Her father had charge of the warehouse of the Bank of

California. The three men were much together. The
detective was a hatchet-faced, unmannerly man; Sontag was handsome. Now, here you can read between
the lines. I know nothing; I say nothing, of any loves
or hates. The trouble began before the alleged robberies of the train . . .

"Such white-headed babies. So white they are almost blue, and back in there in the dim corner the
old grandmother with one of them wrapped up in her
apron—the apron about the brown bare feet, the poor
old withered hand holding tight on to the little feet
to keep them warm, for the little boy was shaking with
ague. In fact the whole family seems to have the
fever—not that Visalia is sickly, but their nerves have
been strung to such a tension this past season that I
wonder that they live at all. Then the grandmother
ceased to rock and the sick baby slept and she took up
a cob pipe.

" 'Would you mind if I smoked, sir?'

" 'Certainly not. My mother smokes when I can
persuade her to take that sort of comfort.'

"So a cob pipe was filled, and breaths of smoke
gathered round the venerable head back in the corner . . .

"At sunrise, the Sierra Nevada mountains flashing
in my face, I climbed up alongside of silent Bill Work-
man, and we dashed away for a sixty-five mile run
and ride up the mountains . . .

"The next day I went out with an old friend and
partner of Evans and walked around the biggest tree
in the world—'General Grant'—a monstrous tree, it

The mountain hideout of Evans, Sontag and Morrell, shortly after the latter two had been caught unaware by lawmen and fled from the scene. In this image, little remains of the cabin save for cookware and the fireplace.

Illustration from the *San Francisco Examiner* of August 5, 1892, showing the destruction of the express car involved in the Collis train robbery.

Geo Contant alias
Santag, under sentence.
Escaped Sept 20 - 88 -
Age 21 - Ht 5 ft 7 3/4
Wt 152 - freckled
flesh hair - black Eyes,
Both shoulders + arms
covered with freckles
Blue scar right knee Cap
Mole on left cheek, Mole
on right side of Chin
$100 - reward,
C J Noser, Warden, Neb. St. Prison

Prison mug shot of George Contant, taken while he served a stretch at the Nebraska State Prison. The image is accompanied by a full physical description.

Smith's identifications for the men standing behind John Sontag, in the famous photo taken at Stone Corral, are not altogether accurate. Left to right, they are: Stingley, Rapelje, Hall, Witty, English, Burns, Gard, Carroll, Stuart. Sontag was later brought down to Visalia in Hall's wagon.

Eva Evans as she appeared in the Evans and Sontag drama.
From an undated newspaper clipping.

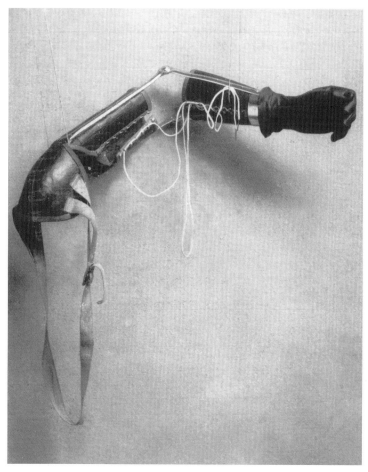

The artificial left arm of Chris Evans, left behind in haste when he escaped from Camp Manzanita with Ed Morrell. It was never returned to him.

Prison mug shot of Ed Morrell, taken when he was transferred from Folsom State Prison to San Quentin. At this time, he had served two years of what would become a fourteen-year sentence.

Portraits of Pelon and Camino, two of the three Apaches who helped track Evans and Sontag throughout the San Joaquin Valley floor and into the Sierra. From an undated newspaper clipping.

SONTAG & EVANS,

(SUCCESSORS TO THOMAS WALLACE.)

Feed and Sale Stable

CORNER ELEVENTH and F Streets,

Modesto, Cal.

—0—

I have just completed the largest Feed Stable in this section of the State and am now prepared to furnish Teamsters and the Transient Traveling Public all kinds of

STOCK FEED

At the Lowest Market Rates. My facilities for keeping Transient Stock are unsurpassed y any establishment in the State.

Chris Evans and John Sontag, respectable liverymen of Modesto, not long before their lives took a considerably different turn. An advertisement which appeared in the *Modesto Daily Evening News* of January 3, 1891.

DIAGRAM OF THE PLACE.

The Location of the Cabin and the Bandits' Position.

Below will be found a diagram of the Stone Corral country, giving a fair idea of the location of the cabin and Evans' and Sontag's positions near the pile of manure:

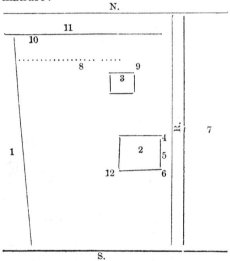

1—The hill from which Evans and Sontag came.
2—The cabin.
3—Straw pile, on ground higher than cabin.
4, 5 and 6—Gard's, Burns' and Rapelje's first position.
7—Wheat field.
8—Where Evans dropped his gun.
9—Where Sontag was found.
10—The bandits' route from hill, along fence, to manure pile.
11—Pile of rocks.
12—Where Jackson was standing when shot.
N—North.
S—South.
R—Road.

Diagram of the Stone Corral fight scene. From the June 16, 1893 issue of the *Fresno Weekly Republican.*

Christopher Evans, in a snapshot taken by his daughter, Ynez, in the living room of her home at Marshfield, Oregon. Evans was then approaching the age of seventy.

The Mussel Slough Settlers: seated left to right are John D. Pursell, James N. Patterson and William Braden; standing left to right are John J. Doyle and Wayman L. Pryor. Photograph taken in 1881, while serving their jail sentences.

Emmett Dalton: "I am sending you a photograph of myself taken about a year ago, dressed and equipped just about as we were in the days of our activity."

Chris Evans is the man in the front row with the dark clothes and long beard who is leaning against the end of the big log. His own family did not know that a photograph had ever been taken of him in his prime, but here it is. The scene is Millwood, near Sequoia Lake, in 1893. The original is owned by Ellsworth Loverin of Three Rivers, whose grandfather, Wesley Loverin, stands in the third row, the third man from the left, with a light shirt and hands on his hips.

Two dark bay standard-bred horses that could travel fast and far.

seems, defiant of nature and of time. It really looks
a little bit in its loneliness and its grandeur like General Grant in his sadder days.

"It was arranged that I should meet Mr. Sontag and
Mr. Evans there on the following day at meridian.
The proprietor of the hotel was to go with me; so you
see there is nothing very secret or exclusive or difficult in meeting these men.

"I had nothing with me but a toothbrush and a comb
and a small package from the wife . . .

"Suddenly I felt the man come out of that tree.
I am used to alert, quick, sudden, sly men. Few men,
if any, have seen more of this sort of thing in these
mountains than I have; but that man came as noise-
lessly and suddenly as one of the chips that fall down
through the broken foliage of the great boughs above ..

"Ten thousand dollars on a man's head, more or less,
puts him at a disadvantage. This man is being hunted
down by all sorts of manhunters, who are eager for
descriptions of him, his manner of dress, and address,
his characteristics, how he carries his arms of defense
and all that. He is already at quite a disadvantage,
hunted all the time, with no place to rest or sleep except up there in the mountains. Not even is he allowed to see his wife and babies without being shot
at from behind barns and fences . . .

"The distance seems long as I recall it, and there we
sat down and I told him all I had to tell. He was sad
and silent and I felt myself soon in the presence of
a man and a brother, and a better man and a bigger
man than myself.

"Everything that I set down here you can accept as under oath . . .

"Evans is a great woodsman, and I think he knows the name and nature of all the trees and their value. You see, he has been hereabouts more than twenty years. He reminds me of gentle John Muir, as I knew Muir nearly a quarter of a century ago. I think he resembles John Muir in appearance as well as manner and love of trees. At Visalia the officers told me to be careful and conceal my long hair as I resembled Chris Evans in the color of my hair and otherwise . . .

"My instructions from the *Examiner* were to go and find out why these men could not be taken.

"I assure you, it is simply because the best men in California, the bone and sinew of the land—such men as were here back in the fifties—don't believe they are guilty, and don't want them taken."

Miller's account seemed so authentic that it sent officers scurrying to the vicinity of the General Grant Big-Tree to pick up Evans' tracks. The joke was on them. Miller's story of the interview was entirely fictitious. His first meeting with Evans took place eighteen years later at The Hights in Oakland, shortly after Evans' release from Folsom. The Evans family did not dare to arrange a meeting between Miller and Evans. The former was being watched too closely by the detectives. Bigelow had managed to secure an interview, but he was less well known than Miller and, besides, he had done it first. The detectives refused to permit any celebrity to fool them more than once. Therefore Miller had to remain in Visalia and content himself with a picture of the General Grant tree given him by Eva, and a description of Chris and his methods, also supplied by her, which was so accurate and life-like that it fooled every one except the three or four persons aware of the secret.

Not everyone admired Joaquin Miller or his defence of the outlaws. The editor of the Visalia *Daily Times* was particularly resentful. When the local boy goes wrong the home community often feels that it is a reflection on conditions there. This editor wrote:[23]

"Joaquin Miller, the Poet of the Sierras, tells in the Sunday *Examiner* of interviewing Chris Evans, one of the Tulare bandits. Miller makes a much abused hero of the fugitive train robber, and takes much pains to show his disapproval of those malicious persons who wish to arrest Evans and Sontag, and put an end to the business of holding up trains and stages. The poet expresses his admiration for the gentleness, bravery, and generally inoffensive character of the bandits, and seems to be imbued with an idea that shooting men from ambush is the most natural and meritorious thing in the world.

"Probably the strait of Evans excites a fellow feeling in Miller. It may serve to recall the time he was a fugitive from justice himself. It excites memories of the time when he was indicted for horse stealing in Siskiyou county, and had the shirt shot off him by the late General Colton, who was then sheriff. After his hegira into Oregon, Miller took to poetry and let horses alone, but it is said he never sees a lariat without instinctively feeling his necktie. Since he has seen and talked with Evans, the public had better have a change of heart. He has only killed people who were trying to rob him of his hard earnings. He is the great and good man much misunderstood."

Miller's sense of timing was excellent. He never stayed in one place long enough to bore people. He also managed to be present when exciting things took place. He went to Dawson during the gold-rush, and reported the bizarre happenings of that wild gold-camp for the *Examiner*.

In the Northland then were young men and women later destined to win fame either as authors or sportsmen: Esther Darling, Jack London, Robert W. Service, Rex Beach, Hamlin Garland, Tex Rickard, and Frank Gotch. The latter was soundly trounced in a boxing match in Dawson by one of Miller's old cronies, Frank (Paddy) Slavin. The latter had been one of the greatest bare-knuckle gladiators in the history of pugilism. He had appeared unheralded in the gold gulches. When Gotch, the young Iowa farmer from Humboldt County, learned the identity of the grizzled old warrior, he had the temerity to challenge him. What had happened in that fight was not pretty to see; it proved that youth need not always be served. Thereafter the handsome young Austrian-German-Indian confined himself to catch-as-catch-can wrestling; in this form of grappling he was never equalled.[24]

Miller was an expert in handling saddle horses and pack-mules. Now, for the first time, he learned about sled dogs. Stories of the size, strength, loyalty, and fierceness of a missionary's lead-dog were circulating throughout the Klondike then. This dog, Jack, thirty-three inches high at the shoulder, weighing two hundred pounds, half St. Bernard and half Great Dane, coal black in color, was the most magnificent canine in harness. Any one who reads Egerton R. Young's[25] autobiography will discover the source material for Jack London's later stories of famous dog heroes and villains: Buck, Spitz, Sol-leks, and White Fang.

Another dog story current then among the goldminers, and later immortalized by Rex Beach, concerned another two-hundred pound dog, half English mastiff and half dusky Alaskan wolf. His owner, a young fur-trapper, was a widower, and left this huge animal in the cabin with his six-year-old son while he trudged through the forest along his trap-line. He was warned that the huge wolf-dog was too fierce and blood-thirsty to be trusted alone all day with a child. One evening, after dark, when the man opened the door to his cabin, he received no welcome, either from child or dog. He lighted a candle and, in great agitation, began to look for his little boy. Then he noticed that the dog, which usually came to meet him eagerly, now lay quietly by the fire-place with blood on his muzzle. The horrified father, unable to find his child, and fearing the worst, swung an axe over the dog's head and split his skull. Then he heard soft sobbing under the bed in a far corner and pulled out the child, frightened but unhurt. And in the opposite corner, he found a big wolf, literally torn to pieces by the loyal dog, which had himself been seriously injured in a fight to the death in defence of the little child placed in his care.

Miller felt at home among the bonanza kings of

the Yukon benches; it reminded him of his early life in the California gold-mines. He was a journalist, but in no sense a tenderfoot. In the eyes of the young hellions who brawled, got drunk, matched their dogs in fights and pulling contests, and panned for gold along the icy streams of the Klondike, Miller was both a legend and an inspiration.

Two years later Miller was in China reporting the Boxer Rebellion. He met Yuan Shi K'ai, Homer Lea, and other officers of the period. He developed a great antipathy for the German commander, Count von Waldersee.

His friendship for the Evans family was enduring. He detested large houses and lived in *The Hights* (he advocated simplified spelling; he named the street-car stop near his place Dimond), a relatively small house, with other still smaller cottages surrounding it in which he placed his mother and other dependents. In one of these Winifred and Carleton Evans were lodged for some time when the health and wealth of the Evans family were at their lowest ebb.

The third reporter sent by the *Examiner* to interview the outlaws was Charles Michelson. His family was of pioneer stock, rich in the traditions of the wild and woolly West, and familiar with outlaws of another era. The father, Sam A. Michelson, a native of Germany and a gold-miner, established a general merchandise store at Murphy's Diggings in the early 1850's. One of his customers was a handsome young miner who often played with the Michelson children. He was of Spanish ancestry, a native of Mexico, and named Joaquin Murieta. One day five American miners, recent arrivals from Missouri, resenting the presence of a Mexican at Saw Mill Flat, attempted to expel him. Joaquin resisted and was beaten into insensibility, and his beautiful young wife was raped by the lusty brutes. She died that night, and Joaquin went mad with grief and rage. One day Murieta borrowed his brother's horse and rode into Murphy's Diggings. A miner claimed the animal, and accused Joaquin of being a horse-thief. His brother Carlos had a bill of sale to show legal ownership, but the miners' court ignored this, hanged Carlos, and horse-whipped Joaquin. Such cruel treatment altered the course of his life and he became a notorious bandit chief.

Michelson's children attended the little log schoolhouse at Murphy's Diggings.[26] The oldest son became a professor at the University of Chicago and in time the intellectuals of the entire world were glad to pay homage to Albert Michelson, the winner of the Nobel Prize, for his success in first measuring the speed of light. The daughter, Miriam, won renown as a novelist, especially for her book entitled *The Bishop's Carriage*. Another son, Charles, the object of this sketch, was born after the parents had moved to Virginia City, Nevada. Although he had the same father and mother, he was nearly twenty years younger than any of the other children.

Charles became a reporter for Hearst in the days when the "Gee Whiz" emotion was at its height. He welcomed the Evans and Sontag assignment, and an-

nounced publicly his intention of invading the outlaw
territory. He did this purposely so that Evans and Sontag would have forewarning. Michelson took with
him James Swinnerton, then a cartoonist for the *Examiner*, and later a famous painter. They wanted both
pictures and a story. Since neither of the outlaws was
ever photographed in his prime, it is a regrettable fact
that no contacts could be established. Michelson and
Swinnerton joined a small posse going into the hills
from Fresno. It was their intention to trail along with
the posse until they had learned the lay of the land;
then they planned to drop out in the hopes of being
picked up by the two outlaws. But it did not work out
that way. Evans and Sontag knew that the two San
Francisco men were in the hills seeking an interview,
but were afraid to get in touch with the representatives
of the *Examiner* because the posse remained too close
for comfort. The plan failed. All Michelson got out
of the trip was a reputation for making super-excellent
flapjacks over an open fire.

Men who were hunting Evans and Sontag had come
to feel, especially after having read the articles by Bigelow and Miller, that the reporters from the *Examiner*
were partisans of the outlaws and not to be trusted.
Deputies vented their spleen and valley editors showed
their antipathy by dubbing Mr. Hearst's paper the San
Francisco *Eczema,* no doubt meaning that it irritated them and made them itch. They had developed
an unholy urge to scratch someone, especially an *Eczema* newspaperman.

Michelson was to have an unexpected opportunity

to write an account about a man who played a unique part in the Evans and Sontag history. After the stage-play had folded up in Oregon, Eva Evans was given a part in a Shakespearian play then being produced in the Valencia Street Theatre. This was in 1894. Going to rehearsal one morning she suddenly heard revolver shots. This was nothing new in her life. She did not know the significance of the shooting until she read the evening paper. A would-be robber had entered the bank at the corner of Market and Valencia, one of those flat-iron corner buildings so common in San Francisco. There were two tellers in the bank; when the bandit pointed a gun at one of them, the other fired at the thug and hit his fellow-worker, a man named Herrick. The bandit ran, but was found hiding in a house on Valencia Street. The captured man gave his name as William Fredericks.

When Eva read this, she hurried to the jail to interrogate Fredericks. Why? Because it was he, under the assumed name of Johnson, who had gone to Visalia, and had carried the guns to Folsom which had been used by George Sontag and his fellow convicts in their attempted break for freedom.

Eva asked him:[27]

"Why in the world did you come back to California? You promised me that you would never return to the Coast."

Fredericks' answer is a sad commentary on conditions during the so-called Cleveland depression:

"I know I did, but dimes are vorse back East den dey are here. So I sought I vould come vunce back. I knew you vould help me get vork, but I could not find you. I asked at several teatres, but no von know vhere you live. I haf been here for two veeks and I haf had little to eat. I am hongry."

Fredericks, his real name, was wanted for his share in the Folsom break, and his fate was sealed when Herrick, the teller, died from his wounds. Eva hired a lawyer, but it was no use. The handsome blonde scion of a German baronial family, the prodigal son who had gone to a far country, was hanged at San Quentin on July 26, 1895. Michelson wrote as follows about what he saw and experienced there that day:[28]

"Fredericks, the murderer who was executed at San Quentin yesterday, was the gamest man I ever saw hanged. . . . It is not a pleasant thing to see a man hanged, and no one wonders as much at the spirit which prompts men to go to executions as those whose business or duty forces them to attend them. I never expect to attend another. Indeed, it was on a promise of the editor of this paper that I would not be required to again perform this unpleasant duty that I undertook the reporting of the execution of William Fredericks.

"Now I am glad that I went. Fredericks was a brute, an enemy of society, all that was vile and malignant, and yet his demeanor on the gallows was such that he compelled a certain amount of admiration. He was as thoroughly self-possessed as any business man going about his regular course and realizing that he must have all his regular faculties alert to cope with difficulties and rivals in the commercial world. Fredericks came into the room with the little procession that has moved from the condemned cells at San Quentin to the gallows chamber so often of late, and he was by all odds the most composed man in all that line . . . He was easy, interested, and debonair. As he passed through the doorway and came into sight of the execution apparatus and the crowd which was waiting to see him die, he cast his eyes about as another man might have done on coming into a strange parlor . . .

"In one of my talks with the condemned man he told me that when he had left the little school in Germany his ambition was to be a soldier, and the career that he had marked out for himself was that of a commander of men . . . Possibly if the boy Fredericks had been given a cadetship instead of being forced by his necessities to go to sea and generally make his way among the hard walks of life, there might have been a Captain Fredericks or a Colonel Fredericks, whose dashing courage would have made him world famous. At all events that is the thought that came to me when they cut his muffled body down."

That was written while Charles Michelson was a cub reporter. In time he gained in stature and dignity, and eventually became a member of the staff of Hearst's New York *Journal*. In 1929 he was appointed director of publicity by the Democratic National Committee; his "smear Hoover" tactics were copied from the Ambrose Bierce attacks on Collis P. Huntington. In 1933-1934 he served as public relations director of the National Recovery Administration (NRA).

The following is an excerpt from an article in *Time,
The Weekly Newsmagazine*, which appeared shortly
after Michelson's death in January, 1948:[29]

"At press conferences, he always sat behind President Roosevelt's big desk, a small, stooped man with
bright, hooded eyes in a seamed face. Behind the
horn-rimmed glasses he looked bored and glum. He
seldom said a word. He didn't have to. As the Democrats' ghostwriter and hatchet man, Charley Michelson got the party's biggest guns to say it for him . . .

"A master of the sly phrase and rankling innuendo,
he painted the Republicans as inept, as the party of
privilege, of the 'corporation lawyer' and the rich in-
dustrialist. He hung the depression around Hoover's
neck and kept it there. He made a mockery of Hoover's
optimism and never let the country forget Hoover's
theme that prosperity was just around the corner. He
never let succeeding G.O.P. candidates forget Hoover's
prediction that 'grass will grow in the streets' if the
Democrats were elected.

"Charley wrote first drafts for many of Roosevelt's
fireside chats. From his littered desk, speeches poured
out through a hundred throats. Senators and Cabinet
members provided the name and the larynx, Charley
the words and the wit. The Republicans cursed him,
called him 'the puppet-master' and 'the greatest silent
orator in America.'

"Charley was a master of timing. He smothered
bad publicity with good. The day the New Deal admitted defeat in its ill-fated attempt to have the Army
fly the mail (ten pilots were killed), the Administra-

tion announced that Andrew Mellon would be investigated for income-tax evasion.

"A sour man with a lurid private vocabulary, Charley never seemed to work. He often needed a shave, spent much time in the Press Club playing chess and dominoes with his newspaper cronies. He held no man in awe. Once Franklin Roosevelt greeted newspaper reporters with the remark that there was no news 'except that Charley Michelson needs a haircut'. Snapped Michelson: 'Somebody's got to economize around here'. Once he told Jim Farley: 'Jim, you're the most honest man alive. You wouldn't steal anything—except an election'."

The foregoing members of the fourth estate have been selected because they were the most important supporters of Evans and Sontag. Their attitude toward the outlaws was based in part on their much earlier hostility toward the Southern Pacific.

Chris Evans and John Sontag were never found guilty in court of train robbery. Their only conviction on this charge was in the tribunal of public opinion, and even there the verdict was not unanimous.

In general the metropolitan press was far more tolerant of adult delinquency than the valley papers. Naturally the latter felt that lawless conditions were a reflection on the life, manners, and morals of the San Joaquin Valley. The big city papers often took time to be facetious; it was not their ox which was being gored. The valley editors seldom saw anything funny in the whole sordid business; their part of the state was getting mighty poor publicity.

The denizens of the valley may have hated the Southern Pacific for its unfair practices, but they resented even more being fooled by a poor laboring man whom they had thought a good neighbor and an upright citizen. Now it seemed, if reports could be given credence, that Evans was neither poor nor upright. If he had stolen and hidden thousands of dollars, then he had deceived them during the preceding years. Some may have been envious of his reputed wealth; others resented being bamboozled. Had Evans been laughing at them? They wondered, and they didn't like it. It was not the money, but the principle of the thing. No one enjoys being the butt of a practical joke, least of all the perennial prankster. Had their judgment of character been faulty? It made many residents of the community squirm, and in their irritation they sought ways of vindicating themselves. They did not want to be considered "saps."

In spite of injured pride, it must be admitted that on occasion even the local papers showed traces of good humor. When a San Jose reporter wrote an article claiming that he had interviewed Chris Evans as the latter was preparing to board a ship bound for Hawaii, a Visalia editor got "a big bang" out of it:[30]

"The statement of the San Jose *Mercury* that Chris Evans was last seen on his way to Honolulu where he will marry Queen Lil and hold up the provisional government, is not confirmed by the latest news from Camp Badger. Chris is much too smart to tackle the Queen Lil proposition with only one arm."

CHAPTER 13

SHOTS IN THE NIGHT

T HE APACHES refused to follow the trail any longer. They collected their pay and went back to the San Carlos Reservation in Arizona. Other men took their places as man-hunters. The officers who pursued Evans and Sontag were honorable men doing their duty. But they were often assisted, or at least augmented, by braggarts from the saloons and pool-halls of the valley towns, who were anxious to collect the blood money for the fugitives, dead or alive. Their sporadic charges into the hills were always futile, and often alcoholically stimulated.

From Sampson's Flat the chase led to Eshom Valley, lying to the southeast; thence to Squaw Valley, ten miles southwest of Sampson's Flat. Emil Tretten, a rancher in Squaw Valley, fed the two outlaws one day, but was afraid to report their presence to the officers. In sparsely settled districts it was dangerous to deny food and shelter to outlaws; it was also equally dangerous to report their whereabouts to posses. During the winter of 1892-1893 the chase lapsed. The man-hunters spent most of their time comfortably in the saloons of Sanger, Reedley, Dinuba, and Visalia. Evans and Sontag eked out an existence in the snow-clad hills. If reports can be believed then the outlaws were well-fed and comfortable. A lumber-jack dropped into Camp Manzanita for Thanksgiving dinner. When he later reached Visalia he told a reporter that he had been royally entertained and the printing of the following menu must have irritated those who were hoping that the outlaws would starve: "Bean soup flavored with bacon, broiled rainbow trout, roast mountain quails, baked sweet potatoes, canned tomatoes, hot soda biscuits, wild honey, coffee, apples, and clusters of Muscat raisins."[1]

Just before Christmas the two men returned to Visalia. S. Sweet & Co. had foreclosed on the Evans home in November, and Molly and her children were now living with Grandmother Byrd. Chris and John occupied a large bedroom in the front part of Mrs. Byrd's house. Ynez was assigned the task of amusing and feeding the younger children, while Winifred served as a lookout. She spent hours in an upper room gazing in the direction of the main part of Visalia from whence danger might come. To the age-old Anglo-Saxon question: "Sister Anne, do you see horsemen?," she could always answer truthfully in the negative. John spent much of his time brooding in the upstairs bed-room which he had previously rented from Mrs. Byrd in the days before becoming an outlaw. He was depressed[2] and told Eva confidentially that he felt hopeless about the outcome. Her father, on the other hand, was cheerful and enjoyed the Christmas holidays immensely. Casual visitors were met at the door in a nonchalant manner by Grandmother Byrd, who calmly entertained them as though no hunted outlaws were within miles of her home. The Evans children had been thoroughly coached, and never revealed, by word or look, the fact that their father and friend were at home.

Aside from a certain shrillness in his laughter, the family noticed nothing in the father's behavior to indicate worry or nervousness. He romped with Carl, the baby, and laid plans for the future education of his children. Eva and he planned that in case of an attack by night the two men would make their escape while the women held the fort. If the posse should come during the day, the grandmother and the children would be sent to the barn, and the four adults would fight it out to a finish. Both daughter and mother were crack shots with rifles, and Evans and Eva believed that Molly would, under pressure, regain much of her old-time skill with the Ballard. But there was not even a hint of trouble. After two weeks of Yuletide happiness, their Merry Christmas came to an end and the two men slipped away to the hills.

It must puzzle the reader, as it does the historian, how it was possible for two men with a reward of $10,000 hanging over them, to remain in Visalia for two weeks without detection. Were the people of Visalia, especially the officers, dull and stupid, or did they like the two outlaws? Perhaps it was felt that "a truce of God" should be observed during the holidays, and that fighting was out of order.

The only person able to keep in constant touch with the two hunted men was Eva. Two reasons explain this. She was clever, and the sheriff's office probably

spent its time watching men rather than the mere slip
of a sixteen-year-old girl. For several months after
their initial flight, she made weekly trips into the
mountains to visit her father and fiance. During all
this time she was their quartermaster corps or service
of supply, bringing to them the things they needed.
Here is how she did it.[3]

Evans owned a little bay mare, a registered thoroughbred, which he had raced as a three-year-old at
the Tulare county fair. Her name was Kitty B. When
it came time for Eva to make a trip to the beleaguered
men, she would impersonate a young cowboy. Appar-
elled in copper-riveted jeans, high-heeled boots, a
brightly colored shirt, and wearing a ten-gallon hat,
she could come and go without attracting undue attention. Kitty B. was kept in Mrs. Byrd's barn, and Eva
would slip over there at three o'clock in the morning
and ride away. At that hour there were no posse
members or special deputies skulking about the premises, and even if a particularly wide-awake and alert
officer had seen the figure on horseback coming down
the road, he would have assumed it was a young cowboy on his way home after a very late poker game in
one of the saloons.

Eva Evans was very proud of her saddle. Her
father, a personal friend of D. E. Walker, then owner
of the Visalia Saddle Works, had ordered it built
especially for her. It was made of hand-tooled leather,
and had a peculiar creak all of its own.

Kitty B. was held down to a slow gait until they
had passed through the oak forest. When the open

plains were reached the little mare was given her head and after that no mounted posse in the state could have caught her. As soon as the foothills were reached Eva was among friends and could come and go without fear. Maggie Rucker, who had provided a hiding place for Grattan and William Dalton at different times at Cross Creek, now performed a similar service for Evans and Sontag. Usually Eva met the two men at Maggie's ranch near Badger, or at the Downing home along Dry Creek. Occasionally she went directly to Camp Manzanita or Fort Defiance.

Camp Manzanita was located along Dry Creek, about three miles from the Downing ranch and a mile above the Hudson Barton mill at Cedar Springs, where Chris and Molly had spent their honeymoon eighteen years before this. The camp was located three hundred feet from the road which led to Evans' Redwood Ranch. Frequently the two men heard the scuffle of horses' hoofs as the posses rode along the road toward the Evans mountain home, hoping to get a shot at the outlaws. To vary the monotony, Evans and Sontag sometimes lay close to the road, screened by dense manzanita bushes, and studied the faces of the unsuspecting man-hunters.

Against a perfectly smooth rock, as tall as a church, they had built their cabin. The fireplace was set against the rock, which formed one wall of Camp Manzanita. The other three walls were built of boards which had been carried up the hill from the Barton mill. The walls were covered with newspapers containing lurid stories of themselves. The men had a saving sense of humor. Any person familar with the foothills of the Sierra Nevada need not be told that manzanita bushes are hard to travel through, and the men felt reasonably secure. But Evans wanted to be doubly safe. So he prepared another camp which was his second line of defense. This he named Camp Defiance.

The first camp was located about three miles upstream from the Downing ranch; Camp Defiance was half a mile downstream from the home of the Downings, his most trusted friends. That meant that the two camps were about three and a half miles apart. Camp Defiance consisted of a deep cave and in times of high water in Dry Creek, it could be entered only by plunging through a water-fall which screened it completely. The opening to the cave was three feet high and seven feet wide. This, with the exception of a narrow space for a small door, was tightly closed by fitting rocks together snugly. Loopholes were provided. Food, ammunition, and a coal-oil stove were placed there. It was impregnable and only treachery would lead to its discovery.

The winter passed pleasantly enough. After the Christmas holidays, Evans and Sontag busied themselves in formulating plans which led to George Sontag's attempt to break out of Folsom. When spring came the men moved over into Eshom Valley and lived with the Yokuts Indians. Here they hunted mountain quails and grouse and enjoyed a change of diet. New shoes and clothes were needed so they went shopping in Fresno; they spent a day and a night there. Molly's uncle, Scott Sanders, who lived along the McCall road between Selma and Sanger, lent them a horse and buckboard. They piled some boxes in the latter to represent farm produce, tied an old canvas over them, and calmly rode into Fresno like two farmers on the way to market. Of course, they had their guns under the canvas as well.

During the spring which followed, many exciting incidents occurred. Eva served as the Intelligence Corps for the little army of two men. Will Smith bought a ticket and planned to take the stage-coach to Sequoia Mills. Evans was informed. Tom Cook, the stage driver, was walking his horses slowly up the steep grade, a mile and a half above Camp Badger, when Evans and Sontag stepped out of the brush and pointed their guns at Cook.

Four frightened passengers were ordered to step out of the stage-coach. Sontag asked Cook:[4]

"Tom, where is Will Smith?"

"I don't know, John. All I know is that he bought a ticket, but he failed to show up this morning. I guess he cancelled it for some reason, but I don't know why. I was supposed to carry five passengers this trip, but only four showed up."

Evans ordered Sontag to frisk the men in the stage-coach for weapons, incriminating letters, and identification cards. John subjected the four trembling men to a careful examination, while Evans covered them with his Winchester. It was soon apparent that the four men were laborers on their way to the lumber mill. After being thoroughly searched, all their possessions, including their money, were returned to them. Evans and Sontag were never accused, even by their worst enemies, of being "sneak thieves." The only charge ever brought against them was that they tangled with two powerful corporations, the Southern Pacific and Wells, Fargo. John Sontag was apparently sorry for the poor workers whom he had frightened out of their wits, and reassured them:

"You boys have nothing to be afraid of. We are only looking for some of these blood-hunters. If Will Smith had been on this stage-coach we would have left him dead in the road. He is trying to swap our lives for $10,000. We have never robbed a person of a cent, and we have never robbed a train. We don't want your money, and this ought to prove to you that we are not petty thieves."

Where was Will Smith on this day, April 29, 1893? He had bought a ticket which should have taken him to Sequoia Mills, but he had failed to show up. Why? Someone stated sententiously a long time ago that God watches over little children and half-wits. Smith had failed to meet his "rendezvous with Death" this particular morning, not because of any adroitness on his part, but because his superior officers at San Francisco had sent him a telegram the previous night ordering him to report to Southern Pacific headquarters in that city the next day. Therefore he had cancelled his trip to the mountains early the next morning, and had taken a train for San Francisco.

At the identical moment when John Sontag was asking Tom Cook for Will Smith, the latter was riding peacefully in the "smoker" of a passenger train on his way to that metropolitan area beside the Golden Gate which Californians to this day call "The City." Smith was to learn later how narrow had been his escape from an ignominious death just above Badger, but at the exact time which was to have been his "zero hour," he was placidly puffing away at a big, black cigar, entirely unaware, as he glanced out of the window at vineyards, orchards, and fields of rustling grain, that a strange coincidence or an omnipotent Fate had kept him from an untimely end.

It is appointed unto every man once to die, but until that time comes no man can die. Smith was to pass away, as all mortals must, and in a far more painful manner than that which might have come to him from a smoking rifle in the hands of either Evans or Sontag. An act of God had saved Smith this day, and he may have felt elated when he returned to Visalia a few days later and learned what had happened. However, within a few short years Smith would be suffering the tortures of the damned, and those who hated him would, with malice, repeat again and again, each repetition exuding a savor all of its own, the old adage: "The mills of the Gods grind slow, but they grind exceeding small."

Shortly after Evans and Sontag had interrogated Tom Cook concerning Will Smith, the two outlaws visited the great lumber mills at Sequoia Lake and had dinner with the lumber-jacks in the vast mess-hall. Among the hard men there they were considered heroes rather than villains. During the afternoon various foremen escorted them through the plant, showing them the entire process of turning huge trees into boards and planks. As the sawyers rode back and forth on their carriages, they waved friendly greetings to the two outlaws. When the latter left Sequoia that evening, after a hearty supper, the burly lumber-jacks bade them a cheery good-bye.

Not long after this visit to the mills, a United States deputy-marshal, J. S. Black, was seriously wounded in the thigh. He and Tom Burns, a detective, had been staying quietly in a small cabin near Camp Badger for four months, hoping to get a shot at the two outlaws. One evening, returning from Camp Badger with groceries, they entered the darkened cabin and some unknown person fired from the inside and Black went down. The assailant then went out through a rear window. Evans was blamed, but always denied that he had anything to do with the shooting. Eva Evans said that Black had "a way with women" and the would-be killer was a lumber-jack, jealous of Black's attentions to his wife. Ed Morrell gave another explanation:[5]

"One of their (Southern Pacific) men, who was brought into the mountains, known locally as Sam Black, claimed to be a Deputy United States Marshal from the Mexican Border. He was a hungry-looking ruffian with notched gun indicating that he had not only killed his man but many men. The side partner with whom he swaggered about had just completed a long term in prison for a heinous offence and both were shunned, dreaded and despised. The climax came one evening after dark in the outskirts of Camp Badger, a lonely mountain settlement.

"Black and his cowardly partner had been watching the cabin of a young married couple. When they discovered that the woman was alone, her husband being away in the logging camps, they forced the door and brutally attacked her. Her screams made them fearful of danger. Both of them quickly slunk away into the heavy manzanita brush before help could arrive.

"In desperation, the mountain people sent word of the tragedy . . . Picked men were ordered into the district to stalk the perpetrators of this new outrage. They lay in wait for Sam and his partner to return to camp, greeting them with heavy fire. The noted gunman fell crumpled up on the trail, while his pal dashed into the underbrush.

"Wounded, the Deputy Marshal crawled into the cabin and under the floor concealed himself out of range of the bullets. Early next morning he was taken to the valley, wounded badly, one leg being amputated as a toll, a reprisal for his cowardly act. But this did not deter him from committing more atrocities, his final and crowning crime being the wanton murder of his employer in San Diego. He was sentenced to life imprisonment, doubtlessly saved from hanging by the influence of the railroad in whose service he had pursued the train robbers."

The stories of the shooting of Black as told by the police, Eva Evans, and Ed. Morrell all differ. Take your choice.

John Holton, who owned a merchandise store at Centerville,[6] set out for the mountains with a six-horse team and a load of hay. Evans and Sontag hailed him a few miles above Squaw Valley; they climbed into his wagon and sat down under the driver's high seat, where they were screened from view by the bales of hay. On the way to Dunlap, Holton was stopped by a posse. Under the circumstances he could hardly be expected to say he knew where the outlaws were to be found. He must have felt for a few moments that he was literally sitting on a keg of dynamite.

One evening William Elam rode horseback up Boyd's grade, due east of Orosi, accompanied by his fiancee, Miss Helen Foster,[7] who was then teaching an elementary school in the foothill area known as Long Valley. In the dusk Elam could dimly see a man standing on a ledge behind a huge rock. What startled Elam was the fact that this man held a rifle, and that it was pointing directly at him. He said later that he felt instinctively like plunging the spurs into his horse and getting away from there pronto. But such an act would have been suicidal and unchivalrous. So he restrained himself, and tried to ride nonchalantly past the point of danger, while the man behind the rock swiveled his gun and kept it aligned on the man on horseback. Elam rode within ten feet of the muzzle of the Winchester. Nothing happened. The presence of a woman no doubt saved his life that night. Sontag, for it was he, realized that a woman on horseback eliminated the possibility of her escort being a man-hunter. As Helen Foster and William Elam rode slowly by the huge rock they noticed through a cleft the figure of a woman dressed in white.

This was Eva Evans on one of her periodic visits to the outlaws in the hills.

In those years it was customary for school teachers to find board and room by rotating from home to home among the parents of the various pupils. When Helen Foster was staying with the Tom Collier family[8] she noticed that one evening the parents seemed agitated. They began to carry food out on the back porch. She learned later that they had been feeding Evans and Sontag.

While each new adventure story which came out of the hills filled the public with a delicious sense of terror, the friends of Evans were not remaining idle. A man of influence sponsored a plan which would have taken Evans and Sontag to a South American country which then had no extradition treaty with the United States. There the men would have been safe and free. Eventually Evans could have been joined by his family. The plan was perfect; money and transportation were waiting; and the language of that foreign land was no barrier to Evans, who spoke Spanish. Many old-time Californians of Spanish stock resided at Visalia, for example the founder of the Visalia Saddle Works and his employees. From men of that type Evans had acquired a vocabulary adequate for all practical purposes. Who was Evans' benefactor? The author asked Evans' daughter, and she replied:[9]

"I will not tell you who this man was. Even when he was outlining the plan to me, he never asked me not to tell anyone but my father. He knew I would not, and I never have. He is long since dead in a far-away land, and few now would remember his name. It was between three people and it still is."

Before this plan could come to fruition, bad luck intervened. Molly Evans was on the verge of a nervous breakdown from the constant worry. For this and other personal reasons, the family decided that Chris and John needed to come home for a family conference. Eva wanted to be the messenger, but her mother's condition and entreaties forced her to stay at home. Instead, a man was sent whom Molly trusted, and he proved to be a traitor. He took ten armed men with him and left them in ambush. He casually asked Chris which road he would take on his way home. Evans told his false friend:[10]

"Over the trail through Wilcox Canyon that comes out at Stone Corral." This man then went back and notified the waiting posse. The next evening Chris and John walked into the trap set for them.

The successful defiance of all constituted authority by Evans and Sontag had become such a scandal in California by that time that finally a United States Marshal, George E. Gard, appeared in the valley. It was the latter who, at the instigation of the "stool pigeon," led a posse of nine men to Stone Corral. It is no reflection on him that he did so; that was his job. Included in the group were Hi Rapelje, a deputy-sheriff from Fresno and a remarkable shot; Fred Jackson, a frontier officer from Nevada; Tom Burns, a detective; Bill English, a constable; and five others.

It was Saturday evening, June 10th, when the members of the posse stationed themselves in the Billy

Bacon cabin near a landmark known as Stone Corral. This is located at the edge of the hills east and north of present Yettem. The cabin was old and abandoned. About a hundred yards north and toward the hills lay the remains of an old straw-stack. An ancient ramshackle barn had been dismantled and the remains of the haymow was about eighteen inches high. Frank Gaines, the owner of the land at the time, had hauled hay to his cattle that day, and had dumped some of the surplus on top of this old straw-stack. The posse members were tired from a previous futile foray into the hills and slept soundly Saturday night and most of the next day. One man remained on guard. This explains why Evans, who sat on the mountain over-looking the cabin, scanning the adjacent plains through his binoculars, saw no signs of life or danger.

Chris, ever suspicious and on the alert, as all good outlaws must be, finally proposed for safety's sake to fire a few random shots into the cabin. He wanted to know if this normally unoccupied shack was really empty. Sontag recoiled from the suggestion, saying nervously that it might contain innocent people. Amorous young lovers were known to have used this cabin as a trysting place on occasion. However, Evans' proposal was not as heartless as it may sound, and later events were to prove that he had been right in theory. Since Evans had won a medal as an "expert rifleman" while serving as a trooper with Custer's Seventh Cavalry, he possessed uncommon skill. He argued that a few well-directed shots, which would make the shingles fly, might "smoke out" all potential foes and friends without injury to them other than fright. But John's squeamishness in the matter dissuaded Chris from his intention. After studying this sector for several hours, Evans and Sontag finally began their descent toward the spring near the cabin. They planned to refresh themselves there before continuing their hike to Visalia.

Rapelje made the following statement immediately after the fight at Stone Corral:[11]

"On Sunday morning, after an all-night tramp (while some members of the posse had spent Saturday night at the Billy Bacon cabin, others did not arrive until early Sunday morning), we came to the cabin mentioned and remained there all day to rest and recuperate. We took turns standing guard. Along toward evening Jackson was on guard and was watching the road in front of the buildings. The rest of us were asleep. I happened to wake up, and, going into the rear room, I espied two men coming down the hill toward the house. I called Jackson. From the appearance of the men and from the number of guns they were carrying we thought them to be Evans and Sontag."

When the two outlaws reached the low straw-stack Evans sat down to rest. It was then about dusk. Sontag and he planned to hide their surplus guns in the straw until their return from Visalia. Evans was sitting in such a way that he presented a profile view to the men watching him from inside the cabin. Gard warned his men not to fire until they were sure of their victims. The path from the straw pile to the

Visalia road lay within a few feet of the cabin. If his men had obeyed Gard's orders, doubtless Evans and Sontag would have walked right by the cabin and could have been shot down with ease. Then this fight would have resembled the one at Young's cabin in reverse; there the officers had been outside, here they were inside. But in all tests of wit and skill, the officers were to prove inferior to Evans.

Jackson, guilty of poor judgment, over-anxiety, or cupidity, fired too soon. Evans, sitting sideways to the men in the cabin, received a nasty wound when the heavy bullet plowed a groove across his back. A fraction of an inch closer and it would have severed his spine. When he whirled to fire, a load of buckshot whined angrily around his head. Three buckshot lodged in his skull, and another gouged out his right eye-ball. He rolled down behind the straw pile and managed to lay down a fairly constant barrage on the cabin. Jackson, whose premature shot had precipitated the battle, went out through the back door and tried to shoot Evans from the corner of the cabin. In aiming he exposed the lower part of his leg. Evans smashed it. The next day it was amputated at the knee. Chris was to say later that Jackson's leg was all that he saw of the posse that day.

The moldy old straw stack was proving a poor rampart. The two outlaws had to hug the ground closely to avoid death. The battle raged for hours.

One of the posse members was a half-breed Huron Indian and a remarkable scout. He crawled out of the cabin and along a creek bed until he was at right angles to the outlaws. From this vantage point he sent a shot through Sontag's chest which pierced the tip of his one remaining lung. With Sontag and Jackson eliminated, it was Evans against nine officers. A bullet shredded Evans' left arm below the elbow. Another bullet ripped his right arm from the wrist to the elbow. His left arm was useless; he could manipulate his right with difficulty. Worst of all, the blood kept gushing out of his empty eye-socket and interfered with his aiming. He was in a tough spot.

An interesting incident occurred during a lull in the battle. William W. Ward[12] of Kingsburg had a cattle ranch in the neighborhood of Stone Corral. A cowboy in his employ named George Boyer died, and Ward was obliged to go to the ranch with a coroner and make provision for the removal of the body. Lewis Draper of Kingsburg owned a light wagon and a fast team of standard-bred trotting mares. Ward hired Draper to accompany him to his mountain ranch. The morning train of Saturday, June 11th, 1893, brought to Kingsburg from Fresno a coroner and a coffin; the former rode in the buggy with Ward, the latter was placed in Draper's spring-wagon. The two rigs turned east on the first road south of the Southern Pacific railroad bridge between Kingsburg and Traver, passed through Monson and the present site of Yettem, and then ascended the hills to the north to Ward's ranch. After the men had performed their duties there, they proceeded on their homeward way. Ward and the coroner preceded the Draper wagon, and reached the valley floor without mishap. Under the circumstances it was natural that Draper should drive more slowly. As he approached the head of the grade he heard rapid firing, then silence. Suddenly both he and his team were greatly startled when two deputies, armed like walking arsenals, stepped from behind a huge rock and ordered Draper to stop. He did!

One of them said:

"Evans and Sontag are lying behind that low straw-stack yonder (about a hundred yards away), and if you try to go on they will shoot you."

Draper was ordered to turn his horses and go back. He protested. To spend the night in the hills alone with a corpse was, to say the least, an unpleasant thought. The other deputy said:

"If you try to go on, Chris Evans will probably send your wagon home with two corpses instead of one."

Draper then attempted to turn his team, but the mares, who were angry because they had been frightened by the sudden shooting, now decided to balk. The deputies had walked up to the wagon, and were standing beside the front wheel. Chris Evans, peering from his hiding place, saw his chance, stepped out with his heavy rifle, and hurriedly fired three shots. Due to his mangled left arm, he was handicapped and inaccurate. Two bullets splintered the spokes in the front wheel between the two deputies, the third scarred the thill.

The high strung mares, slightly un-strung by the previous shooting, were now promptly re-strung, and exercising the prerogatives of their feminine persuasion, changed their minds about balking, and departed forthwith. Their exit was so sudden that the seat of the wagon jumped off its hinges, and fell back on the box containing the body of Boyer, but fortunately the double-tree was made of tough old hickory, and a real horseman held the reins.

In the midst of the sudden turmoil another deputy behind another rock shouted:

"Hey, wait a minute. I've got a wounded man here (Fred Jackson); take him to Visalia!"

The team was gaining momentum at every bound, the bullets were whining angrily, and to stop would have been both impossible and suicidal. Draper called back through the din:

"Got one corpse; can't use another!"

He drove unscathed through an enfilading fire, managed to turn his team at the foot of the grade a half mile away, and traveled the intervening thirty-five miles to Kingsburg at a rate of speed not customary in the transportation of cadavers. Years later Ward was to say that Draper had jumped into the coffin and had ridden down the hill with the dead man. This was a facetious exaggeration.

After blanketing his horses, Draper left the livery stable without comment. The next morning an irate stable-hand accosted him and related with gusto his emotional re-actions during the night when he had occasion to move Draper's wagon and discovered a dead man looking up at him. Draper had known Evans before the latter became an outlaw. After Evans had been taken into custody, Draper visited him in the

Fresno jail. He told Evans about the fracas at Stone Corral. Chris replied soberly:

"Lew, I did not know it was you in that wagon, but even if I had, it would have made no difference to me at that time. I was shooting to save my own life."

After the exit of Lew Draper, the battle of Stone Corral continued with unabated fury. The first shot was fired just after sun-down, but the summer evening was clear, and the shots in the night reverberated throughout the hills. During the next few hours the posse fired one hundred and thirty rounds.

When daylight was not far away John told Chris to leave. He said:

"Chris, I'm done for. Get away if you can walk. These hell-hounds will be upon us as soon as it's light."

Evans did not want to leave his friend, but there was nothing he could do for him. Another bullet had smashed through his right arm and he could no longer handle his rifle effectively. Sontag, by this time suffering excruciating pain, begged Evans to take his revolver and give him the "mercy shot." The latter naturally refused. Taking good-bye of John, Evans started back-tracking toward the Perkins home in the Elderwood district of Wilcox Canyon. Mrs. Perkins' daughter, Jane, had married Molly's brother, Perry Byrd, and the two families were supposedly good friends.

If there is any reader who has doubted Evans' courage and endurance, his achievement that night should dispel such an attitude. The deep gash in his back was bleeding so profusely that his boots were half-filled with blood. His left arm was so badly mangled that it would be amputated two days later. His right arm had been perforated by a Winchester bullet. Three buckshot lay imbedded in his skull. Later it was to be learned that they were lodged against the membrane surrounding his brain. Because of them Evans was thenceforth to suffer one continuous, maddening headache. Eventually they were to work through the membrane and press against the brain itself; this condition was to produce palsy and partial paralysis. Years later, when a famous surgeon removed the buckshot, he put a stop to the headache, but the operation came too late to cure the palsy and paralysis.

Worst of all, as far as that particular night was concerned, Evans' right eye dangled against his cheek, suspended at the end of the ocular muscle. Evans' vision was understandably blurred. So, in the darkness, he often blundered against trees. His pursuers, the next morning, saw many evidences of his head-on collisions along the way. At one place he had crashed into a tree with sufficient force to knock him down. At another place he had fainted, fallen face down in the gravel, and had lain there unconscious for a long time, judged by the pool of blood that remained.

To throw the posse off the trail he tried to roll down a hillside over the tops of a thick growth of manzanita bushes. He succeeded. But at the foot of the hill his ocular cord became entwined in the brush and, with agonizing pain, he fumbled with his one remaining hand to disentangle himself. It was a ghastly night.

In such a condition and under such circumstances that man walked seven miles over rough mountain trails to the Perkins home. When he finally reached his destination he had strength enough left in his right arm to manipulate the pump handle in order to secure water to assuage his feverish thirst. He then climbed up an outside stairway which led to the attic in the Perkins house, and lay down on a bed. It had been a hard day!

If the reader doubts the truth of the statement that Evans rolled down a small hillside over the tops of manzanita bushes, then he will have to find some other explanation why the posse lost his trail. Many of the latter were experts in tracking fugitives, and yet they admitted that Evans' tracks and blood-stains vanished in thin air. Ed. Morrell wrote this:[13]

"Delirious and maddened by thirst, the hunted outlaw tumbled into Wilcox Canyon. His trackers marvelled afterward that such a thing could be possible, for here all further trace was lost. The desperate man had literally rolled down over the top of thick patches of manzanita, blotting out his trail by acres of ground.

"Once again the shrewd Indian scout of old demonstrated his marvelous endurance. His mind had cleared for a moment and he realized that he was leaving a plain trail of blood for his relentless pursuers. He had resorted to strategy and as a result the man-trackers stood baffled on the brow of a hill looking aimlessly around a sea of manzanita."

The next morning Al Perkins, the youngest son in the family, and then about twenty years old, discovered blood on the pump handle and on the rack a bloody towel. He followed the red trail up the stairway. Evans was still conscious and told Al:[14]

"Please go and tell Eva I am in trouble. She will take care of me. I won't bother you long. I'll be all right in a few days."

Al's mother sent word to her older son, Elijah, who lived half a mile away. The latter, accompanied by his son, Elmer, soon arrived and helped to dress Evans' wounds. Elijah, who was later to be portrayed as a low comedy character in the stage play, gave the following account of what happened that day:[15]

"Mother sent for me and I went up immediately. I live about a half mile from my mother's place. When I was in the room I saw Evans lying on the bed and he was a horrible sight. He was covered with blood, and the shot in his eye gave him a ghastly appearance. I remarked:

" 'Well, Chris, you are in a pretty bad fix, ain't you?'

" 'Yes,' he responded, 'and I want you to dress my wounds.'

"I made a splint and put it on his arm, washed his eye, and dressed his other wounds as best I could. He said when he left Stone Corral that he went to the cottonwoods to get some water, but when he got there the creek was dry. It is one and three-fourths miles from Stone Corral to my mother's, but the way he came he must have walked six or seven miles. I told him that he was now too badly shot to make any further resistance and that it would be impossible for him to get away; that he could not remain at our home for we could not afford to harbor him. I advised him to give himself up and told him that I thought it would be better for him, his family, and all concerned to have the officers come and take him. He would not agree to it, and said he would be all right in three weeks. I then asked him if I should go for his wife to take care of him and he said yes. Then he said:

" 'No it wouldn't do for her to come. She would be followed by the officers if she left town.'

"I then told him I did not understand why he wanted to make any further resistance. He answered that it was of no use to borrow trouble; he would soon be all right. I concluded that the only thing for me to do was to come to Visalia and notify the officers."

Toward evening the Perkins family decided that some action would have to be taken with respect to Evans. His presence was both unwelcome and dangerous, and his physical condition demanded medical attention. Therefore Elijah Perkins saddled his horse and set out for Visalia. The Evans family said later that he secured Evans' consent to surrender on the understanding that Molly should be notified first. This would have enabled her to go to the sheriff's office and collect the reward offered for Evans' capture. Elmer Perkins said that his father made no such agreement; the officers would never have permitted such an arrangement. Perkins arrived at the sheriff's office about 11:30 in the evening of June 12th.

Sheriff Kay was out of town, and William Hall, under-sheriff, received the news. He procured a fast

team and two-seated buggy and drafted Elijah Perkins
to do the driving as he knew the road to his mother's
house better than anyone else. Hall was accompanied
by George Witty and Joe Carroll. The latter was a
newspaper correspondent, who was deputized for the
occasion.[16]

During the day which was now drawing to a close,
rumors had been circulating rapidly. Marshal Gard
at Fresno had been informed that Evans might be
found at the Perkins home. He appointed Rapelje a
United States deputy marshal, and sent him, with
Sheriff Scott and deputy-sheriff Peck of Fresno, to
make the arrest. They took the train to Visalia, hired
a team and carry-all there, added Tom Burns to the
posse, and quietly set out for the Perkins ranch at about
9 o'clock in the evening. Since they were unfamiliar
with the roads, especially at night, they made poor
time and were passed by the Hall posse some time
during the night. A third rig, carrying two correspondents and two deputies, sustained a collision with
a sheep corral and dished one of the wheels.

Elijah Perkins proved to be an expert horseman
and, besides, he knew the roads. He took a short-cut
over the hills which shortened the trip by five miles
and arrived first at his mother's home. Al Perkins
was offered $100 if he would go up the stairs and dis-
arm Evans. He brought back word that Evans would
surrender to Hall. Later the officers conveniently forgot to pay Al. While Hall and Witty were helping
Evans to put his clothes on, and Carroll was interviewing him, a free lancing group of man-hunters arrived.

The latter included William Stuck, Harry Stuart, and one other. A few minutes later Rapelje, Peck, Scott and Tom Burns, driving lickety-cut, tore into the Perkins yard. Both groups felt cheated, and resented Hall's remark:

"This house is in Tulare County, and Chris Evans is my prisoner."

Guns were drawn and another battle was narrowly averted over the body of the seriously wounded man. Evans restored some semblance of sanity by begging:

"Gentlemen, fight it out later over the blood money. I'm suffering terribly. Get me to a doctor."

Aside from the first-aid rendered by the men in the Perkins family, Evans' wounds, which had been inflicted in the evening of June 11th, had received no attention. It was now early in the morning hours of June 13th. Hall and his deputies placed Evans in a light wagon owned by Al Perkins which served as an ambulance. Chris suffered agonies during that drive over rough mountain roads. He had a large and glowering escort. Besides Hall and his men, the other two posses also tagged along. On the way to Visalia the carryall with the dished wheel was encountered, and it also fell into line and followed the procession. Evans was placed in the Visalia jail about 5:30 in the morning of June 13th.

The matter of the reward created bitter feeling and recriminations were hurled back and forth. Wells, Fargo & Co. and the Southern Pacific had offered $5,000 for each man, dead or alive. The State of California had added $600 for each man, so the total amount was $11,200.[17] Just how this blood money was later divided is uncertain now. A Visalia paper stated that Marshal Gard was given $5,000 for his share in the Stone Corral battle. The Fresno officers kicked because they felt that they had been robbed of both the reward and the glory:[18]

"Fresno officers are very indignant at what they consider ungenerous conduct on the part of Tulare county officers in the arrest of Evans. Sheriff Scott and his deputies are severe in their disapproval. They say that the officers from Fresno county have done all the fighting and planning which has led up to the capture of the outlaws, and when all the fighting and all the danger was past, the officers from Visalia rush in and arrest the men, and not only claim the reward for the same, but what is of more importance, they claim the honor also.

"The particular subject of complaint is in regard to Evans. There was a division of work last night agreed to between Sheriff Scott of Fresno and Sheriff Kay of Tulare by which Scott was to go to Wilcox canyon, and Kay was to search the swamps near Visalia and guard Evans' house, to catch him if he should go home.

"In conformity to this, Scott, with his posse, went to the mountains, but after they had left, Kay learned that Evans was wounded and helpless at the house to which Scott was going, and Kay's deputy, Hall, set out and reached there just ahead of the Fresno posse, rushed up the stairs, and arrested Evans while the Fresno men were at the door. Now they claim both the reward and the glory of capturing the outlaw, who had been driven in by the Fresno officers.

"This morning the posse from Fresno returned and a more indignant set of men would be hard to find. One of them said:

" 'The next time we go into Tulare county to catch men that the officers there have failed for months to capture, it will be a cold day. Had it not been for Rapelje and Jackson, both deputy-sheriffs from Fresno, Evans and Sontag would still be roaming Tulare county, as they have done for the past ten months. It seems pretty hard now for our men to be robbed of the reward. It is not the money so much as the credit of the capture that we want.' "

George Byrd insisted that the reward should be paid to his sister Molly, as Evans had so stipulated at the time of his surrender. However, no one seemed to pay any heed to his contention.

When news began to spread through Visalia that Evans was in jail under the care of Dr. Mathewson, it created a sensation. Men gathered in groups to discuss the situation. A correspondent wrote:[19]

"Generally the people rejoice that the end has come. The warfare has disgraced the county and has done the entire valley incalculable harm. This is everywhere admitted, even by those who do not think it is wrong to steal from the railroad company.

"Here and there one hears the expression: 'They undoubtedly deserved to be shot down, but it is hard on their families.' The reply comes as quickly: 'It was pretty hard on the men whom they shot dead and wounded, and on their families, wasn't it?' That usually ends the colloquy."

When Evans was carried into the Visalia jail, Sontag was already there. The posse, unable to follow Evans' trail, had returned to Visalia with John. The latter had lain unconscious by the straw-stack most of the time after Evans had left Stone Corral. The chill of the morning dawn revived him and he tried to commit suicide. His hand was unsteady[20] and the first bullet from his revolver tore across his temple; the second went through his face just back of the nose. He did not regain consciousness until the posse stood over him.

Jackson, who had been wounded by Evans the previous evening, had been taken to Visalia by Rapelje and Hall. They had reached the county seat about midnight. They added George Witty, deputy-sheriff, and Bill English, constable, to the party and hurried back to Stone Corral, where Gard had remained on guard all night. Burns had tried to follow Evans the previous evening and was picked up by the returning posse about a mile from the William Bacon cabin where Gard was still dubiously eyeing the straw-stack for signs of Sontag. Other men scouting in the immediate vicinity were Jud Elwood; Luke Hall, owner of an adjoining ranch; Harry Stewart, a newspaper reporter; Joe P. Carroll, also a reporter; George Stanley and William Stuck. When daylight arrived these twelve men moved cautiously in on the straw-pile and found Sontag unconscious. While they stood around him he opened his eyes and feebly asked for water. The decencies of life were temporarily held in abeyance while E. M. Davidson, a photographer, grouped the posse back of the mortally wounded outlaw. This old photograph, still extant, a gruesome thing which can only appeal to morbid minds, shows nine men who were in at the kill: Jud Elwood, Hi Rapelje, U. S. Marshal George Gard, George Witty, Thomas Burns, William Stuck, Joe P. Carroll, Harry Stewart, and one other about whose identity old-timers disagree. He was either Bill English, George Stanley, or Luke Hall.

The last named, mentioned elsewhere as the man whose children had been nursed by Evans when they had had scarlet fever, volunteered to take Sontag to Visalia in his "sporting wagon." Gard accepted this offer, and Hall went to his ranch to prepare for the trip. Some members of the posse were detailed to escort Hall to Visalia. The others then tried to follow Evans' trail but soon lost it.

The news that Sontag had been captured spread like wild-fire throughout the county seat. Men neglected their customary tasks that day to stand on the street corners and discuss the battle and its implications. Where was Evans? Visalia remained wide open that night, because most of its adult inhabitants did not bother to go to bed. No one knew what news the next hour might bring. At dawn the emotions of the inhabitants were further titillated by the momentous tidings that Evans was also in the Visalia jail. Now the man-hunt was finally over. Or so they thought.

Later that day Molly and Eva Evans were admitted to see their men. A Visalia reporter described the pathetic meeting:[21]

"Mrs Evans broke down for a few minutes after entering the cell. She had to stop and rest twice on her way up the steps. She passed around to the right side of the cot, sat down on the edge, and buried her face in her handkerchief, murmuring some inarticulate words. Chris said, 'How do you do, Mollie?' She stooped and kissed him warmly.

"Nothing more was said for a minute or two, during which time Mrs. Evans wept bitterly. Then she recovered her composure and, touching his arm all wrapped in splints, asked Evans if it was broken. Chris replied that he guessed it was. Mrs. Evans then raised a large piece of cloth over his right eye, all swollen, discolored, and closed, and inquired if it was shot out.

" 'No; oh, no!' replied Chris in a careless, reassuring tone. Mrs. Evans then asked if she could see her husband alone. 'I think, Mrs. Evans', the Sheriff replied, 'that I had better stay with you.'

"All the others then retired, and for ten minutes the three remained alone in the cell. At the end of that time, Eva Evans arrived and was shown up. She entered the cell, and, without a word, kneeled at the side of the cot, placed her arms around the head of the wounded outlaw, and showered kisses upon his face."

When Molly went to see her husband, Eva had gone into her fiance's cell. She took his hand and with the other she stroked the furrowed temple grazed by the bullet. Sontag had been shaved and his head wounds dressed. Hardly any words were spoken. What could one say? She said later:[22]

"There was more there than a broken body. I saw a broken heart."

The same newspaper quoted above stated:[23]

"Lovers met and talked for a few minutes this afternoon. Eva Evans was admitted into the room where Sontag lies. The interview lasted about eight or ten minutes. Only a few were present besides the two. They were both visibly affected, and neither spoke for some moments after shaking hands. It was the meeting of two lovers—a sad meeting, after a separating. She held his hand in one of hers, and with the other gently rubbed his forehead. It was such a meeting as might take place between very dear friends."

Evans' arm had been amputated that morning before he saw either his wife or daughter. Apparently he was covered by blankets in such a way that Molly did not notice it. The family always asserted that his arm could have been saved. When Molly left the jail after her first visit a man with a morbid sense of humor gave her a neatly wrapped bundle with the remark: "Your husband's clothes." When she opened it later she screamed and almost fainted. It contained a soggy mess of blood-soaked clothing.

The daughter was permitted to spend the first night in her father's cell. When she left him in the morning, he told her:

"Eva, don't carry on so; I'm not dead yet."

But Eva, loyal little trooper that she was, had reached the end of her tether. A friend, waiting to take her home, noticed that she talked wildly. A buggy ride around the town failed to soothe her, and she was taken home, where she blew a fuse. She had to be held forcibly in bed for the next thirty-six hours before her brain cleared.

While lying on their cots in the Visalia jail a steady stream of inquisitive people came to peer at the wounded outlaws through the wicket. After a few days Evans and Sontag were lodged in the Fresno jail, and received the same unwelcome attention there. They must have felt like two wolves in a cage. After Sontag was able to answer questions, he was interviewed by several reporters. The following is a general summary of his statement as printed in the various newspapers:

"Smith and Witty knew that I hated the Southern Pacific Railway Company and that I never lost a chance to tell people how much dirt it had done me. When they came back to the Evans house after having taken my brother George to jail, I figured that they planned to frame me. That is why I ran Smith off the place. Chris had warned me several times never to surrender to railroad 'dicks', because he was sure that they would beat me up some day on general principles because they had heard me express my hatred and contempt for them and their rotten organization.

"When the two officers came to the house I remembered what Evans had told me. He had also warned me to be more careful and not to talk so much, because some day the 'shacks' would get a-hold of me on a trumped-up charge and give me the third degree in order to prove me guilty of some crime or other. I wouldn't let them get away with it, and when Smith, condemn him, reached for his gun, I let him have both barrels."

There is no doubt that Sontag died with a bitter hatred in his heart for the Southern Pacific. Can a mighty and impersonal corporation hate? If so, the Southern Pacific must have hated John Sontag.

When news reached Minnesota that Sontag had been wounded, the following news item under a Mankato date-line was printed in San Francisco:[24]

"The news that John Sontag had been captured and seriously wounded at Visalia, California, yesterday, created considerable excitement here (Mankato). His parents were notified and the mother is broken-hearted over the terrible life her son has chosen. The right name of the bandit is Contant, Sontag being the name of his stepfather. George, who is serving a life sentence, has a wife and children in this city. The Sontag boys were born in Mankato, and John always was considered a good boy. He was the last one suspected of adopting the life of a bandit, but George frequently got into trouble here.

"John went to Visalia about twelve years ago. He went into the livery business with Chris Evans and several years later began a life which has long been notorious and brought him to grief. John Contant is about 32 years old and is unmarried. Their family connections in Mankato are respectable and law-abiding citizens.

"The stepfather is wealthy and is the proprietor of the Sontag Hotel. While (John) Sontag and Evans were here a year ago last winter, John took his mother on a trip East (*to Connecticut?*). During their absence it is supposed that Evans and George held up the train at Kasota (half-way between St. Peter and Mankato, Minnesota). Should he (John) die from his wounds, Sontag will be brought here for burial."

When the mother of the Sontag brothers learned that they were in trouble she left Mankato for California. Her arrival at Visalia came at a tragic moment. George had just made his unsuccessful attempt to escape from Folsom, and was lying there seriously wounded. John had just been removed to the Fresno jail in a dying condition. Mrs. Sontag developed an intense hatred for the entire Evans family. A combination of causes may explain her attitude. Valley residents often were heard to say that Evans had been a fine citizen until he began to associate with the worthless Sontags. The mother, hearing such remarks, flew to the defense of her offspring and asserted that they had been good boys until they had been led astray by an evil, older man. Then she was disappointed to learn that Eva, her son's fiancee, was not a Catholic. She said openly: "They are bad people —all of them." She may have been ignorant and bigoted, but she had suffered much. George Sontag was to say later that it was the unkind treatment accorded his mother by the Evans family which led him to turn State's evidence against Chris. That may have been an excuse for his action, but it indicated that an unpleasant clash of personalities had taken place between John's mother and his closest friends in California. Before Mrs. Sontag left Visalia for Fresno, she frankly told Eva what she thought of the Evans family. The pitiful scene of an aged mother hovering over the cot on which lay her handsome, wayward, and dying son was made to order for the "sob sisters" of the newspaper fraternity. They made the most of it.

Eva Evans went to visit her father and lover in Fresno. John was then dying of peritonitis. As she stood by his cot he looked up at her with his beautiful, brown eyes dulled with a pain which was both physical and mental. Then he took her hand, laid it against the beat of his throat, and closed his eyes. He refused to open them again. Perhaps he could not endure the agony of gazing upon the face of the one he loved. She never saw him again.

Shortly after his death an unsigned poem of seventeen stanzas appeared in a Fresno paper. The two concluding stanzas follow:[25]

> "Came that last and desperate battle,
> In the blackness of the night,
> Flames from rifles lit the ledges
> In the dawn of morning light.
>
> All was silent. It was over.
> Far away beneath the shade
> Of that rugged desert cedar
> Lies the bandit Sontag's grave."

John Sontag died on July 3rd. He was buried the next day in the Calvary Cemetery, due west of Roeding Park. There were no mourners present. As the body of John Sontag rode in solitary state to its final resting place, the people of Fresno were celebrating the 4th of July in the noisy manner prevalent during the gay, old nineties. Along the streets and all the way out to the graveyard gigantic firecrackers were hissing and exploding. As Sontag was lowered into his grave the sound and the fury was like unto that of a pagan Roman holiday.

CHAPTER 14

THE SHOW MUST GO ON

DURING the summer of 1893 the American people in general, and the Evans family in particular, were suffering from the hard times. Grover Cleveland, then president of the United States, was being blamed for a depression somewhat similar to that which was to come later during the administration of Herbert Hoover.

Chris Evans was in jail during that very hot summer of 1893. The outlook for him was very dark at that time. His health was bad, he had lost an eye and an arm, he was without funds to hire lawyers, and he was facing a court trial which might well result in the death penalty. One day Bill Hickey, a Southern Pacific railway detective, told Eva:

"We are going to hang your Dad!"

This callous threat made her so furious that she made a vow that if her father were hanged, she would personally shoot Hickey, and then kill herself.

It is sometimes darkest just before the dawn. It proved to be so in this case. When not a ray of hope was discernible, a man named R. C. White, a San Francisco playwright and producer, made Molly and Eva an offer. He had just completed the writing of a stage-play entitled *Evans and Sontag* which he planned to present at the National Theatre in San Francisco. He thought it would make money, but believed that if Molly and Eva would consent to join the cast and play themselves that they would prove drawing cards and attract bigger audiences. Therefore he offered them, contingent upon their accepting parts in the cast, 25% of the net receipts.

Molly was not enthusiastic over the offer. She was rather timid about becoming an actress at her time of life. But Eva was eager to try it. Was there ever a young lady in her teens who did not secretly believe that she was potentially a great actress? Eva liked to recite poems and do impersonations. She loved to dramatize herself. Here was a golden opportunity for advancement and a career; besides it would provide the money needed to hire lawyers for her father's defense. So she managed to overcome her mother's scruples and objections and they went to San Francisco. At the suggestion of Mr. White they took the little children along; he thought it would be good publicity. It was.

The family was installed in an apartment on Harrison Street near the corner of Eleventh. Molly and Eva rehearsed with the professional cast for only one week before opening night. The original cast in this lurid melodrama, *Evans and Sontag,* as produced at the National Theatre, is listed below:

Chris Evans	.	.	.	Mortimer Snow
John Sontag	.	.	.	Clyde Hess
Lige Perkins	.	.	.	Charlie Reynolds

Eva Evans	. . .	Herself
Mrs. Evans	. . .	Herself
Grandmother Byrd	. .	Julia Blanc
Wily Smooth		
(Will Smith-Villain)	.	Frank Pugh

On the opening night the SRO (standing room only) sign was hung out long before the doors were opened. The San Francisco *Examiner* for September 19, 1893, printed the following account. The lengthy review is quoted because it shows the spirit of the times and the occasion. The headlines read:[1]

"Like the roar of battle. The Evans and Sontag drama at the National Theatre a perfect volley of musketry. Eva Evans given a genuinely enthusiastic reception and proves to be an actress. An immense assemblage. The Visalia tragedy reproduced behind the footlights before as large an audience as the National could hold—Mrs. Evans plays her part listlessly, but her daughter displays considerable dramatic talent and makes a hit—six acts of bloodshed."

Then followed a blow-by-blow account of the battle centering around Evans and Sontag:

"At 7:30 o'clock last evening the street outside the National Theatre on the corner of Eddy and Jones looked as it used to when the building was known as the Wigwam and there were big glove contests on.

"It was the opening night of the new melodrama, *Evans and Sontag, or the Visalia Bandits,* and the fact that the wife and daughter of Chris Evans were to take the leading parts was sufficient to pack the theatre until it seemed as if the walls would bulge out and split at the corners. By the time the curtain rose it would have been a physical impossibility to squeeze another human being into the place. The seating capacity of the house is said to be 2,200. If this is the case, there were fully 2,800 people present when the curtain rose on the Visalia home of the Evans family.

"It was a curious mixture of an audience, too, that gathered to see the recent tragdy repeated on the mimic stage. One saw many faces that are usually only visible at the Baldwin first nights, and a good half of the orchestra chairs were filled with men and women who two nights before cheered and clapped their hands from the three dollar seats of the Grand Opera House, when the curtain fell on the last act of *Louis XI* and Henry Irving made his farewell speech. Hundreds of the people present do not enter a theatre once a year, but the Visalia battles are still fresh in the public mind, and to even see there some of the family of the famous outlaw proved too strong a temptation to be resisted. As for the regular patrons of the blank-cartridge school of acting, there was not one absent. They came early and they settled down in their seats with the delightful prospect of three or four solid hours of gunpowder and red fire.

"*The audience came to yell*. The curtain was late in rising, but no more so than an opening night warrants, and the audience contented themselves with the pleasurable excitement of seeing an occasional seat in the gallery give way with a crash under the weight of three or four occupants, and only once or twice

were the indefatigable efforts of the orchestra drowned
by the customary whistling and stamping of those
that felt the play ought to begin. The audience came
prepared to enjoy the play, and it was all that they
could do to keep their enthusiasm under control.
When the curtain finally rose, disclosing a brilliant yellow landscape with a real picket fence and the Evans
cottage just visible on the left, the gallery and half
the orchestra rose to their feet and let out a pent-up
howl of anticipation that started the shingles. Lige
Perkins and the mother of Mrs. Chris Evans were
discovered in earnest conversation, but the applause
was so loud and long drawn out for fully five minutes
that the dialogue was carried on in pantomine. Perhaps this was just as well, for Lige Perkins, a low
comedy part, was played by an actor who forgot a
good half of his lines, and filled in the gaps by stating that he desired his buttons 'gol-darned' until the
monotony of this expression rather palled.

"The stars appear. Then the audience quieted down
and waited with open mouth and uplifted feet for
the appearance of the stars of the evening. Mrs. Evans
entered first, and a yell went up that could have been
heard on Market Street. Her lines could not be heard,
but no one seemed to mind. Then Eva Evans entered,
and the storm broke and the gallery rocked back and
forth in a pure frenzy of joy and emitted whoops like
a calliope. Eva's opening speech is a strong one, and
she waited until there was a dead silence and then
said:

'How do you do. I hope you're well.'

"And once more the gallery expressed approval in the usual way. Then came the villain, Wily Smooth, who is supposed to represent Will Smith, the railroad detective, and whose make-up was not unlike the original. He is of course in love with Eva, who repels his advances with a scathing denunciation of the detective industry. The audience greeted each verbal uppercut with approval and made it evident that they were thoroughly in harmony with her anti-railroad sentiments.

"Eva Evans is a self-possessed little body, and after her excusable nervousness wore off, she put a great deal of spirit into her lines and seemed to enter into her part with real enjoyment and a good deal of appreciation. Her careful pronounciation of the 'Tos', 'Ofs', and 'Thes' suggested elocution as it is taught in the country school, but she spoke with more or less feeling, and her measured denunciation of the villainous Smooth captured the audience. Of course, John Sontag appeared just in time to save Eva the trouble of requesting Smooth to 'unhand her', and the baffled detective retreated in confusion. Then Evans and Sontag depart for the mountains and the scene closes in.

"*Revengeful Mussel Slough.* The next two scenes represent four inhabitants of Mussel Slough in brigand's boots and red cloth masks who deplore their wrong and then hold up a canvas train by tearing a hole in the side and burning a pan of red fire, while they form a tableau. In act two, still at the Evans home, Eva Evans again denounces Smooth in more or less bitter terms, and Smooth retaliates by hiding proofs of the Collis Train Robbery in the Evans orchard. The Sheriff's posse comes to arrest Evans and Sontag, the shooting begins in real earnest, and the outlaws escape in a buggy, or rather, strike a tableau expressive of escape, and the curtain falls.

"The powder burning part is now fairly under way and for the remainder of the piece the action of the play sounds like the fireworks part of a Chinese New Year. The stage is continually invaded by men in boots, red shirts, and heavy black beards, who continually run across Evans and Sontag, with a good deal of revolvers, rifle practice, and considerable mortality subsequent. Eva abandons the elocution school as her opportunities increase, and does some Davy Crockett effects, barring a door with her arm while her father and lover escape, that reduces the gallery to a perfectly breathless condition.

"*The rapid whiskers.* Then the scene changes to Sampson's Flat. A little over a month is supposed to have elapsed and the mountain air has had such a beneficial effect upon Sontag that he has easily raised a beard a foot long. The shooting now scarcely lets up for a minute, and Andrew McGinnis and Victor Wilson are killed. A year elapses and Eva, in boy's clothes, rides across the stage to rescue her father and John Sontag with $200. The applause that had been fairly hurled at her since the beginning of the play seemed to spur her on and she played this scene with real dramatic ability. When it is remembered that she is only sixteen, and up to a week or so ago was totally ignorant of anything connected with the stage, her work was really surprising. Mrs. Evans was very nervous and spoke her lines and no more, but Eva really acted, and had the audience with her from the opening scene.

"The last act consists of little besides gun-firing and tableaux. It is divided into seven scenes and ends with the tableau of the death of John Sontag.

"Behind the scenes. Behind the scenes Eva Evans all but ran the piece. She was as excited and happy as a girl at her first ball, and she was genuinely triumphant over her success. She could not keep still a minute and was all over the place at once, talking, laughing, and even dancing with delight. Mrs. Evans moved around in a sort of daze, pleased at her daughter's success and happy at the prospect of earning the money she needs so badly. She has gone through much, however, in the past year and things nowadays hardly rouse her from her listless hopelessness, and she only smiled a sad little smile when Eva hopped off her horse after the fifth act and flung her arms around her.

" 'I'm not a bit nervous now', said Eva last night about the middle of the play, 'But I tell you it made me sick when the curtain rose and I thought of going on before all those people.'

" 'I don't believe I know much about acting yet, but I really like it very much indeed. I think I would gladly become an actress—that is if there were money in it. I like the scene where I bar the door with my arm

best, and the one in which I wear boy's clothes on horseback, but I enjoy most defying Smooth and the railroad. That makes me thrill all through.'

"Then she fled into her dressing room and audibly
requested some one to help find her trousers."

After the show Mr. White, the producer, told Eva
in the presence of the rest of the cast:[2]

"I'm pleased beyond words with you. You are not
an actress yet, but you will be, and your voice is a
marvel. I could hear every word you said in the last
seat in the gallery, and you seemed to be making no
effort to pitch it. I wish I could have heard the rest of
the company like I did you."

The play was the rankest kind of melodrama, but
the audience liked it. What it lacked in subtlety and
depth, it made up in blood and thunder. One effective
bit was added to the play after Eva joined the show.
She told Mr. White that Luke Hall, whose children
had been nursed by Evans when they had scarlet fever
during the threshing season, had rented his bloodhounds to the officers who were trailing Evans and
Sontag. Naturally Eva resented what she considered
his mercenary motive and unappreciative attitude.
However, Hall may have argued that he was only
trying to help in the maintenance of law and order.
At any rate, Mr. White, more interested in dramatics
than in debate, added a scene to the play which showed
Mortimer Snow (Chris Evans) staggering weakly
across the stage croaking hoarsely "Water! Water!
Water!" And in the distance could be heard the bay-

ing of Hall's trained bloodhounds, leading the officers
ever closer and closer. It made the audience shiver and
develop goose pimples.

One day Mrs. Evans sent little four-year-old John
Christopher to Mr. White with a note. The latter lived
around the corner on Eleventh Street, but the child
failed to make the turn and kept on down Harrison
until he reached Fifth. By this time he was hope-
lessly lost, and it was there that a policeman picked
him up and took him to headquarters. The reporters
of the various newspapers made much of the story and
some said accusingly that it was a publicity stunt. It
had all the value of one, although it was not planned
that way. Chris Evans read about it, and wrote Molly
an indignant letter, saying the big city was no place
for little children. When the letter arrived his wife
had already left for Visalia with John Christopher.
When the show went on the road all the other children
were also taken to Grandmother Byrd.

The play was shown in San Francisco for one month
and then went on the road. It invariably played to
full houses. After a while on the road it would return
to San Francisco for a return engagement. This pro-
cedure was repeated several times. The play was presented in Oakland, Los Angeles, Sacramento, Stockton, and again and again in San Francisco.

When Evans went to trial the play was being shown
in the San Joaquin Valley towns north of Fresno.
Under-studies took the places of Molly and Eva who
were required to appear in court as witnesses. After
the trial they hurried to rejoin the cast. The girl who

substituted for Eva could not ride a horse, and the attendance fell off. This proved that Molly and Eva were the real drawing cards. They were playing in Santa Rosa when the verdict of the jury was announced. Molly and Eva had hoped for an acquittal, but felt that life imprisonment was preferable to the death sentence. Now, at least, they could begin to work for a pardon.

About 7 o'clock in the evening of December 28, 1893, the Associated Press at San Francisco began receiving over its telegraph the startling news of Evans' sensational jail-break. That same night the actors in *The Count of Monte Cristo,* a serious dramatic production, took advantage of the excitement created by these dispatches to give Chris Evans some free and favorable publicity. In one scene the prisoner was shown trying to dig his way out of his cell. When the jailer caught him in the act of pulling out bricks, he asked jocosely:[3]

"Why all the hard work? Why don't you take a tip from Chris Evans and just walk out?"

The audience roared with laughter and applauded loudly.

Eva Evans went to San Francisco and began work on the new play which the occasion demanded: *Evans & Sontag Up to Date.* Scenes were added which showed Ben Scott, the jailer; the shooting of John H. Morgan, and Ed. Morrell's heroic defiance of evil men. A newspaper reported:[4]

"Mrs. Chris Evans, with her six youngest children —two girls and four boys—left Visalia for San Francisco this morning. On Saturday evening, at the National Theatre, the revived Evans and Sontag play will be given to the public. Eva and her mother will take the same parts they had in the old version, while the younger children will be bunched on the stage whenever the occasion calls for a display of tow-headed children.

"It is thought by some Visalians that Chris himself will essay to slip in and take a hand after the play gets well on the road up the valley."

During those gay, old nineties any member of the Evans family was considered a celebrity. San Francisco had its first World's Fair during the winter of 1893-1894. A popular song of the period listed all persons of prominence that would be seen there:

"Eva Evans will be there,
With her 18-carat hair."

The play was in Oakland when news came that Evans and Morell had been captured. The next time Eva saw her father he was an inmate of Folsom.

Mr. White booked his show for a series of performances in the cities of the Sacramento Valley. From there it was taken into Oregon. In the latter state the attendance was poor. Evidently the people there were not interested in San Joaquin Valley outlaws.

Finally the show was scheduled to appear at Heppner in eastern Oregon. This little town lay about forty miles south of the Columbia River, and had railway connections with Heppner Junction, lying along the river. The train crew resided at the junction. The branch train which made the run between Heppner

Junction and Heppner usually left the latter place at 9:30 in the evening. Mr. White asked the conductor if he would hold the train until the play was over that night. The latter good-naturedly consented:

"Sure; we got lots of time. We'll all go and see the play. We usually go down early so the boys can get home early. But they won't mind staying a little later to-night."

When the conductor agreed to do this favor for Mr. White and the cast, he did not know that Governor Sylvester Pennoyer was on the train stumping the state for re-election. The latter naturally wanted to leave on scheduled time. The conductor knew the danger of fudging with the timetable when a "big-shot" politician was on board. So the poor man was afraid to hold his train, and unintentionally double-crossed the players. The result was that Mr. White and his cast were left stranded. Then some more of that bad luck which seemed to hound the Evans family appeared. The Columbia River overflowed its banks that night; it was the greatest flood in the history of that river. The roadbed from Heppner Junction to Portland was washed out; and Portland itself was under water for nine blocks up from the river front. The players at Heppner were marooned for weeks with no chance to get out. To make matters worse, White had been losing money on the play for weeks and had no funds with which to pay the members of the cast. To cap the climax, Eva Evans broke down from internal injuries sustained when the run-way in the Hazzard Pavilion at Los Angeles crashed and the horse and she went down in a heap. Later she had a similar experience in Oakland. Her new horse, a spirited animal, was startled by the foot-lights and backed across the stage into the canvas and wooden scenery. Horse, rider, and stage settings went down together. Eva was knocked unconscious, but managed to finish the performance. Three vetrebrae in her back were pushed out of place and she was able to continue her work only because her doctor gave her morphine shots. She was paying for it now at Heppner. She was bed-ridden for weeks. Good Samaritans had to come to her aid. Molly and Eva had arrived at Heppner in May; it was not until August 9th that they could take the train over the newly laid rails which took them from Heppner to Heppner Junction to Portland.

Molly returned to her other children in Visalia. Her acting career was now definitely ended. Eva remained in Oakland in hopes of getting stage work. She succeeded. This was the summer of 1894 and the Cleveland depression was at its height or depth. The Evans family finances had never been in worse shape. Chris was in Folsom, George Byrd was working on a ranch for his board and keep, Ynez was cooking on another ranch for harvest hands, trying to make enough money to feed the children who were being cared for by Grandmother Byrd.

Eva went to see her father shortly after her return from Oregon. Molly and she had lacked nourishing food during their months in Heppner. Chris was not thriving under prison conditions. He was an out-door man; for him incarceration was almost as bad as death. Therefore father and daughter were mutually shocked at what they saw.

Chris Evans had always taught his children that truth was one of the cardinal virtues. During this interview Christopher and Eva lied gloriously to each other. They were feeling fine, and everything was lovely. Then they laughed, but it was the "laughter which keeps one from bursting into tears."

CHAPTER 15

LET GEORGE DO IT

GEORGE Sontag was a broken man. As he lay on his cot at Folsom his nerves were jumpy, his heart was fluttering, his shattered leg was throbbing painfully, his spirits were low, and his health was generally bad. His brother John was dead and out of his misery. His friend Evans, awaiting trial at Fresno, would doubtless be convicted for the shooting of Beaver, Wilson, and McGinnis. There were witnesses to all of these killings, and Evans had frankly admitted that he had shot them in self-defense. Mulling these things over in his mind led George to make a momentous decision. He would save his own skin, and hurt no one else. So he informed Warden Aull that he had a confession to make. And it was a honey!

However, before George would talk he made certain demands. He was no fool. He presented a certain general and all-inclusive proposition to the proper officials, and then said in effect: "Take it or leave it!" They decided to take it. A deputy warden at Folsom was later to reveal the terms laid down by George. Specifically he demanded six things.

First, his attractive young wife and two little sons should be moved from Mankato, Minnesota, to Sacramento, California.

Second, he should be permitted to spend one week-end each month with them. While George was in the Fresno jail his baby daughter had died. He may have been a scoundrel in some ways, but he was an affectionate father. He grieved over the loss of his little girl with the golden curls, and was filled with an increased tenderness for the remaining members of his family.

Third, since his wife and sons were dependent upon relatives for their support, George demanded that enough money should be provided for their upkeep. By this he stipulated that a furnished house should be provided, the rent paid, the groceries purchased, and a comfortable living made available.

Fourth, after a decent interval he should be granted a full pardon.

Fifth, George refused under any circumstances to talk to Will Smith, whom he hated.

Sixth, he would recite his confession to two men: J. B. Hume, a Wells Fargo detective, and J. B. Wright, a division superintendent of the Southern Pacific.

These terms were accepted and, strange to say, they were all carried out to the letter. Warden Aull brought Hume and Wright to the prison, escorted them into George's room, and left them there. These two men, together with a professional stenographer who took down the story, were the only three persons present when George related his version of preceding events with respect to train robberies and his alleged part therein. The following is a synopsis of his story as he subsequently repeated it to the jury during the trial of Chris Evans.

His brother, John Sontag, arrived at Mankato, Minnesota, some time in May, 1891. This was after the disastrous fire at Modesto, which had destroyed Evans' livery stable. George and John spent the summer hunting and fishing together. One evening John told George confidentially how Chris Evans, one of his California friends, and he had robbed the trains at Pixley and Goshen, out in the San Joaquin Valley. It was easy money. John tried to interest George in future ventures of a similar nature, and George and he planned the Ceres hold-up while still in Minnesota. John returned to California, but George was delayed and did not get there in time to take part in the attempted robbery. Chris and John tried it without George, and failed.

John then returned to Minnesota for a second visit, and helped George rob a train near Western Junction, just out of Chicago. This was in November, 1891. They were very, very successful, and managed to get away with $4,800. However, George was disappointed that they could not remove the entire $100,000 in the express coach; John lost his nerve and hurried away too soon. George was the little hero in the affair, but tried to make the jury understand that he could hardly be expected to remove the rest of the money and do the job all by himself.

The next spring, 1892, John and George returned to California together, and George met Chris Evans for the first time. The three men then went back East and tried to rob a train near Kasota, located between Mankato and St. Peter, but failed. George did not explain what went wrong there; either the express-coach carried no money, or the men fumbled the job. Then the three musketeers went back to California and succeeded in their attempt at Collis, where they secured about $50,000, according to George. The amount given in this case was false, as later testimony clearly proved during the trial of Chris Evans. George went into great detail with respect to his description of the Collis holdup. He knew what the prosecution wanted and needed for conviction, and he gave it to them.

George said he had met Chris Evans in a saloon on the west side of Fresno during the afternoon of August 3rd. There the two men had completed plans for the hold-up that night. According to legend, but not mentioned in court, Chris Evans always planned his robberies with the Sontags while sitting in a rowboat in the middle of Tulare Lake. Any reader who has visited Tulare Lake, even now in 1950 with the fast automobiles in use, will testify that it is a long way from all centers of population. To have driven there in that horse and buggy age, sixty years ago, would seem an unreasonable precaution to take; surely men planning illicit operations could have found a safe and secret meeting place, without fear of eavesdroppers, much closer at hand.

George made no reference to clandestine meetings on Tulare Lake; he merely stated that Chris walked from Fresno out to the Rolinda School. At eight o'clock John Sontag harnessed his horses and drove slowly across the tracks to the west side of Fresno, where he picked up George. The two brothers then rode to the Rolinda School, and Evans rode with them from that place to a point within a mile and a half of Collis. Chris and George walked the rest of the way into town, and John, who was still lame, took the team back to the Rolinda School to wait for the pay-off. In the meantime Chris and George hid along the tracks of the Southern Pacific until the passenger train arrived. Then they put on their masks, and climbed undetected into the coal-car or tender.

After the hold-up, which George described with true histrionic ability and handled with a master's touch, the three men rode back to Fresno by way of the Gordon Ranch, where George watered his matchless steeds, Button and Joe. This act may sound like kindness to animals and a praiseworthy act on the part of George, but was as necessary at that time as filling up the gas-tank under similar circumstances would be today.

At Fresno, George boarded the train for Visalia and at Goshen transferred from the through-train for Los Angeles to the little branch-line road which served the county seat. Chris and John rode home in the Bequette buggy, and reached Visalia by a long and circuitous route; they approached the Evans home from the east to make it appear that they had come from the mountains. The Bequette horses had travelled ninety miles between eight in the evening and eight in the morning. The two men arrived at the Evans home about eight, and John returned the team to the Bequette stables about eleven. The owner testified later that his horses showed signs of hard driving. No wonder!

Men who grew up during the horse and buggy age may question the possibility of two horses travelling so far in so short a time. Young men who have known only automobiles and trucks don't know enough about the matter to discuss it. The author interrogated three men in whom he has the utmost confidence.

One of them, Norman Parks, a quarter-breed Sioux Indian and a Montana rancher, who shipped thousands of horses to France during World War I, said that he had known horses good enough to do it. On one occasion he drove two trotting mares, hitched to a light buckboard, from his ranch in Montana to the nearest railway station, a distance of forty-five miles, in four hours. He fed, watered, and rested his horses for one hour, and then drove them back in four hours. The total elapsed time was nine hours and the distance travelled was ninety miles. It was a bitterly cold day, but no snow had fallen. The ground was frozen hard, and the horses wanted to trot fast in order to keep warm.[1]

Sam B. Kerner, a Dinuba rancher, is authority for the statement that his father-in-law, Jack Salyer, and William Ward, both of Kingsburg, drove a span of trotting horses from Fresno to Bakersfield in one day. The winding country roads of the period, not laid out in as direct a line as present Highway 99, made the distance travelled that day approximately one hundred and twenty-five miles. Salyer and Ward left Fresno early in the morning, stopped three times to feed, rest, and water their horses, and arrived at Bakersfield late in the evening.[2]

The two horses driven by Sontag had to contend with unfavorable climatic conditions. In August it is very warm in the San Joaquin Valley, and the team had trotted between fifty and seventy-five miles on August 2nd, depending upon John Sontag's route. The night of the hold-up it did another ninety miles, if George's story were true, but the weather at night in the valley is ideal and would cause no ill effects to livestock. But these horses had been asked to do a repeat performance with only one day of rest. Were there such animals in California then? Yes.

This writer asked William Elam about the Bequette team; he knew the two horses well. They were foaled in the foothill country and grew to maturity scampering up and down the steep hills. Their environment was excellent; what about their heredity? These rangy, dark bay animals, trained to the saddle as well as to harness, belonged to that famous breed of livestock known to horsemen as trotters, Hambletonians, or standardbreds. For this kind of work they are the toughest horses in the world. This particular team, according to Elam, was the fastest and the most enduring one in the San Joaquin Valley at that time.[3]

Members of the Bequette family still residing at Visalia stated that these two horses, named Joe and Button, whose merits were so hotly debated in court, were brothers, both sired by the famous trotting stallion, Ben Franklin.[4]

If the prosecution lawyers were correct in their contention, then the Bequette horses had trotted ninety miles that night. From Collis (Kerman) to Fresno three men had ridden in the buggy, and from Fresno to Visalia, presumably by way of Reedley, Dinuba, and Yettem, two men had been the passengers. In addition there had been two bags of silver coins which had weighed another two hundred and fifty pounds. The total weight of men and money placed in the Bequette buggy that night had amounted to at least seven hundred and seventy-five pounds for a part of the way, and six hundred pounds during the rest of the journey. Was this possible? The owner was interrogated about his vehicle. Bequette testified that this particular buggy was a custom-built three-passenger rig, and able to carry such a load. He called it "an extra stout buggy." However, when it came to motive power, the defence lawyers maintained that not even those famous steeds of antiquity, Pegasus and Bucephalus, could have gone that distance with such a load in the time allotted.

Whatever the truth of the matter may be with respect to that horse and buggy age, the fact remains that if credence can be placed in the confession of George Sontag and the deductions of the many detectives assigned to the case, then this was the answer to the question: "Who robbed the trains?"

The sworn testimony of several reputable citizens was to verify many points in George's story. James M. Leslie, the young man who has already been referred to as the member of a bear hunting party guided by

Evans, was a personal friend of the latter. And yet he assured the author that he believed that Evans was guilty of train robberies. Leslie had become acquainted with Chris while serving as foreman of the ranch owned by Dr. James Long McClelland of Selma. This place was located along the McCall Road, due south of Harry Nelson's Selma Stock Farm and across the road from the Franklin school. McClelland, a physician and surgeon, resided in Selma. He had married Molly Evans' sister, Sophia Byrd, who was also a medical doctor. According to Dr. J. H. Wagner[5] she enjoyed an even more extensive practice than did her husband. Women doctors were scarce in the early 1890's; that Molly Evans' sister had been educated in the field of medicine indicated that the Byrd family possessed brains, social vision, professional ambition, and an outlook far in advance of the times. Chris Evans and Dr. J. L. McClelland, having married sisters, were often together. Evans frequently spent the night at the McClelland ranch, and was well acquainted with the men who worked there.

In time McClelland sold his property to E. R. Pease, a hardware merchant of Visalia, who thereupon leased the ranch to Leslie. Since Pease was also a friend and neighbor of Evans, the latter continued to visit the ranch from time to time. After the Modesto fire, Evans sent his four remaining horses to the Pease holdings where they were placed in a pasture. One day, when Leslie was absent, Clarke Moore came from Visalia and took the horses away without paying for the pasturage. This annoyed Leslie at the time as he knew from past experience that it was often hard to collect such bills after the livestock had been removed. Therefore he hurriedly wrote a letter to Pease explaining the situation. Pease arrived a few days later with the money. He told Leslie that Evans had paid him promptly. In all his personal relations Evans was as honest as the most exacting could desire. However, one thing seemed peculiar to both Pease and Leslie. Evans had paid his bill with greenbacks. Paper money was as scarce in California during the 1890's as the proverbial hen's teeth. Its possession was always an indication that a man had come from the Eastern states recently. In this case the two men remembered that the $5,000 stolen at Pixley had been greenbacks. Had Evans hidden it, and used it carefully and at long intervals? Or had someone else robbed the trains, and had Evans innocently come into the possession of this money? Who knows?

About six o'clock in the evening of August 2nd, Leslie was returning to the Pease ranch with a wagon and some ranch laborers. When he reached the crossroads beside the Franklin school, he met Evans. Leslie hailed him, and asked:[6]

"Chris, do you want a ride?"

"No, I'll walk. It isn't far."

Leslie told the author that Evans was the greatest walker he had ever met. He thought nothing of a twenty-mile hike, even when horses were available. The man had tremendous nervous and physical energy. This evening he told Leslie that he had come from Sampson's Flat that day, but did not say in what manner. He had appeared at the ticket-window of the railway station at Kingsburg, and the agent had informed him that the train for Fresno had already left. Then he walked due west from Kingsburg along Conejo Avenue until he reached the Franklin school where he was intercepted by Leslie. He then asked permission to stay at the Pease ranch during the night. He stated that some legal matters had arisen over the ownership of his mine and he planned to go to Fresno the next day to discuss the matter with his lawyer, Mr. Coldwell. The latter verified the fact that Evans did see him on legal business during the afternoon of August 3rd.

Evans was in no hurry to leave the Pease ranch the next morning. Leslie said he loitered about the place until about 10 o'clock, at which time he started walking along the McCall Road toward Selma. Leslie was driving into Selma that morning and offered Evans a ride, but the latter declined. Leslie assumed that Evans had planned to rob a train and did not want to implicate his friend by being seen in his company. As it was, Leslie got into trouble because of Evans' presence at the Pease ranch during the evening of August 2nd.

The following incident will show that the best of men were subject to arrest in those days for train robbery. The subsequent career of James M. Leslie as a leader of uncommon ability and unblemished reputation must make his surveillance by the railway detectives seem absurd. It was merely a lucky circumstance which saved him from the possible fate of Evans and

Sontag. It was quickly established that Evans had been
with him the night before the robbery. It looked suspicious. Shortly after the robbery Leslie received a
letter from Evans. The detectives were watching the
mails and knew about it. At two o'clock in the morning following the receipt of this letter, John Thacker
appeared at the Pease ranch and demanded the surrender of this letter. Leslie refused. However, he took
it out and placed it on a table, and told the detective
that he might make a copy of it. This was done. There
was nothing incriminating in it. After the Modesto
fire, Evans had not only sent his remaining horses to
the Pease ranch, but had shipped to it several halters,
fifth-chains, and other equipment. In this letter he
asked Leslie to send the fifth-chains to Visalia.[7]

Courtship saved Leslie from a court trial. Before
the officers served a warrant on him it was proved un-
officially that Leslie had been visiting his fiancee the
evening of the Collis robbery. His future wife as well
as the other members of her family thus provided him
with the alibi which prevented any further annoyance
by the police.

Another good citizen who verified a portion of
George's confession was Bart Patterson[8] of Dinuba.
He told the author that he was employed as a ranch
hand at the Gordon Ranch at the time of the Collis
robbery. This place was located half-way between the
Rolinda School and the present Central Union High
School. About half an hour after the hold-up George
came to the door of the bunk-house, where the young
employees were playing poker, and asked permission

to water his horses at the ranch trough. George's presence in the vicinity with a team was thus proved, but since none of the men at the ranch went outside, they saw nothing of any other men.

While George admitted his full share for the responsibility of the Collis hold-up, he swore that he was not present when the trains were stopped at Pixley, Goshen, and Ceres.

When this story was released, how did it affect Evans, his family, and the prosecution? Let us take them one at a time.

Evans never said a word, not a word. Not then nor later. He saw George at the trial, but naturally had no chance to say anything to him then. Whether Evans was guilty or not guilty of train robberies, it must have been a strain on George to re-tell his story in court under the single piercing eye of his former friend. He must have felt like a heel.

George was taken back to Folsom to resume the serving of his sentence. After a "strange interlude" in the mountains, Evans followed him. It was suggested by some officials that it might be safer for George to be transferred to San Quentin, as Evans might try to exact vengeance. But nothing ever came of either the suggestion or the vengeance. Chris and George met only once after the trial. Evans won the respect of the warden and his assistants, and was eventually placed in charge of the surgical supply room in the second story. The instruments stored there would have provided hideous weapons in an attempted jail-break. It speaks volumes for Evans' integrity that he was chosen

to guard these from other convicts. One day a man
started to mount the stairs which led to this room.
Evans stopped in front of him, and said:[9]

"No prisoner is allowed to go up these stairs."

"Whose orders?"

"The Warden's."

"Well, I'm going up."

"Oh, no, you are not."

"Who is going to stop me?"

"I am!"

For the first time George took a good look at the
man standing a few steps above him, and saw the man
he most feared in this world. He quailed. The prison
doctor, who had stepped out of an adjacent door, had
heard the colloquy. He said later that the low, intense
voice of Evans cut like a knife, and made his spine
tingle.

How did Eva and Molly react to the story? A good
account was published about them in the *Examiner*:[10]

"Mrs. Evans and Eva were on the stage at the
National Theatre when word was brought of George
Sontag's confession.

"The girl had just finished one of her denunciations
of Wily Smooth, and George Sontag, an injured innocent in the play, had been taken off to prison.

"Mr. White would not let them be told about the
confession for fear that it would so disturb them that
they could not go on with the play. Everybody else
knew it, however, and the other characters looked on
the two as if a great calamity were hanging over them.

"After the performance, George's confession was

read to them. There were smelling salts and restoratives handy in case the effect was serious. They listened to the long story and both broke out with a laugh.

" 'I don't believe he ever said it,' cried Mrs. Evans. 'It is the most arrant nonsense I ever listened to.'

" 'Yes, I believe he said it,' said Eva, rather more seriously. 'Poor George! I guess he has got down to a point where he would lie, even about himself, if he thought it would do any good. He wants a pardon and hopes to get it by this means. There was a time when George wouldn't have done this.'

" 'This so-called confession will not affect our plans at all. His saying these things does not make them true, and I do not believe anybody who understands the situation will take any stock in the statements.'

" 'I would do as much for George now as ever,' said the girl softly: 'But, oh, I am sorry that he is so broken down that he would tell such stories, even for the sake of liberty!' "

How did the prosecution lawyers receive George's confession. With glee! It tallied exactly with the theories which the detectives and law-enforcement officers had propounded. Some accused George of concocting a story which would dove-tail with theirs. At any rate, the prosecution lawyers planned to make George their star witness. His arrival in court created a sensation. George was dapper, handsome, and crippled. It was a scene a moving picture director might well crave. The casual observer was apt to miss the evil-looking eyes and the sinister appearance of the man. His testimony made a favorable impression on the jury.

But after the lawyers for the defence got through with him on the witness stand, he did not look so good. Here is some of the testimony from the court record, Mr. Hinds cross-examining:

"You have been in the penitentiary before, have you not?"

"Yes, sir." (In Nebraska).

"For how long?"

"Two years."

"Would you lie again if you thought it would benefit you?"

"Yes, I would lie again, if I thought I could gain my liberty by doing so."

"When did you begin to tell the truth in this case?"

"When I was on my couch in Folsom, wounded. I was in the train robbery and I told all about it."

"And you would lie again, if it would be of any benefit to you?"

"Yes, I told you I would lie again if I could gain my liberty by it."

The defence lawyers were pretty rough on George. When they were through with him he had been forced to admit that he was a liar, a loafer, a perjurer, a philanderer, a traitor, and a two-time convict. He willingly admitted that his brother had always been good to him, and yet he also had to admit under prodding that he was accusing that brother, who was dead and could not defend himself, of murder and robbery. He also admitted that Evans had been a good friend. And now he was putting that friend's neck into a noose. It did not make George look so good.

However, George may have reasoned that John was

beyond all injury, and Evans beyond redemption. Or he may not have reasoned at all. And then he had been promised much at a time when his life held so little of hope. The promises were kept. His wife and two sons were safely established in a cozy home at Sacramento, and George spent some time with them each month. His leg healed nicely, although he was to limp the rest of his natural life. His health began to mend; George began to feel better.

But Fate could never be kind to George for long. One day, when his older son, George, Jr., was playing in the railroad yards at Sacramento, he was run over by a switch engine and instantly killed (the Iron Horse again!). The mother, heart-broken by the accident, took her remaining child, John, back to Mankato.

When the officials, who were trying to solve the train robberies, were in need of evidence they had reasoned that if George could and would furnish it for a price, then let George do it! He had done it. Whether he had lied or had told the truth, no one will ever know. It is a matter of personal opinion. He had kept his part of the bargain. The officials, to their credit, were to keep theirs. They had told George that after a decent interval, he would be pardoned. He was. But when that potentially happy day finally arrived, it did not prove to be an entirely joyous occasion for George. Just before he was granted his freedom, he received word that his wife had died!

CHAPTER 16

GENTLEMEN OF THE JURY

CHRISTOPHER EVANS had been captured in the early morning hours of June 13th, at the Perkins home. He had been taken to Visalia where his left arm had been amputated. Shortly thereafter he had been placed in the Fresno jail to await trial. He spent the summer of 1893 there. His wife and daughter were away with the show earning the money with which to pay for the services of two first-class lawyers, S. J. Hinds and State Senator G. G. Goucher. The trial opened on November 20th. Molly and Eva were present, having left their parts in the play to under-studies. Judge M. K. Harris presided. The lawyers for the prosecution were W. D. Tupper and H. H. Welsh.

Nine days were required to secure a jury. The first venire of a hundred names yielded only two possible jurors. Apparently every person in the state had heard of Chris Evans, and had formed an opinion concerning him and his troubles with the law. Three hundred names were called before twelve good men and true could be secured. Prosecution and defense vied with one another in hurling challenges and offering objections.

Much of the testimony heard during the trial of

Chris Evans was a repetition of that which had been given during the trial of George Contant (Sontag). It was practically the same case tried a second time.

Evans was being tried for murder, and yet the first witness called was George D. Roberts, the express messenger, whose shoes had mysteriously been blown off his feet when his express coach had been dynamited at Collis. Hinds jumped to his feet and addressed Judge Harris:[1]

"We object, Your Honor. Our client is not on trial for the Collis train robbery. He is accused for a murder committed more than a year earlier. The question is incompetent, immaterial, and irrelevant."

Hinds argued his point eloquently for one solid hour. When he sat down Judge Harris promptly overruled him. The court held that all evidence pertaining to train robberies was admissible since it was pertinent to the case of *The People of the State of California vs. Christopher Evans.* If it could be proved that Evans had robbed trains, then his resistance was inexcusable and a heinous crime. On the other hand, if it could be shown that Evans was innocent of wrongdoing with respect to train robberies, then his resentment of the bullying tactics of Smith and the uncalled-for firing by Witty of his revolver in the Evans home was understandable. These were mitigating circumstances, which would have to be considered. Also, a motive might thus be established for the shooting of Beaver, Wilson, and McGinnis.

When Evans entered the court-room the first day of the trial he did not look like a vicious criminal or a dangerous railway bandit. He was pale and wan from his illness and several months in jail; his left sleeve, empty now, was pinned across his breast; and his right eye was missing. The courtroom was packed with spectators who had come to gloat over Public Enemy No. 1; they went away filled with pity.

Roberts finally was permitted to give his testimony. He told about the use of the bombs, and the injuries sustained by himself, the express coach, and the locomotive. In order to cripple the engine, the bandits had blown off the arm on the left main pin. However, the engineer managed to pull his train into Fresno. Roberts was an honorable man and would not swear to anything about which he was not certain. Sixteen months had elapsed since the Collis hold-up. Having been the victim of the concussions of two bombs that night, he must have been a trifle shell-shocked at the time. Roberts did not prove entirely satisfactory to the prosecution since he refused to unequivocally identify Evans as the short man at the scene of the Collis robbery.[2]

One of the most brilliant and resourceful detectives in the state then was John N. Thacker. He had played a prominent part in the unmasking of Black Bart (Charles Bolton). He was the second witness called. According to his testimony, he had gone to the Chris Evans' home three weeks after the Collis robbery, and had dug up two bags containing $2,000 worth of Peruvian silver dollars. He had located the sacks by prodding the ground with a long, slender steel rod. His assistants were James Hume, Frank Burke, and

Vernon C. Wilson. This testimony did not meet with unanimous approval among the people. Some accepted it as good evidence; others wanted to know why no neutral observers or witnesses had been taken to the "diggings." Scott Gillum told the author that he, and many other old-timers, always believed that the two bags were "planted" in the Evans yard. No one ever saw the officers dig in the yard, and this led many persons to wonder how they could have escaped the keen eyes of Grandmother Byrd and the little tow-headed children who were always playing around the yard, not to mention the inquisitive loafers who were usually "snooping" in the vicinity. Goucher cross-examined Thacker:[3]

"When did you dig up that coin?"

"I think it was about the last of August."

"What did you do with the money?"

"We put the coin-sack into a gunny-sack, and the gunny-sack into a box, and took the box to J. B. Hume, at Fresno."

"Was Evans at home when you found the money?"

"I think not; I did not go into the house to look for him. Nobody was at home so far as I know."

"Did you take pains, when you found the money, that nobody but employees of the Southern Pacific and Wells, Fargo were present?"

"We did not take pains for any such purpose."

"Well, was anyone present when you found the money, except employees of the Southern Pacific and Wells, Fargo?"

"No, none others were present."

Most of the men and women who had occupied the witness stand during the trial of George Contant (Sontag) during the previous year, were called a second time.

Frank Bequette of Visalia told the jurors that John Sontag had rented a team from him on August 2nd of the previous year. He had brought it back[4] two days later, but the owner had no way of knowing where his horses had been. They were as nearly played out as horses of their calibre ever permit themselves to be. The only man who could have told the truth about their peregrinations during those days was John Sontag, and he was dead.

James M. Leslie repeated his testimony with respect to Evans' presence at the Pease ranch during the night of August 2nd. This established[5] the fact that Chris had not been at Sampson's Flat at the time, and that he had been within striking distance of Collis. However, this evidence was not damaging to Evans since he had stated from the outset that he had been in Fresno on August 3rd to see his lawyer, N. C. Coldwell, about his mining property. The latter verified this statement of his client.

John Armstrong, owner of a stable in Fresno, repeated his story that John Sontag had placed the Bequette team in his barns in the afternoon of August 2nd, and had taken it out about 7:45 in the evening of August 3rd. When the lawyer for the defence suggested that Armstrong might have been mistaken in his identification of Sontag, the former replied:[6]

"Evans and Sontag were often in the Fresno dis-

trict buying horses. After such purchases they often
left their livestock with me. I knew both men well;
Sontag was no stranger to me. It was he, and no one
else, who left the Bequette team in my stables on
August 2nd."

The high-light of the trial came when George Sontag was ushered to the witness stand. He may have
been a villain but, like so many other rogues, he could
win the love and admiration of little children, dogs,
honest men, and lovely women. Men suffering from
inferiority complexes apparently feel at ease with innocent children and fawning dogs; the need for being
on the defensive disappears, and they secure the attention they crave. George's confession had been released
some time before this, and now he was to repeat it in
the presence of Chris Evans. Under the gentle direction of the prosecution lawyers his story rolled smooth-
ly to its logical conclusion.

Another titillating moment came when Eva Evans
took the stand. Her fame as an actress, and the courageous fight she was making in her father's behalf,
had won for her a great deal of admiration. Then,
too, her lover had died, and there was a certain amount
of pathos involved. Eva, as well as her eleven-year-old
sister, Winifred, testified that the trouble started, not
over train robberies, but over the insulting and profane
remarks tossed about in the Evans home by Will
Smith. Any father who reads this would probably
resent two strange men entering his house without
permission, especially if one of them cursed his
daughter and the other fired a pistol in her general

direction. The two girls were given a long and tough cross-examination but it failed to shake their story. They stuck to it. Their testimony made a deep impression on the jury.

Will Smith denied that he had made the remark attributed to him. Since the two daughters of Evans, as well as the detective, were under oath, it was up to the jury to decide who was telling the truth.

John Coffee, a mountaineer and a friend to Evans, gave his account of a visit to Jim Young's cabin two days before the gun battle there. Wilson and his posse appeared, and the marshal boasted that he would shoot Evans and Sontag on sight, and threatened Clarke Moore, also present:

"If you are with Evans when I shoot him, I'll kill you too. You have helped him elude us several times. I warn you not to be so friendly with the outlaws from now on."

Clarke Moore corroborated the statements of Coffee and added his damaging bit against Warren Hill, a Fresno deputy sheriff and Sanger constable. The latter had offered Moore $50,000 if he would betray Evans and Sontag. Just where this money was coming from was not made clear, but the inference was that the Southern Pacific and Wells, Fargo would consider this amount well spent in the liquidaton of Evans and Sontag.

The defense lawyers managed to have read into the record several articles which had appeared in the Visalia papers, which expressed a fear that the two outlaws would be lynched if captured. The lawyers for the defense argued that it would therefore have been useless for the two outlaws to surrender. They might as well be shot by officers while resisting arrest as hanged by the mob. What else could they do but fight? So argued Messrs. Hinds and Goucher.

After days of wrangling over train robberies and other related subjects, the trial finally reached the fight at Young's cabin. A large map showing the cabin and its immediate surroundings had been prepared and was hung on the wall in such a way that the jurors could study it. An officer diagrammed for them the successive steps in that fatal battle.

The climax of the trial came when Christopher Evans took the witness stand. This was what the audience in the court room had been waiting for with impatience and some apprehension. In the estimation of many people, he was the chief character in a drama equal in derring-do to the exploits of Robin Hood, Dick Turpin, Joaquin Murieta, John Tolberg,[7] Tiburcio Vasquez, Black Bart, Jesse James, and Bob Dalton. Evans gave his version of the fight at Young's cabin simply and clearly. He said it had been a case of killing or being killed. What would the jurors have done in such a case? Or the reader? Evans denied categorically the entire story as told by George Sontag. One of the two men was lying. It was up to the jury!

Frank Burke, the handsome half-breed Indian detective, stated that the two Apaches and he were the only ones who had fired at the outlaws that day. Pelon and Cameño Dulce were not present at the trial. Presumably their outspoken contempt for certain members of the posse made their presence unwelcome by the prosecution.

Will Smith turned out to be one of the best witnesses for the defence, although he did not plan it that way. It was perhaps an inadvertence on his part when he testified that McGinnis' gun had one exploded cartridge in it. This verified the contention of Evans that he had been forced to kill McGinnis because the latter had first shot Chris.

At the beginning of the trial Warren Hill appeared in court with two big revolvers strapped to his waist. His artillery attracted so much attention that the defence lawyers protested to the judge. They argued that Hill's parading around heavily armed was prejudicing the jury; the impression was being created that plans were being laid to free Evans by force. Judge Harris ruled that Hill would have to disarm.

The Bank of California, for whom Evans had worked for many years, sent several officials to the trial. They all testified that he had been a man of probity, integrity, and honesty. It was brought out at the trial that the train robbers had never molested private passengers or the United States mails. The object of attack had always been a corporation.

Several character witnesses from Visalia were called by the defence. The testimony of one of them received special attention in the Fresno *Expositor*:[8]

"Joseph Thomas of Visalia came next. He had lived in Tulare County since 1857 and has known Evans for about twenty-five years. He also gave Evans

a good name and a reputaton for industry and work:
'In fact,' said the witness, 'he was a leader in work'."

" 'Did you ever know him to have any fights?'
asked Mr. Tupper (for the prosecution.)"

" 'I did.' "

" 'You did, eh?' "

" 'Yes, do you want the particulars?' asked the witness of the lawyer."

" 'I will ask you for what I want,' said Mr. Tupper,
'don't be too willing'. "

" 'I am not too willing; I thought you might want
to know,' replied the witness."

" 'No, I don't want to know the particulars of the
fight, but whom was the fight with? You can tell
me that'."

" 'A man named Bigelow'."

The newspapers sensed a story at this point. Since
the facts were not permitted to be brought out in court,
the reporters concocted their own distortions. In one
story Evans had beaten a man to death; in another,
Chris had been tried for manslaughter, but had been
acquitted because no doctor had been called prior to
the man's death, and so the evidence was inconclusive.

According to many old-timers, this is what had
happened:

During the year 1875 a worker in one of the lumber
camps in the mountains amused himself by writing
filthy doggerels about various women of his acquaintance. Evans, whose worst enemies admitted that morally he was as pure as the driven snow, said:

"If that dirty cur ever turns his rotten mind on anyone dear to me, I'll wring his neck."

At that time no one knew the author of the obscene verses. His compositions were posted in conspicuous places and were naturally unsigned. One day a foul poem was tacked to the fence of the corral where Evans kept his horses. The general theme of this epistolary effusion, addressed to Chris Evans, was that Molly's first baby had arrived before she had been married nine months. The man with the poetic ability and unclean mind stated that "Molly, who belonged to the tribe of Byrd, had left to roam with another herd." Evans was naturally enraged and began to look for the perpetrator of the outrage. Other men in the camp were also infuriated over similar writings and the guilty man decided to leave camp. Evans managed to waylay the culprit, and made him confess, and then proceeded to give him an artistic beating. After the man had been battered into abject submission, Chris gave him a final twist of the neck which the victim testified well-nigh killed him. Evans was arrested, and tried in the superior court at Visalia. Judge Clark was willing to overlook the whipping, but ruled that the twist of the neck was unnecessary and fined Evans one hundred dollars. That was a huge sum in those days, and Chris lacked even a portion thereof. But Grandfather Byrd, a chivalrous Southerner, gladly paid the fine for his son-in-law.

Howard R. McGee of Dunlap, a personal friend and defender of Evans,[9] gave a slightly different slant

to the story. He said that Chris accosted the man as
he was fleeing from the camp in the mountains. Evans
had a shotgun and the man threw up his hands and
shouted:

"I am unarmed."

Evans then threw away his weapon and yelled:

"So am I."

Then he proceeded to beat the poet mercilessly
and ended the struggle by jumping up and down on
the prostrate man. He literally "tromped" him to
death. According to McGee, the man died later from
internal injuries. This is the version of the affair as
told in the mountains at the present time. The man
died some time after the beating, but whether as a
result of it or of other causes no one now can tell.

Evans' willingness to fight for the weak or helpless
was illustrated by another fight near Hanford. McGee
stated that a group of threshing hands were returning
from an evening spent in that city. A huge man
amused himself by tormenting a small boy in the
wagon. Evans told the driver to stop his horses because there was going to be a fight. The other men
were astonished when Evans challenged the giant,
but were even more amazed when the smaller man
cut the big man down to his own size. When the
threshing camp was reached McGee gave the big fellow first-aid treatment and wrapped him up in his
blankets. In the morning the defeated bully and his
blankets were gone.

While most of the Visalia reporters were hostile to
Evans because they felt that he had given their city

bad publicity, all of them agreed that he had been an exemplary citizen prior to his accusation as a train robber. S. B. Patrick, editor of the Visalia *Times*, was quoted as follows in an interview:[10]

"I have known Chris Evans since 1873, and have always looked upon him as an industrious citizen, who promptly paid his debts, and was honorable in all his business transactions.

"He generally struck me as being a rather peculiar fellow; while he was generally very quiet, at times he was quite jovial. He surprised me on many occasions by his extensive knowledge. He was only a laboring man, yet he seemed to be remarkably well informed. His education was evidently limited, yet he displayed a knowledge of, and an acute insight into, the affairs of the world that was remarkable in a man of his class.

"So far as I know, he had no bad habits. I do not think he ever drank, smoked, or gambled, or had any doubtful acquaintances."

The actual trial of Christopher Evans lasted fifteen days after the jury had been selected. The jurors were locked up at 5 o'clock in the afternoon of December 13th. They must have had a tempestuous meeting.

There were six things for the jury to consider:

First, Evans had killed Beaver, Wilson, and Mc-Ginnis. This was admitted. The defense had merely sought to prove that the provocation had been great. It had been a case of kill or be killed. Any Western jury could appreciate that.

Second, the prosecution had tried to prove that Evans and Sontag had robbed the trains and that

Evans and/or Sontag, who was now dead, had also killed Gabert, Radcliff, and Christiansen. No proof.

Third, if point No. 2 were true, then Evans and/or Sontag were responsible for the wounding of Bentley, Haswell, Lawson, and Roberts. No proof.

Fourth, Evans had seriously wounded the two Witty brothers and Jackson. Again it had been a case of kill or be killed.

Fifth, the prosecution had tried to prove that Evans had shot Sam Black in the cabin near Camp Badger. No proof.

Sixth, if Evans had planned the attempted jail-break at Folsom, he was indirectly responsible for the killing of Williams, Wilson, and Dalton, and the serious wounding of Abbot, Duffy and George Sontag. No proof.

The prosecution had sought to show that Evans and Sontag were directly or indirectly responsible for the death of nine men, and the serious wounding of eleven. There was no argument about the total number of men killed and seriously wounded. Somebody had been mighty careless with firearms. Evans had admittedly accounted for three dead and three wounded. Had the homicides been justifiable? A second question remained: Who had shot the others?

The Visalia *Times* reported on the 14th:[11]

"The jury in the case of the outlaw, Chris Evans, charged with the murder of the United States Marshal Wilson and McGinnis at Sampson's Flat, disagreed this morning after being out sixteen hours. Judge Harris refused to discharge the jury, and sent them back. About half an hour later, they returned with a verdict of guilty of murder in the first degree, fixing the punishment at life imprisonment."

The jury reached its final agreement at 10 o'clock in the forenoon of December 14th.

This verdict did not please one Visalia editor, who wrote as follows in the *Daily Times*:[12]

"The jury in the case of Chris Evans have rendered a most outrageous verdict. By what method of reasoning they arrived at the conclusion that Evans ought not to be hanged, we are at a loss to imagine. There never has been a more heartless murderer in the State of California; and his punishment should have been death.

"If such a thing were possible, he should have been ordered hanged for murder committed while robbing the train at Goshen; he should have been hanged for a similar crime when the Pixley robbery occurred; he should have been hanged for robbing the train at Collis; he deserved hanging for shooting George Witty at Visalia; he should have been hanged for killing Oscar Beaver; he should have been hanged twice for the double murder of McGinnis and Wilson; he should have been lynched for trying to assassinate Black at Camp Badger. In spite of these crimes, nearly all of which were brought to the attention of the jury, they found him guilty and fixed the punishment at imprisonment for life. It is such miscarriages of justice that make law-abiding people resort to lynch law, and the jurors who rendered the verdict ought to be ashamed of themselves."

Christopher Evans was taken back to his cell to await sentence. He was not downcast. Evans was one of those rare persons subject to premonitions, or forewarnings. He told his daughter Eva on many occasions:

"They will never kill me!"

They never did.

On the other hand, John Sontag was depressed and told his fiancee on his frequent visits to Visalia:

"I will never get out of this alive. Your dad is always cheerful, and talks hopefully about our future plans. I always agree with him, but I know that my days are numbered."

They were.

Chris believed that no barriers built by human hands could restrain him. When his time came, he would simply walk out into God's great out-of-doors. He did. He wasn't licked yet. In the parlance of the prize-ring, he had not thrown his Sunday punch.

James Hume, the wizard among the detectives, said:

"Chris Evans could always be expected to do the unexpected."

He could and he did!

CHAPTER 17

MOUNTAIN INTERLUDE

DURING the weeks following the trial of Chris Evans the show featuring his career was presented in the San Joaquin Valley towns north of Fresno. It closed down for the Christmas holidays, and Eva went to visit her father. On one of these occasions he told her: "Get me a gun and I'll do the rest."

Chris Evans was in poor health at this time, and the Evans family was permitted by the sheriff's office to send in food with which to supplement the prison fare. A young waiter working in Stock's restaurant,[1] which provided this food, went by the name of Ed Morrell. He had spent some time during the summer of 1893 in the Fresno jail on a misdemeanor charge, and had met Evans. Morrell had developed an intense admiration for the older man. There are men who are naturally hero-worshippers; Morrell seems to have belonged to this type. Such men, whether they live in a democracy or an autocracy, will blindly and unthinkingly follow a popular leader, be he saint or sinner, rogue or reformer, devastator or builder. Of such is the strength of a Hitler on the one hand, of a Roosevelt on the other. Like these national figures, Evans was endowed with that magnetism which Stewart Edward White defined as "a certain magnificent foofaraw of the spirit."[2] Any man possessing such a personality needs little else to succeed, and lacking it, his efforts are usually futile, no matter what other qualities he may have. Such leaders are never required to explain any errors of action or judgment which they may commit.

Detective James Hume, who investigated Ed Morrell's career, stated that the latter was born in Liverpool, England, and that his real name was Ed Martin. He had landed at San Francisco and shortly thereafter he had been sent to San Quentin for a two-year stretch on a charge of grand larceny.

Morrell told a different story. He claimed that he was born in the coal-mining district of Pennsylvania. His mother was a widow and the boy[3] was sent into the pits at the age of nine to open and shut the doors which regulated the ventilation as the mule-drawn coal-cars came and went. His early life resembled that of Jack Simpson, the hero in George A. Henty's *Facing Death*. He finally ran away from the poverty and squalor of life in the coal-fields. For a time he worked in Jersey City, and later reached Liverpool as a seaman. There he took a boat for Australia via Italy. After many strange adventures "Down Under", he reached San Francisco and admitted that he had served time in San Quentin.

From this point the stories of Hume and Morrell flowed togther as one. On March 27, 1893, Ed was released and, at the request of a lifer named Hutchinson, went to Fresno to help the latter's family take the necessary steps to secure his pardon. Hutchinson's son, Jim, and Morrell became cronies; a mutual friend of these two was a young fellow named E. E. Deck. In the eyes of the police, all three were unsavory characters.

Morrell, who had met Eva Evans at Stock's restaurant, often expressed his liking for her father and resentment at the verdict of the jury. One day, when he was indulging in his customary tirade, she asked him:

"Would you do anything to help my father?"

"Try me, that's all, just try me."

She then suggested that he place a revolver under the napkin in addition to the customary food, and try to carry it past the jailer. It was a routine performance for Morrell to carry the tray into the corridor; Evans was then let out of his cell and permitted to eat his food there. Usually there was no inspection of the tray.

In order to make everything click, certain deep-laid plans had to be formulated. Finally the evening of December 28, 1893, was set for the attempted jailbreak. The following closely related events took place in quick order. Either they were planned that way, or they formed an unusual train of coincidences.

The morning train from Porterville to Fresno on that date carried as a passenger E. E. Deck. He appeared before the conductor in a seemingly agitated frame of mind, and asked permission to speak to the latter confidentially. Granted this favor, he proceeded to volunteer the information that a wild and reckless band of hoodlums had planned to rob this particular train on its way back to Porterville that evening. He admitted that he was a member of this gang, but had lost his nerve and wanted to break away from it. The robbery had been planned in Si Lovern's saloon at Visalia. Deck said that this train was expected to carry a large amount of gold in payment for recent shipments of fruit, garden truck, and poultry. Deck had something there. The conductor knew that his train was scheduled to carry such a shipment that evening. He wondered how Deck knew about it. The latter's story worried the conductor, who began to suspect danger.

When the train reached Fresno the conductor made a report of the threatened robbery to the sheriff's office. Deck was promised immunity from arrest if he would accompany the officers and identify the would-be robbers. When the train left Fresno that evening at 5:30 there were secreted on board Deck and four deputy-sheriffs: Bedford, Peck, Timmins, and White. Sheriff Jay Scott had gone to San Luis Obispo to bring back a prisoner. Was it a coincidence that practically all of the officers were out of town the same evening that Chris Evans planned to walk out of jail? The Fresno *Expositor* did not think so:[4]

"Not only did Evans disperse his own confederates to the best possible advantage, but he succeeded in disposing of the forces of the sheriff's office in a way that must show once and for all that Chris Evans is the deepest planner, the most perfect in his schemes of all the criminals who have come to the front in this State or anywhere else."

Ironically enough, it was Mrs. Chris Evans who was to prove the biggest obstacle to the success of the venture. She knew nothing of the plans under way. She had worries enough without this added burden. Molly decided to choose this particular evening as the time when she would visit her husband. Eva tactfully tried to dissuade her. The mother asked the sixty-four dollar question:

"Why?"

The only answer which occurred to Eva at the moment was:

"Oh, because."

This has been defined as a typical woman's answer because, like a Mother Hubbard, it covers all and touches nothing.

Molly Evans arrived at the jail shortly before six o'clock in the evening. While she was visiting with her husband in the corridor, Ed Morrell arrived with his meal. Ben Scott, a brother of the sheriff, was the jailer that night. After admitting Morrell without inspecting the tray, he went back to his office. Molly Evans, unaware of impending events, was horrified when she saw the contents of the platter. Besides the dinner, she saw a revolver, which in a sense was to serve as dessert. She neither screamed nor made any comment when Evans slipped the weapon into his pocket, but continued to chat with her husband while he ate his meal. After his repast, Evans was ready for action. Morrell called:

"Hey, Ben, come and let me out."

The good-natured and unsuspecting Scott unlocked the door and was flabbergasted when Evans and Morrell aimed revolvers at his midriff and told him to turn over the keys. Mrs. Evans fainted. Scott gasped:[5]

"My God, I can't do that. All the other prisoners will get out, and I will be lynched. You might as well shoot me now."

Evans was a reasonable man even in his supreme moments. So he said:

"All right, Ben, lock the door after us, and then come along."

With trembling hands the jailer obeyed, and then marched ahead of the two armed men. They went out the front way and then back of the court-house. They walked along Mariposa Street until they came to M Street; here they encountered S. H. Cole, a former mayor of Fresno, in front of the Christian Church. He was added to the procession.

One thing favored the jail-breakers on this particular evening. It was about 6:30 of a cold, dark evening in December, and the tule fog, almost as black as coal smoke, was swirling about the streets and buildings. They continued their march along Mariposa until they were half-way between N and O. At this point was located the Adventist Church, and standing at the hitching-rack on the north side of this edifice, was a fine team of horses. If Morrell can be believed, then he had arranged for his friend, Jim Hutchinson, to leave this trotting team there with a wagon loaded with provisions and ammunition. On the other hand, Eva Evans told the author that the two men merely planned to appropriate the first good available team. At any rate, the horses they needed stood waiting for them in front of the Adventist Church.

Good fortune deserted Evans and Morrell at this point. John D. Morgan, then constable of Fresno township, and destined later to serve as the city's chief of police, had met a friend, W. M. Wyatt, in front of the church. Both of these men, whose wives were out of town, had planned to attend the chicken dinner given by the ladies of the Adventist Church. Since they had arrived rather early, they were standing outside conversing. The arrival of the procession of four men, two of them with their hands in the air, aroused the curiosity of Morgan and Wyatt. In the thick, soupy fog, it would have been easy for Evans and Morrell to slip away, but the latter impulsively shouted:[6]

"Hands up."

Morgan, wearing a long overcoat buttoned up to his neck, was unable to get at his gun. Therefore he obeyed orders. Wyatt, a former Texas ranger, thought it was a robbery, and began to throw his money on the sidewalk; he even tossed his watch into the gutter. Morrell, having disarmed Morgan, turned his attention to Wyatt. The latter, in a token of surrender, did not raise his arms over his head as is usual in such cases, but held them straight out from the shoulders. This amused Morgan then and later. Morrell, young and inexperienced in the technique of a highwayman, foolishly turned his back to Morgan. The latter, used to handling law-breakers, quickly grabbed the slight, young man in a vise-like grip. He could have batted Morrell's brains out against the church wall, but had no desire to pollute the sanctuary in such a manner. He was merely trying to stop the nonsense.

Since it was early in the evening men and women were still promenading up and down the sidewalks. Thus far no one had become aware of the excitement being enacted in front of the church. Evans, who feared capture at any moment, acted quickly. He ordered Morgan to release Morrell, and when the officer hesitated, Evans fired. The bullet narrowly missed an artery when it smashed through Morgan's shoulder. Following this explosion at close quarters, the high-strung horses broke their halters and ran away.

Scott and Cole, taking advantage of the confusion, disappeared in the fog. The two outlaws, also making use of the low visibility, ran down the alley between O and P streets to Tulare. They kept on to the corner of Mono and Q where they intercepted Benny Cochrane, a boy delivering newspapers. The latter was driving a horse hitched to a Petaluma cart. In this make-shift rig, the two men rode until they reached the flume of the Hume Lumber Company, about twelve miles away, and in the immediate vicinity of Sanger. A board-walk had been built alongside this flume, and the two men walked on it into the mountains.

The person most to be pitied this evening and in the days that followed was not Evans or Morrell, fugitives; nor Morgan, the wounded constable, who had been taken to Dr. Maupin by Wyatt; nor Molly Evans, who had been found in a fainting condition in the jail and kept there for several days. It was Ben Scott, the jailer, whose excessive trust in the goodness of human nature was to make the sheriff's office the laughing stock of the nation. For weeks thereafter, when the jailer appeared on the street, flippant youngsters would "wise-crack":

"There goes Scott, who lets his prisoners go scot-free!"

When the jailer's brother, Sheriff Jay Scott, returned with the criminal he had gone to fetch from San Luis Obispo, his grief and rage must have been truly homeric. It certainly was not his fault, but critics are not often reasonable. The sheriff may have drawn comfort from William Hazlitt's statement: "Nothing is more unjust or capricious than public opinion." James Hume, representing Wells, Fargo & Co., stated that his firm and the Southern Pacific had spent about $30,000 and three lives to capture and convict Evans. Now he and his employers were through. Thenceforth Sheriff Scott was to draw generously from his own purse in an attempt to capture the outlaws. His term in office was not to prove profitable financially.

The four deputies who had been sent on a fool's errand to Porterville, were notified by telegraph to come back. The wire reached them at Reedley, but they could get no train at that place, so they went on to Porterville and a special locomotive took them back as far as Sanger, where they left it to follow the outlaws.

An attempt was made to form a posse at Sanger, but the residents there merely laughed at the officers. They still remembered the condition of the posse which had passed that way after the fight at Young's cabin. So they sarcastically told the deputies to do their own man-hunting; that was what they were paid for.

Deck, who had told the cock-and-bull story of the proposed train robbery, was arrested. It was charged that his ruse in luring the officers away from Fresno at the psychological moment, amounted to a conspiracy.

The team which had run away when Evans shot Morgan was found, wind-broken and bogged down in the soft, muddy river-bottom of the San Joaquin River, fourteen miles west of Fresno. It was identified as one of the best teams from the Woy & Shield livery stable, and had been hired that afternoon by Jim Hutchinson, the pal of Ed Morrell and E. E. Deck. Not far from the wrecked wagon was found a bag belonging to Jim which contained cartridges. He, too, was arrested as an accomplice. He admitted that he had rented the team and had used it to go hunting that afternoon. After his return to Fresno, he had tied the horses in front of the church, while he performed some errand. During the fracas, the horses had run away and he had been unable to find them. Later Jim's wife and four other members of his family were also arrested. Eventually they all, including Deck, were released. The brains and spark-plug in the clever and successful jail-break was Eva Evans. Strangely enough, she was not suspected, interrogated, or arrested. She calmly returned to her work as an actress. The unexpected turn of events made the stage play more popular than ever, and it drew tremendous crowds.

Evans and Morrell finally reached the Hume Mills,

deep in the Sierra Nevada. Lumbering operations had closed down for the winter, but a few tough, hardened men remained at the mills as caretakers. Among them the outlaws were safe. Finally Evans and Morrell went down to the Downing ranch for supplies. It had been a dry winter, and no snow had fallen. Therefore Bill Downing was still able to go down into the valley for food and other provisions. But the trouble with an open road is that it runs in both directions. If Downing could go down, the officers could come up. Hence it was deemed unsafe for Evans and Morrell to remain with the Downings, and it was decided that they should occupy Camp Manzanita. Since this place was surrounded by a dense growth of manzanita bushes, which are virtually impenetrable, it was a secure hide-out. Besides, it had a fire-place which would enable the men to keep warm during the long, cold winter months.

Shortly after they had moved into Camp Manzanita, Ed Morrell, no slouch as a story-teller, claimed that he heard a weird scratching in the chimney one night and then, out of the smoke and flames, bounded a snarling black demon in the shape of a cat. This diabolic-looking beast landed on the cot where the exhausted Evans lay asleep. Morrell, petrified for the moment by the sudden appearance of this fiend incarnate from the region of fire and brimstone, quickly "snapped out of it," and reached for his Winchester, hoping to save the life of the older man, but to his amazement, this savage, smaller edition of a black panther, snuggled up against Evans and began to purr. When Evans awoke some time later, he told Morrell that this was the cat Sontag and he had tamed the previous winter. Apparently it had remained in the vicinity after the two men had disappeared following the fight at Stone Corral in June; it was now January. Since the doors and windows were tightly closed, the cat had used the chimney as an entrance and exit. The leaping flames in the fire-place this particular night had no doubt given the cat a surprisingly hot reception. Morrell asserted that the feline continued to use the big chimney, fire or no fire; it had no use for an open door. The next morning Morrell saw a big bear approaching the cabin, but was prevented from shooting it by Evans, who hurriedly warned Ed that Bruin, house-broken as a cub by Sontag the previous year and now grown to respectable size, was the cat's playmate and friend. Had Morrell killed the friendly bear it would have been a case of mistaken identity. The cat hunted for the bear and the latter furnished company and moral support. If one can believe all this, Evans and Morrell had a sort of Garden of Eden enjoyment out of their animal friends that winter.

The small children in the Downing family had known about Camp Manzanita during the days when Evans and Sontag had occupied it. They had been warned never to tell anyone about its location, and they had kept the faith. However, after John Sontag had died and Evans had been placed in jail, the youngsters deemed that the time for silence was over. Many an adult would have felt likewise. So, in a moment of exuberance, they had shown the hide-out to a young relative by marriage named Walter Kirkland.[7] When Evans, accompanied by young Morrell, suddenly appeared at their home, like a man risen from the dead, the poor "kids" knew that they had made a mistake. But they were afraid to tell their parents for fear of dire punishment. Who can blame them? They hoped that Kirkland would keep his mouth shut. He didn't!

In the meantime all sorts of ridiculous stories kept coming to the sheriff's office. They all had to be sifted and investigated. One never knew which one might yield pay-dirt.

One man in particular was a pain in the neck to the sheriff. His name was Marion Childers.[8] He had been in jail with Chris Evans and an intense mutual dislike had developed between the two. All old-timers have agreed that morally Evans was decent and as clean as a hound's tooth. Childers did or said something to Evans which led the latter to tell the jailer that if Marion did not keep away from him he would kill the young man. Evans refused to speak to Childers again, and his hatred seemed out of the ordinary. Perhaps Marion was a pathological case. Shortly after the latter had been released from jail, he scurried into the sheriff's office and said that Evans was hiding in Frank Dusy's barn near Selma. The house on this ranch had a high cupola and from it a fugitive, or anyone else, could easily scan the surrounding plains. The story sounded plausible. A posse was sent there. A Selma resident, who investigated this part of the Evans episode, wrote about the occasion as follows:[9]

"One chapter of the Sontag and Evans page in

Fresno County's history was written here. When Evans escaped from the Fresno jail, the sheriff and his deputies thought he might have sought refuge in the towering cupola to secure an excellent view of the surrounding territory and the approach of the officers. Evans was not found in the cupola, but he was thought to be hiding in the barn and here an amusing incident in the life of a brave sheriff and his deputies was written. While approaching the barn, Dusy was used as a shield for the approaching officers."

The officers laid down a barrage on the barn, and then charged. It was empty. The only near casualty in this celebrated "battle of the empty barn" was a reporter from the San Francisco *Chronicle,* who had been invited to attend the obsequies of Chris Evans. Instead he almost experienced his own demise, as a coiled rattlesnake, on guard in Dusy's barn, assaulted him with rattle and fang. The poor startled "city slicker" was saved only by a generous internal application of the best known antidote of that period.

The highly chagrined officers, thoroughly disgusted with Mr. Childers, kicked him off the place. But the young man was persistent. He tried again. The next time he appeared at the sheriff's office he had an even more fantastic yarn to spin. He related with gusto how he had encountered Evans and Morrell near Goshen. They had tried to shoot him, but had succeeded only in killing one of his horses. A special posse was hastily formed. When Tice, agent for Wells, Fargo & Co. at Fresno, was loading his Winchester, a magazine containing sixteen cartridges exploded, wounding him severely. The other men boarded a special train which whirled them the thirty-six miles to Goshen in thirty-five minutes, a record run for that time and distance. The posse members were then taken to the scene of the shooting and a horse, lying beside its team-mate, was offered as evidence. It was dead all right. A veterinary examined the animal carefully, and then stated that it was his professional opinion that the wound which had led to the demise of the gallant steed could only have been inflicted by a man standing on the seat of the buggy and firing down into the horse's back.

A psychoanalyst would no doubt have a name for a character like Marion Childers, but it would not be a more fitting description of him than the epithets applied to him that day along the Goshen road by the members of the Fresno posse.

Other incredible reports kept pouring into the sheriff's office. A Petaluma paper stated that Evans and Morrell had been seen in that city. A San Jose reporter[10] wrote that he had interviewed Evans, who was at that time boarding a boat for Honolulu. Chris confided in the newspaper man, and told him that he was on his way to Hawaii to marry Queen Lilioukalani. So ran the story. This led a Visalia editor[11] to write that Evans was too smart to tackle Queen Lil with only one arm.

More reliable stories were told by reputable men in the mountains. Both Harvey and Fred Akers, cattlemen, reported that they had at different times fed the outlaws. Newton Demasters said he had rowed them

across Kings River one evening at a point some miles
north above Centerville.

One evening Elijah Perkins' son Elmer,[12] who had
been riding the range all day, reached his grandmother's home and found the women-folk in an agitated
frame of mind. Evans and Morrell had been there
that afternoon and had appropriated a horse and cart.
During the course of the conversation, Evans had an-
gered Mrs. Perkins by remarking: "Well, another
blood-hunter[13] died with his boots on." This was a
reference to Al Perkins' death, who had been crushed
when a huge boulder tipped over and pinned him underneath; only his feet protruded. Mrs. Perkins resented the remark and "bawled out" Evans for making it. The members of the Evans family were under
the impression that Al had "double-crossed" Chris,
but Elmer Perkins told the author that their belief
was not based on the facts in the case. Al had always
been friendly to Evans, and had never done him any
harm. However, what disturbed Grandmother Perkins
the most this particular evening was Evans' threat that
he was going to Visalia to kill Elijah, her son, and
Perry Byrd, her son-in-law. At that time Elijah was
working some land he owned near the county seat;
Evans hated him because it was he who had reported
Evans' presence at the Perkins home to the sheriff's
office. Chris also hated Byrd because he believed that
Perry was the man who had lured him into the trap
at Stone Corral.

To allay the fears of the women and warn his father
and uncle, Elmer mounted a fresh horse and rode at

break-neck speed to Visalia. He told the writer that he expected at any moment to catch up with the two outlaws; and feared that he would then be shot. But he met with no difficulties along the way, and arrived in time to warn the two men. It developed later that Evans had not set out for Visalia; his threat had been a bluff.

During the evening of January 11, 1894, George A. Leon, the station agent at Fowler,[14] and three other men, were sitting beside the stove in his office. A masked bandit entered and relieved the men of $20; A. A. Vincent, a local resident, and Howard Harris, an insurance agent at Fowler, were passing the depot at the time. They stopped to watch the performance through the window, and were invited to enter by the genial bandit who waved a pistol in their general direction. They contributed an additional $40. The robber then marched the six men to the Kutner-Goldstein store. While pilfering the till, he was interrupted by the arrival of Charles Ochs, the local constable, and another man. The startled officer hastily fired two shots. One struck the section foreman, Pat Lahey, in the arm; the other, lodged in the shoulder of H. A. Mulligan. The bandit shot Ochs in the hip and the latter fell to the floor and rolled out through the open door.

Mrs. Jim Hutchinson related that she had hired a livery rig at Kingsburg and had driven eastward to a point half a mile beyond Clarke's Bridge. Here she had met Evans and Morrell, who were riding in a cart on their way from Reedley to Traver. This was on January 15, 1894. Morrell told her about the Fowler hold-up:[15]

"We got around in that quarter, and were awfully hard up for money. I concluded to make a raise, and I did it. The newspapers said I held up seven people and got $70. The fact is, I held up four besides those at the depot and store, and got $150. I was pretty closely cornered at the store and it looked for a minute as though I was in for it. But after I had knocked the officer out of it, I made a run and jump, shooting as I went, and the others scattered like ducks."

Evans told Mrs. Hutchinson on this occasion that the Fresno officers had treated him kindly, and that he would not shoot them unless they pushed him too hard. He expressed appreciation for the fair treatment accorded Molly after his escape. She had been found unconscious in the jail corridor and was held for several days. However, Sheriff Scott believed her statement that she had neither planned nor aided in the jail-break, and she was sent home to her family.

A San Francisco paper printed an estimate of Evans shortly after he had returned to the mountains:[16]

"With all of the strange characteristics of Evans, and his many inconsistencies, there was one trait which always stood out in bold relief from the darkness of his life's background. That was his strong attachment for his children. That was but natural, but he seemed to think more of his little children than most men do. Probably his being away so much from them of late and the knowledge that they held him innocent and loved him, was the reason for his strong affection for

his white-haired babies. His feeling for them amounted to idolatry. Sometimes the children were admitted
to his cell and he would catch as many of them in his
arm and his piece of arm, as he could, and if he was
left with them for hours he never grew tired of playing with them. He has six children younger than Eva.

"Chris Evans in many ways stands alone in the annals of crime on this coast or in the United States. It
is safe to say that no one person, not even members
of his own family, understood him. He said: 'There is
no power on earth or heaven that can defy fate and
fate is on my side. Man has no control over his own
destiny. Men are only machines. When the thought
strikes me and tells me to act, then I act. I may be
in this jail two or three years, but I will get out at
last.' There never was a man in jail here in Fresno
who so attracted people."

Ed Morrell maintained that he made a trip to San
Francisco while Evans[17] remained at Camp Manzanita.
The former went to Visalia, stayed with a friend there
over night, and then rode horseback by way of Hanford to Sunflower Valley in the Coast Range. Here
he procured new clothes and, dressed in the height of
fashion, he took the train for San Francisco, where
he made arrangements to have a schooner wait for
Evans and him in the Santa Barbara Channel. This
boat was to take them to the South Pacific. Chris was
not in favor of the plan; he preferred seeking safety
in the Chihuahua mountains of Mexico. After this
business deal had been completed, Morrell went to the
theatre to see the new presentation of the show starring

Molly and Eva. The cast was excellent, and the pitch of excitement reached its climax when the actor representing Morrell was shown holding up Ben Scott, the jailer. A beautiful woman, sitting next to Morrell, turned to her elderly escort, and said:[18]

"Oh, daddy, I could kiss that young man. He is my ideal of a real hero!"

Morrell lost his head for a moment, and blurted out:

"Miss, the opportunity is here! You can kiss me right now!"

When the young woman poised her right hand as if she planned to slap his face, Morrell decided to walk out of the theater. He returned by way of Goshen to Camp Manzanita where he was to meet new and exciting adventures.

The harassed officers, anxious for a clue, went from hither to yon, but most of the information they received proved to be figments of the imagination. Finally L. Parker Timmins and Charles Boyd, deputy sheriffs, went to Camp Badger. Timmins, in order to lighten the load for his horse, decided to walk up a steep hill. He took a short-cut over the ridge and when Boyd, riding in the cart, reached the top of the grade, he saw a cabin with Evans standing in the door-way. The latter called out:

"Come in and be sociable."

Boyd did not respond graciously to the invitation, and Evans fired at him. The shot gouged out a sliver from the cart seat, and the horse became temporarily unmanageable. Timmins, observing the incident from the top of the ridge, opened fire long enough to permit

Boyd to escape. The two officers then hurried back to Reedley and telegraphed news of the battle of Slick Rock to the sheriff's office. Eva Evans told the author that her father knew nothing of this fight. She insisted that either another man shot playfully at Boyd, or else the two men fabricated the story to create a little excitement. Ed Morrell gave another version. He said that Boyd got away, but that he had quite an exciting afternoon with Mr. Timmins.[19]

"He was zigzagging, now running wildly, clearly at a loss which way to go. He had his choice, straight across the range, up it , or down it. At last he took the latter, plunging down through thickets of manzanita, with every little while a bullet from my long ranged Winchester screeching a strange sound to his ears as it whizzed by.

"I played with him, teased and tired him, drove him over rocks and rough ground and through dense thickets of scratching manzanita and chaparral. Behind, and all the time just a little above him I could see every move. Hour after hour he worked his way down the brushy mountainside heading toward the stage station at Dunlap and dodging in and out to avoid the spattering lead which hit about him.

"My fire frustrated his every attempt to hide under the clumps of bush for rest. The man was wild-eyed, panting for breath. He had cast away his rifle. All caution was gone. Heedless of the tearing manzanita he now plunged head foremost through the thickets, his pace quickened every little while by more random shots.

"Climbing to a high ledge of rock where I could overlook the entire mountainside below me, I took up an easy position to rest and watch the antics of my frightened game. My ammunition was nearly gone, but I still had enough left to use for a parting salute.

"These last I directed with careful aim, striving to knock him over by a leg shot, but he was a moving target and hard to hit. The sun was setting and darkness would soon put an end to this struggle. I ceased firing and watched him as he disappeared far down the mountain and out of sight."

Eva Evans always insisted that the fight at Slick Rock was all fiction; Ed Morrell, no doubt, fictionized parts of it.

The following account is based on a description of that episode by three eye-witnesses still living: Walter Robison of Badger; and his brothers, George of Auckland, and Earl of Dinuba. As small boys they stood on the porch of their father's house and saw Evans and Morrell drive up in a one-horse cart to the Dan St. Clair home, a furlong away. The two outlaws were given breakfast, and then Evans stepped out on the porch from where he discovered Timmins and Boyd riding in a buckboard (not a cart). They were on the other side of Sycamore Creek, and headed in the direction of the St. Clair home. Evidently they were following the trail left by the horse and cart appropriated at the Perkins home. When they reached the little stream, Timmins got out of the embryonic vehicle, and approached the St. Clair house on foot. Just then Morrell walked out on the porch and, with boyish enthusiasm fired hurriedly at the deputy sitting in the rig. Boyd whirled his horse and tore down the mountain road at a dead run. Timmins headed for the brush. Evans and Morrell walked rapidly toward his hiding place. This was a reckless thing to do as the deputy easily could have killed them both; why he failed to do so is still a mystery. Timmins kept retreating from one clump of brush to another, and Morrell pursued him for a short distance. Evans, who had not fired a shot, casually strolled back to the St. Clair dwelling. Eva Evans was correct in saying her father had taken no part in the so-called battle of Slick Rock. Ed Morrell could truthfully say that he had chased the deputy, but he doubtless added some frills to the story.

Boyd, madly driving in the direction of Reedley, was astonished when he arrived to find Timmins already in town. This tale was elaborated to show how fear had lent seven-league boots to Timmins' feet; the truth was that a man in a hurry and a fast team had given him a ride.

As a result of the report telegraphed from Reedley to the sheriff's office, a posse was sent into the hills. Bill Henry, accompanied by Ed Miles, went to Reedley and picked up L. Parker Timmins, the opponent of Ed Morrell the previous day. These three deputies then followed Walter Kirkland to Camp Manzanita, the location of which had been revealed by the Downing children.

Chris Evans and Ed Morrell were sitting in front of the fire-place at night-fall. Chris was engaging in his favorite pastime, reading aloud. Suddenly he heard a twig snap outside. Evans ran out of the house without putting on hat or coat. Morrell, who happened to have his coat on at the time, picked up his hat as he ran. Evans was also minus his artificial arm, which he had put aside as the stump still pained him. Bill Henry fired at Evans, and said later that he saw Evans' hair fly. The deputy was sure that he had creased Evans' scalp.

The two outlaws ran behind the tall rock against which the cabin had been built, and disappeared in the gloaming without firing a shot. The first snow-fall of the season was on its way, and this soon developed into a blizzard.

Ed Morrell made this part of Evans' career replete with dramatic encounters and gun battles. All the approaches to Camp Manzanita[20] were mined. If Morrell can be believed in this case, then Evans had anticipated much of the technique of World War II. Just when and by whom all this intricate machinery had been installed, he did not make clear. At the beginning of the attack, Ed ran out and pulled the lever behind the big rock which was supposed to have released a charge from the batteries sufficient to rip the entire mountainside loose on the posse, but nothing happened. Time and the elements had corroded the mechanism.

The deputies tried to follow the fleeing men, but the blizzard raged with increasing fury and they were unable to endure the torment. They gave up. Evans was again to prove of tougher fibre than the men who were chasing him. The forces of law and order comforted themselves with the thought that a crippled man, without hat, coat, or shelter, would soon die from exposure. The storm raged with unabated anger for twenty-four hours. When it finally broke and the wind subsided Evans and Morrell staggered into Eshom Valley where the Yokuts Indians once again provided food, warmth, and rest for an old friend. Later the two men returned to the Downing home and learned how they had been betrayed.

Before the deputies returned to Fresno they had burned Camp Manzanita. Evans' artificial arm had been taken back to the jail and placed in the museum as an exhibit. In spite of the protests of the Evans family, it was never returned to Chris.[21]

The "scorched earth policy" of the deputies made existence from this time much harder for Evans. All the old-timers who have been interviewed have been unanimous in saying that there was nothing glamorous in the subsequent career of Evans in the hills. Miss Helen Foster, then a young school teacher in a mountain school in Long Valley, and later the wife of William Elam, said his troubles with the Southern Pacific were at best a sordid affair. Picture him at this period of his life, a crippled old man, minus an arm and an eye, skulking in the hills, asking for a hand-out from the mountain dwellers. His companion now was no stalwart figure like John Sontag, but a callow hash-slinger without much training or aptitude for the task at hand. A transcript of his record shows that some of his education was based on a two-year enforced attendance at San Quentin, and a summer session in the Fresno jail.

Ed Mainwaring's wife, the former Constance Bigelow, told the author the following:[22]

"They (Evans and Morrell) had a hard time in the winter, because it was cold in the mountains. John Crabtree kept them for sometime, and then they stayed with us at Sampson's Flat. At this time they were just ahead of the posse, and Evans was very weak and ill."

In response to certain questions she sent the following information:[23]

"I have often wondered why we sympathized with Evans, when you realize what a dreadful thing it is to stop a train and endanger lives. And now that I am old I do not think crime should be romanticized. But it was exciting to have Evans and Morrell under our roof at Sampson's Flat. It was more like a story than reality. We had gone to Sampson's Flat for my younger brother's health, after living in San Francisco for twenty-nine years. A log cabin was very romantic even if it was hard. My Aunt Lucy always read to us out of the Bible and we had a short prayer at the beginning of the day. So before breakfast she took the Bible and opened it at random. Evans and Morrell were both very polite, and sat with folded hands, as we all did. She read: 'Now Barabbas was a robber' and the rest of the verse. Her voice faltered a bit, but she went on bravely, and then we all kneeled and she prayed for their safety. Evans thanked her with tears in his eyes."

Ed Morrell referred in his autobiography to Aunt

Lucy,[24] and related how she and her husband cared for Evans and him after the fight at Camp Manzanita. Morrell verified Henry's statement that Chris had been wounded in the scalp. The two outlaws remained with the Mainwarings for several days. Chris was so weak and handicapped by his lack of an arm, that he had to be helped up the ladder which led into the loft where his bed was located.

Shortly after the fight at Camp Manzanita, Bill Downing went to Visalia a second time to get supplies. At that time Molly and Eva were away with the show. S. Sweet & Co. had foreclosed on the Evans home the previous November, and had then rented the property to Mr. and Mrs. J. V. Brighton, former residents of Los Angeles. Grandmother Byrd had been caring for the six small Evans children, but she was getting old and tired. Therefore Molly hired the Brightons, who lived next door, to care for the youngsters, and the latter went back to the house which had been home in happier times. Downing went to see the children and was told that Carl, the baby, was sick unto death, and that if the father wanted to see his little boy alive he must come home at once. Downing was not permitted to see Carl, but believed what he was told and innocently conveyed this sad message to Evans.

Just who were the Brightons? According to the Los Angeles *Times*,[25] Brighton, who was slightly crippled, was a skillful detective sent to Visalia by the Southern Pacific. The San Francisco *Chronicle*[26] stated that he was merely used as a decoy by the United States Marshal, George Gard. It is immaterial now whether Brighton planned it that way, or was the tool of other more clever men. The important fact is that Evans walked into a second trap.

Chris was above all an affectionate father. He went to Visalia to see his little son. Morrell said afterwards, perhaps with prophetic hindsight, that he had "smelled a rat," but loyally, as always, he followed his chief. Evans' paternal instinct was to prove fatal. When the two outlaws arrived in Visalia, shortly before daybreak, Brighton told them that Carl was much better. Evans said later that he knew then that the caretaker was a traitor, but he felt that killing him would not undo the mischief. Besides, both Evans and his daughter, Eva, believed that the real villain was Perry Byrd who, they said, dominated Brighton and had told him what to do.

Daylight revealed that the house was surrounded by a posse supplemented by a large mob. Sheriff Kay was in command. Evans, on his return to his old home, could not complain about either the enthusiasm or the size of the reception committee. Under the circumstances he would have liked less of both. While the members of the mob assured all and sundry what they intended to do with the outlaws, Sheriff Kay could find no one fool-hardy enough to approach the house with a message. Morrell was an unknown quantity, but everyone feared Evans, even if he was minus one arm. The posse did not want to fire into the house as it contained, in addition to the outlaws, Mr. and Mrs. Brighton and the six small Evans children.

The first message sent in to Evans read as follows. "Chris Evans:—Surrender, and we will protect you. If not, we will take you anyway. E. W. Kay, Sheriff." The bearer of this note was an eight-year-old boy named George Morris. It seems a shameful thing now that a mere child would be sent on such an errand, but it was known that Evans loved little children and it was thought he would do the youngster no harm. The latter soon returned with Evans' answer. In the meantime the little boy's grandmother, Mrs. Henry Morris, had appeared on the scene. She quickly rescued George from the clutches of the posse and mob and took him home. The grandmother was both frightened and angry over the use made of her little grandson. Who can blame her?[27]

Since no other babes or sucklings were available to serve as runners into no-man's land, it was necessary to solve the situation in some other way. Walter A. Beason, a young man about town, apparently had more intestinal fortitude than any of the other adults present that day. He told the sheriff that he would carry a note to Evans for one dollar. The sheriff accepted Beason's offer, and wrote:

"Mr. Evans:—You have a chance to surrender. Surrender now without being hurt. If you give up to me, I will protect you and let the law take its course. I will disperse this mob if you say so, and will meet you. E. W. Kay."

Beason walked toward the house with this note held over his head as a white flag. Before he had time to knock on the door, it was swiftly opened, and Beason was jerked inside. He was retained as a hostage, and little nine-year-old Joe Evans opened the door and walked toward the posse. It must have been a tragic sight to observe a little child bearing a message from his outlaw father to the waiting sheriff. But children were walking that day where grown men feared to tread. The mob, always cruel, was unmindful of the pitiful scene, and swooped down on the child and rushed him to the officers. Evans knew the presence of a mob spelled danger, and asked Kay to disperse it. Another note was given to Joe, who carried it back to his father, and finally Kay and Hall met Evans and Morrell on the front porch. The four men then rode to the jail in a closely guarded wagon. Along the way there were occasional shouts of "Hello, there, Chris," and he replied in kind. But in spite of evidences of good-will and gentle raillery, the officers were nervous.

Talk of lynching developed among the rabble in the saloons.[28] The fastest standard-bred team in Visalia was hitched to a light wagon and Evans and Morrell were taken for a ride. In the parlance of modern racketeering, to take a man for a ride is synonymous with murder. But on this occasion the two outlaws were taken for a ride to save their lives. George Witty, deputy-sheriff, was the driver; Sheriff Kay, who had received Evans' surrender on the latter's front porch, watched the prisoners; and Sheriff Scott of Fresno, peered into the darkness on the alert for possible pursuers. The members of the mob mounted their horses and chased the fast trotters. The latter lived up to their reputation as the fastest Hambletonians in that part of the valley, and good Hambletonians are the best horses in the world for the task assigned them that night. The cow-ponies of the mob were not evenly matched in speed and bottom, and their riders were unable to approach the wagon in a compact body. Morrell wrote later that the situation became so serious that the two sheriffs took the handcuffs off the two outlaws and gave them their guns. Then the wagon was stopped, and the officers and outlaws turned to face the mob, which dispersed in great confusion. No one else recalled such an incident. The mob which, after the fashion of dogs and little children, will chase anything that runs, dropped out of the race at Goshen for liquid refreshments. This wild ride occurred during the night of February 19, 1894.

At 1:30 in the morning of the 20th, the two outlaws were safely lodged in the Fresno jail. Evans, found guilty by the jury, had not yet been sentenced. At first it was decided to call him before the court during the afternoon session, which normally convened at two o'clock. But the mounting tension in the city led the authorities to change the hour. They did not want to take any chances with either the mob or the resourceful Chris Evans. So Judge Harris decided to pass sentence on the outlaw at ten o'clock in the forenoon. The sooner the famous brigand was on his way to Folsom, the better everyone in a position of responsibility in Fresno would feel.

As Christopher Evans stood before the bar of justice he heard Judge M. K. Harris say:[29]

"Christopher Evans, a grand jury of Fresno County

found against you an indictment charging you with the murder of one Vernon Coke Wilson. To that charge you pleaded not guilty. You were tried before an impartial jury of your countrymen, who found you guilty of murder in the first degree and fixed the penalty at imprisonment for life. Have you any cause to show why the judgment of the court should not be pronounced against you?"

Evans shook his head, and sat down. Then he arose again while the judge pronounced the following sentence:[30]

"No cause having been shown why sentence should not be pronounced against you, now, therefore, the judgment of this court is that you *Christopher Columbus,* be confined in the State's prison at Folsom for the period of your natural life."

The judge's error in sentencing the wrong man broke the tension in the court room. Even Evans laughed. The judge quickly corrected himself and the short comedy was over.

As Christopher Evans stood before the judge and heard the fateful words, he may have recalled that it was the 20th day of February. On this date, forty-seven years before, he had been born at Bell's Corner, in the province of Ontario, Canada. And to what end? It was certainly a unique birthday present that Judge M. K. Harris had handed him. It may safely be assumed that few men in history have been presented with life imprisonment on a birthday anniversary.

Sheriff Scott, accompanied by Hi Rapelje, Henry Scott, and L. Parker Timmins took Evans to the railway station at 11 o'clock. A crowd of more than 2,000 persons were there to see the great outlaw board the train for Folsom. This was about ten percent of the total population of Fresno at that time. This showed the interest Chris Evans had aroused in the general public. When he was released seventeen years later[31] he was met at the gates of Folsom by one daughter and a lone newspaper reporter. Thus time marches on and public interests change.

CHAPTER 18

IT IS FINISHED

IF EVANS' part in this story has been a tragedy, then in a certain sense Morrell's trial turned out to be a farce. He had helped Evans to walk out of the jail, but he had killed no one. He had joyously and blindly followed his hero into the mountains, and his defiance and outwitting of the officers had made them smart. The young man needed a lesson. So he was tried for horse stealing, then a serious crime in California. Benny Cochrane's horse and cart had been taken by the two outlaws and used in the wild drive to Sanger. The jury deliberated for ten little minutes, and gravely announced that Morrell was guilty of highway robbery, and recommended life imprisonment. He got it.

Morrell's hero-worship of Evans had proved disastrous. But he was young, and served only nine years of his sentence. The first five years were spent in Folsom; the next four in San Quentin, where he became a trusty. Then he was pardoned and began life anew. His experiments with thought transference and spiritualism while in solitary confinement aroused the interest of his friend, Jack London, who subsequently wrote a book based on Morrell's experiences which he called *The Star Rover*. After his release Morrell devoted himself to prison reform and his book, *The 25th Man,* was sponsored by the American Crusaders who were striving for a new penology. He appeared on the lecture platform throughout the country, and old-timers who heard him, said that he had a pleasing appearance[1] and was an eloquent speaker. His skill in awakening public opinion led to many needed reforms.

After all the outlaws discussed thus far had been buried, either under the sod or behind the bars, Southern Pacific trains continued to be molested. This led defenders of Chris Evans to argue that perhaps these other men had been guilty of the train robberies of an earlier date as well as those committed after Evans and Sontag had been placed in cold storage. Who knows?

Much of the lawlessness rampant in the valley, especially in Tulare county, from 1884 to 1900, centered around the rise and fall of Traver. Flush times there attracted not only fine, law-abiding citizens, but rogues who had no speaking acquaintance with the seven cardinal virtues.

The story of Traver is one of the most hectic episodes that can be told[2] in relation to the life and times of Evans and Sontag. A group of capitalists organized the 76 Land & Water Company and financed a colonization project on 30,000 acres lying along the left bank of Kings River. The town, named after Charles Traver, one of the directors, lay about five miles south of Kings River. It was one of the late arrivals among the towns located along the main-line of the Southern Pacific. A townsite of 240 acres was surveyed and lots offered for sale on April 8th and 9th, 1884. The sales on these two days amounted to $60,000. Sixty days

later the newly born town of Traver contained a post-
office, an express office, a railway station, a drug store,
an implement store, two merchandise stores, two lumber yards, two hotels, two barber shops, two livery
stables, three large saloons (later increased to fourteen), several bawdy houses, and a picturesque Chinatown on the west side of the railroad tracks.

The seamy side of life cannot be ignored in a true
portrayal of these early wheat towns. Hundreds of
laborers employed by the 76 Land & Water Company
in its warehouses, on its ranches, and in construction
work on the ditches and canals, made Traver their
headquarters. These men were paid every Saturday
night at the office in Traver; their pay, in most cases,
was freely spent in the town the same evening in the
various saloons and gambling houses along Front
Street.

The mining town of Bodie, which had given birth
to the expression "the bad man from Bodie," had been
founded by Waterman Body in 1859. It was a typical
wild mining camp, located ten miles north of Mono
Lake and fifteen miles east of the Sierra. When mining petered out there, most of its inhabitants flocked
to Traver. Professional gamblers, prostitutes, and gun-
men made Traver look like a typical frontier mining
camp. Games of chance were played day and night
without interruption. Two hundred packs of cards
were often used in a single game. Dice were thrown
at two hundred dollars a shake. Five hundred dollars
in twenty dollar gold pieces were usually stacked at
one time on the table.

One of the officials in the 76 Land & Water Company wrote this about those picturesque times in Traver:[3]

"There were more than a half-score of saloon and gambling hells, together with other places of evil, that were running unrestricted in that wide open town. Hundreds of laborers, employed in the warehouses, at the ditch camps, and on the ranches, collected their wages every Saturday night, and the scene witnessed along Front Street on Sundays beggars description. Scores of men would stagger up and down the street trying to keep track of all the gambling games that were running, and the drunkenness would increase as the day advanced. Crowds would assemble where an exciting game was in progress, and not only fill the building but extend clear out across the sidewalk, forcing pedestrians to take to the street.

"'Two places 'across the track,' where men without self-respect and women without shame congregated, served as a legalized way-station on the road to ruin. The resorts mentioned, one of which was a dance hall, housed fifteen to twenty women. At that time there were no speed regulations in California that applied to traffic on the highway to perdition except the single one strictly enforced against every owner of an empty purse."

The boisterous life prevalent during wheat-growing days was a direct result, like so many other evils, of idleness. After the men employed on a bonanza farm had completed the seeding in the spring, they were practically unemployed until harvest time. Even then the climatic conditions made haste unnecessary. Where should they go and what should they do during the early summer months? Traver and the other wheat towns beckoned. The saloons and the gambling "joints" offered amusement. During the long, tiresome wait incidental to the delivery of grain, the teamsters wanted solace and they found it in the saloons.

Out of all this turmoil emerged many reckless characters capable of trying anything, especially if it had never been tried before. For many of them, to rob a train, steal a cow, or kill a brother was all in the night's work, and just a lark.

In 1886 Worth Brown, a Traver cowboy, visited the neighboring town of Kingsburg,[4] and engaged Pete Simpson, the constable, and Jim Allison, his deputy, in a gun battle. Brown was quick on the draw, and shot Allison in the jaw. This annoyed the deputy, and he retaliated by shooting Brown through the lungs. Both men recovered. This was a relief to Allison as several of Brown's friends had vowed to kill the deputy if Brown died. Late in the evening of September 2nd of the same year Worth shot and killed his brother, Luther, over a woman's favor. Worth Brown was sent to San Quentin for life, and died there from tuberculosis of the lungs, presumably induced by the wound inflicted by Allison years before.

The postmaster at Traver, Lyman B. Ruggles, had at one time represented Yolo county in the California legislature. He was a reputable citizen, but his son John had trouble with the law and served time in the penitentiary. At the time of his release he was about thirty years of age. He induced his nineteen year old brother, Charles, to help him rob a train near Redding in Shasta county. The express messenger was killed and $3,000 was taken. During the fracas Charles was shot in the jaw, and two days later he required medical attention. His story was not plausible enough to prevent his arrest. John was also picked up, and the two men were placed in jail to await trial. A mob smashed the door one night and hanged both brothers to a telegraph pole. As the train rolled slowly into Redding the next morning, the passengers were horrified to see two corpses dangling in front of their windows. Both brothers were brought back to Traver for burial.[5]

One night the southbound train out of Goshen was boarded by a masked bandit. He crawled over the coal in the tender (this was in the days before oil had came into use as fuel), and entered the cab of the locomotive. There was a deafening roar, and the bandit gave a convulsive start, and slid slowly to the floor. On his face there was the look of an overwhelming surprise. He had not known that Vic Reed, a deputy-sheriff, armed with a sawed-off shotgun, was riding in the cab that night to see the passenger train safely through the wild and lawless Tulare County. Reed, later a prominent banker at Lindsay, and a nephew of Thomas L. Reed, the founder of Reedley, had fired a double-barreled shotgun at the bandit's belly with devastating results. The dead man was identified as Johnny Keener, the young man who had accompanied Scott Gillum to the Sam Ellis home for dinner on the

Sunday when Evans and Sontag had been uninvited guests.[6]

The train was halted at a point south of the present Visalia airport, and a search made for other would-be robbers. Jim Lee, a Visalia resident, was picked up for questioning and turned State's evidence. Aside from Keener, who was dead, Lee named as accomplices Joe Anderson, and two brothers, Charles and Johnny Johnson. Jim Lee's wife, a sister of the Johnson boys, had a reputation none too good, and may have been partly responsible for Jim Lee's downfall. Some years before this she and her first husband, John Marriott, had been arrested and tried for the murder of her father who, according to the daughter's testimony, had repeatedly forced her to submit to incest. Although most of the community felt that this was a trumped-up charge against the old man in order to secure his property, no conviction had been obtained. Later Marriott had died and his widow had married Jim Lee, who was now turning State's evidence against his wife's brothers. Honor among thieves is said to be the usual thing; in this case honor was conspicuous by its absence which proves that either the men accused were not thieves or else they were of an unusually low type. The Johnson brothers left for Florida and no proof of misconduct was found against Anderson.

The next attempted hold-up involved a prominent Visalia business man named Josiah Loverin. He operated a bar and hotel well known in the valley at that time. Si, as he was always called, had been born in Iowa in the 1840's, and at an early age had accompanied his family, devout Mormons, to Utah. He had grown to manhood in an environment romantically described in *The Riders of the Purple Sage* and in the Hopalong Cassidy stories. At different times he had been cowboy, prospector, and lumberjack, and for a time he had driven the stage-coach between Bodie and Carson City. In the early 1870's he had engaged in a shooting scrape with a rival over a girl's affections and Si, not the expert marksman he was to become later, had aimed at the bully who was trying to molest his sweetheart and had shot the girl in the thigh. This must have proved rather painful to the woman and mortifying to Loverin. Some time during the late 1870's Si, with three of his brothers, had moved to Visalia. During those years extensive lumbering operations were being carried on in the adjacent mountains and Si had won fame as a logger; he was said to have been the best in the West. He had also attracted attention as a fighter; the Americans usually fought with their fists, but Si had effectively imitated the French-Canadian lumberjacks who, according to Ralph Connor's *The Man From Glengarry*, always went into action *a la savate*, which means that they had educated feet.

The correct spelling of the family name is uncertain. To Si it was always Loveren; to Wesley, who died from gunshot wounds inflicted by a negro during an election at Visalia, it was Loverin; Ben, fatally injured in a gun-fight in Arizona, couldn't spell; Knot, killed in a gunfight in Nevada, had no opinion one way or the other; and Claus, the only one of the brothers who lived peaceably, spelled it Loverne.

In time the Southern Pacific railway directors developed a great antipathy toward Si Loverin (the accepted spelling of the family name in recent years). He had been a close friend of Chris Evans and John Sontag; he had taken care of the Evans family when Chris had been a fugitive in the mountains; he had furnished the guns used by George Sontag and his fellow convicts in their attempted jail-break at Folsom; he had served as a "fence," so it was said, for $500 worth of half-dollars taken by Evans and Sontag from a Southern Pacific express coach; he had gone into the hog-raising business with Chris Evans as a partner, and this mountain enterprise had been tied in with train robberies in some mysterious fashion, so it was asserted by men both observant and shrewd; he had often been heard to quote Evans to the effect that the latter was being blamed for robberies he had never committed; and his big saloon, admittedly a tough spot, was an ideal hang-out for men who might want to plan a train robbery or any other heinous crime. For these various reasons it is apparent why Si Loverin's name and place of business were anathema to the directors of the great railroad.

Into this social pattern moved a young woodchopper named Dan McCall. The oak forest surrounding Visalia provided plenty of work for men with strong backs because wood, then the only available fuel, was in demand, and the land needed to be cleared before it

could be farmed. Another chopper named Britt detested the heavy work and complained bitterly to McCall about his blistered hands. The latter replied:
"If you want to get money the easy way, and have any guts, why don't you help me rob a train?"
This was a challenging thought. One thing led to another, and it was finally decided that on the evening of April 19, 1896, they would attempt to remove the treasure from the express coach of the Southern Pacific passenger train. Britt had decided to string along, as he put it later.
McCall's preparations for the robbery were thorough. He bought new clothes, had a barber trim his beard in such a way that it covered an identifying scar, and developed a deep interest in religion, which was a hypocritical cover-up for things to come.
Britt, a coward at heart, soon lost his nerve, and told all to an influential citizen at Visalia. The latter advised Britt to provide Sheriff Merritt with all the details of the proposed hold-up. The sheriff told Britt to go along with McCall and see the robbery through; to do otherwise would have aroused the latter's suspicions.
McCall had planned that Britt and he should rob the northbound train out of Tulare. Since Britt was now reporting McCall's plans to the sheriff's office, several deputies were sent there to board this train. However, McCall found out in some way that deputies would be on this particular train and at the last minute switched his operations to the southbound train out of Goshen. Two deputies, Draggett and Reed (the latter

was the same man who had terminated Johnny Keener's career), quite unaware of McCall's changed program, took this train at Goshen in order to reach Tulare where they expected to transfer to the supposedly threatened northbound train which would also have on board the posse sent there from Visalia.

McCall and Britt boarded the train at Goshen and walked along the top of the coaches. Britt, who was behind McCall and hoping to become a hero and win the approbation of good citizens, fired at his partner but missed him. McCall, thinking it was an accident, turned around and cautioned his false friend:

"What's the matter with you, Britt? Are you nervous? Be careful, or you'll hurt someone!"

After this admonition, the unsuspecting McCall turned and stalked nonchalantly ahead. Britt had had enough; he jumped off the train.

The deputies, riding in the cab, were warned by Britt's shot, and were on the alert. When McCall started to slide from the coal-tender into the cab, the two deputies opened fire. McCall, surprised and fatally wounded, was certainly no coward and managed in his dying moments to shoot Draggett in the hip and Reed in the arm. However, his resistance was short-lived as the first blast from one of the shotguns had torn McCall's body in such a way that his liver was found lying in the coal-car, and the rest of his torso rolled out of the locomotive cab.

The train was stopped, as on a previous occasion, near the present Visalia airport, and again men went looking for accomplices and evidences of collusion.

According to one account, Si Loverin's horse and buckboard were found tied to a tree near the right-of-way; it was asserted later that Loverin had been seen driving through Visalia earlier in the evening with one horse and that this was the same animal found later near the scene of the attempted hold-up. The result was the arrest of Si Loverin and Charles Ardell, his partner in the liquor business, on the charge that they had placed this horse and buckboard along the railway tracks south of Goshen for the purpose of hauling away the loot.

At the trial the prosecution lawyers offered as Exhibit A the gun taken from the body of McCall; it was identified as belonging to Si Loverin. The defense argued that this proved nothing, as Loverin owned many rifles and revolvers which were stacked in a rack in his saloon. He was in the habit of lending a gun to anyone whom he knew. The testimony of witnesses for the prosecution that Si had driven a certain horse named Birdie through Visalia in the direction of Goshen the evening of the robbery was largely devaluated by the sworn statement of Si's ex-wife, who had no reason to like or defend him, that the quadruped in question had never left his home pasture that night.

Britt, star witness for the railway, admitted that McCall had never mentioned Loverin as a partner, nor had he included him in his plans. The defense attorneys emphasized the keen interest the Southern Pacific directors were showing in the case and their evident desire to liquidate Si Loverin and his liquid-dispensing place of business.

The most telling testimony was not admitted as evidence. Another man's wife could have told the court where Si Loverin had been during the entire night of the robbery. He had been in bed with her! The officers who had arrested Si made no bones about the fact that in the early morning hours following the excitement near Goshen they had gone to a disreputable part of Visalia then known as Spanish-town and had found Loverin asleep with his sweetheart. Just why this information was withheld from the court is uncertain. It may have been due to Loverin's chivalry and his desire to take the rap rather than squawk; fear of an irate husband may have been a deterrent, although this would not have been in keeping with Si's well-known indifference to physical danger; certainly the railroad lawyers would not have relished having the minor crime of cohabitation substituted for the major one of train robbery.

The woman in the case was anxious to tell all; presumably she loved the man who was sent away to San Quentin for life. Si Loverin had not been a party to the hold-up, but his horse and buckboard had been in bad company that night. The injustice of it made him bitter and despondent and while in the penitentiary he made one attempt to commit suicide.

As the years rolled on many old-timers, sincerely believing that Si Loverin had been wrongly convicted, continued to work for his release. Judges in subsequent years were to say that they could not possibly understand how he could have been found guilty on the evidence submitted.

Finally, after having served sixteen years, his case was reviewed by Governor Hiram Johnson, and Si Loverin was granted a parole. He came home to meet many new relatives and to see a countryside which had undergone a tremendous change. A son of his brother Wesley took him to his foothill cattle ranch at Three Rivers and there Si lived for many years, a great favorite with his nephew's little children.

Only once did the old pugnacious spirit of the frontier show up in the otherwise jovial and kindly Si Loverin. A Salvation Army man had testified that he had seen Loverin at the time of the hold-up and had identified him as one of the would-be robbers. The integrity of the witness was of such a nature that his sworn testimony had proved most damaging to Loverin's case. Shortly after the latter's release the Salvation Army officer, motivated either by fear, a guilty conscience, or a feeling that he had made an honest mistake, sent word from Fresno that he wanted to talk with Si; the latter sent back the terse and fiery answer:

"If I ever see you I'll kill you!"

This threat was taken seriously and the follower of General Booth, knowing Si to be a man of his word, departed for the eastern seaboard forthwith.

Two men, Walter Hunsaker of Visalia and Jim Rivers of Goshen, worked incessantly to secure a pardon for Si Loverin. Rivers, facetiously known as "the mayor of Goshen," and well-known as a horseman, was to win fame in subsequent years as a rodeo entertainer. He and various members of the Loverin family operated pack-mule trains from Three Rivers into the mountains for the benefit of visiting sportsmen. On one occasion James Rolph, then governor of California, was a guest. When Rolph returned from his highly successful quest for deer, bears, and golden trout, he handed Si Loverin a full and free pardon.[7]

A well-organized group of men then operating in the valley was known as the Forty Thieves. Its members, said to have included among others, John Marriott, Jim Lee, and the Johnson brothers, stole grain, cattle, money, and anything else of value which they could find. It is now known that on at least one occasion certain members of the band had assaulted a Southern Pacific express coach. One night O. S. Brewer, residing two miles north of Traver, investigated a trail herd passing his ranch in the dead of night. The cattle carried the brand registered in the name of Billy Ruth of Squaw Valley. Brewer's suspicions were aroused and he telephoned officers of the San Joaquin Valley Cattlemen's Association. It was learned that the cattle had been stolen and the two drovers, Avery Marlar and Jack Works, were arrested at Mussel Slough where they had driven the herd for slaughtering. To the disgust of law-abiding citizens, they were given a light sentence. Harrison Peacock, who owned a livery stable at Traver, and later founded a chain of creameries and ice-cream manufacturing plants still bearing his name, was appointed a deputy-sheriff. He laid the groundwork which led to the arrest of the Forty Thieves and their subsequent conviction. [8]

Traver, during its heyday, had three newspapers:

The Traver *Tidings* owned by Hayes & Starring; the Traver *Advocate* edited sucessively by F. V. Dewey, F. A. Zeigler, and Harry Hurst; and the Traver *Tribune,* edited by James McDonald. From their files can be gleaned many kernels of truth regarding life in the raw during that period. One evening Carol S. Hayes, one of the editors of the Traver *Tidings,* went to visit a young lady at Lemoore. While they were sitting on the porch looking at the family album, some unknown person fired a load of buckshot through the screen porch, and Hayes slid to the floor and across the Great Divide. A cousin of the young lady was arrested for the murder, but acquitted for lack of evidence.

Shortly after Evans had been sent to Folsom, a man named Will Porter[9] was indicted for irregularities in connection with his work in the First National Bank at Austin, Texas. It is now known that another man, a friend of Porter, had taken the funds, but Porter took the rap. He refused to testify against his false friend, and his proud reserve made it impossible for his attorneys to do much for him. His running away to Central America made him appear guilty. While there he met two train robbers, Al and Frank Jennings, who had skipped out of New Orleans with $32,000 in cash, the amount left from their most recent escapade.[10]

Eventually Porter and the Jennings brothers arrived in Mexico City. They took rooms in the exclusive Hotel De Republic. One evening a grand ball was given in the lobby of this hotel which was attended by Porfirio Diaz, then President of Mexico, and many other notables. It was a formal affair. When the men were dressing, Al was dissuaded from putting on his shoulder scabbard. But he felt lost without his gun, and returned later and slipped his Colt into his trouser's belt. This act was to have profound consequences.

The most striking couple on the floor that night was a Spanish don, faultless in looks, dress, manners, and breeding; and his fiancee, a compelling, red-haired, blue-eyed beauty of uncommon personality. Will Porter, a handsome Southerner, hailing originally from North Carolina, was unusually magnetic. He could not resist flirting with the girl. When she danced past the place where the little group of strange Americans stood, Porter smiled at her and she responded. At the end of the dance, the don, the finished product of centuries of social training, inwardly raging but outwardly courteous, asked Porter to desist from any further attentions to his fiancee. Al Jennings knew the breed; he told Porter to be careful. But Porter merely laughed. During the next dance the red-headed charmer deftly dropped her mantilla near Porter. He picked it up and returned it to her at the end of the dance. Thereafter things happened with deadly celerity.

The don slapped Porter's face so hard that it left four livid welts on his cheek; Porter bounced four knuckles off the don's nose; the latter came in swinging with a stiletto in his hand; just before it reached Porter's throat, Al Jennings fired in the don's face; the Spaniard was dead when he hit the floor; and the three Americans escaped. It was a tragic ending to the grand march.

Al and Frank Jennings and Porter took a small steamer at Mazatlan, and finally arrived in San Diego. They disappeared somewhere in California, and before they finally emerged at Oakland, another train had been robbed in the San Joaquin Valley. This is what happened.

One evening the northbound train out of Goshen was stopped by two masked men at Cross Creek. The express messenger heard them walking on the roof overhead, but thought they were hoboes. They climbed into the coal-car, held up the engineer and the fireman in the same manner as other hold-ups had been staged, left the main part of the train on the Cross Creek bridge, and forced the engineer to drive the locomotive and express car two miles up the track toward Traver. Here a group of men and a buckboard awaited them. The expressman said he had lost the keys, but a stick of dynamite forced the safe open.

A rancher named Adam Heimrod, living south of Traver, heard the explosion and rode down to the tracks on his burro to investigate. He lay prone in the grass while the men in the party passed; he recognized those in the buckboard as well as the men on horseback. They were all residents of the community. He made a mistake and twitted some of them about the hold-up one day in Traver. They let him know that any revelations on his part would result in instantaneous death. He decided to take no chances, and did not sleep in his own house for a year. He bought a fierce watchdog, tied him in the yard at night, placed his blankets on top of a huge haystack back of the barn, and slept there. For a year he took his Winchester to bed with him every night.[11]

The Southern Pacific sent guards from Fresno to the scene of the hold-up to watch the property which the bandits had thrown out of the express coach. Crates of chickens, sacks of mail, and thousands of silver dollars had been hurled out on the right-of-way; only gold coins had been taken. Until the debris could be cleaned up, it was necessary to watch it. The next morning the school children at Traver were very excited, and pleaded with the school-teacher to dismiss school so that they could go to the scene of the excitement. But no dice! The men who robbed the train were said to have taken their spoils to the Harry Burke saloon where, in an inner room, they divided $70,000 in gold.

John Sontag was not suspected this time; he was dead. His brother George and Chris Evans were not blamed; they were both in Folsom. The Dalton boys were not accused; they were all dead, excepting Emmett, and he was in Leavenworth. Question: Had the guilty men robbed trains before this? Who knows? The technique was the same as in previous hold-ups. These men needed money; they took it from the Southern Pacific no doubt to square accounts over excessively high shipping rates on grain, and they never borrowed money in this way again. So much is certain. Some of them derived little good from their ill-gotten gains, although one man, poor at the time, invested his proceeds in good farm land, became a respected leader in the community, and died honored and respected at Kingsburg in 1937.

The men who robbed the train near Traver were never caught. Lew Draper, whose team had run away from the fight at Stone Corral, and his wife's brother, Henry Burris, had been hunting coyotes the day of the robbery. They had used a team and buckboard. One of their horses was unshod. The seven men who robbed the train that night had also used a buckboard drawn by two horses, one of which was minus shoes. This coincidence led Will Smith to interrogate Draper and Burris, but nothing came of the investigation. The integrity of the two men under surveillance was too well established to make them seriously suspected.[12]

In the meantime Porter and the two Jennings brothers left Oakland for San Francisco, but they never got there. When the ferry-boat was getting ready to dock, Al discovered Captain Dodge, the chief of the Wells, Fargo detectives, standing near by. He hissed a warning to his comrades, and they remained on the boat and returned to Oakland, and eventually to Texas. Al and Frank held up a bank while Porter waited apprehensively for them in a room in the Plaza Hotel at San Antonio. The two brothers walked out of the bank with $15,060, and bought a ranch. Sometimes it is as easy as that. Porter went with them to their new property, but left Texas shortly thereafter. He never helped the Jennings gang rob trains, although Al said he held their horses on one occasion.

The Jennings boys were captured some time after they had failed in a bold attempt to rob the Rock Island flyer in broad daylight. When Al arrived at Columbus to begin the serving of his sentence in the Ohio penitentiary, he found Will Porter already there as an inmate.[13]

Since no officers ever learned the identity of the men responsible for the Traver holdup, they tried to pin the guilt on men who were innocent in this particular case. The Wells, Fargo detectives knew that the Jennings boys and Porter were in California, and were hot on their trail. Will Smith, representing the Southern Pacific, also began to look for them, but the outlaws left the state so quickly that no detective had time to pick them up. Shortly thereafter they were swallowed up by the penitentiary at Columbus; they were to remain there for many years. When they were finally released other detectives and other problems held sway.

When Porter had completed his sentence he went to New York where, some years later, Al Jennings was to join him. The former had by that time become one of the most famous short-story writers in the world; he was known to millions as O. Henry.

Porter had adopted this cognomen because it had been his pet name among his intimate friends down in Texas. One of the latter, a girl named Lollie Cave, owned a plebeian-looking tom-cat which proudly refused to come when called. His haughty disdain in the matter amused Porter who solemnly christened the cat "Henry the Proud" after a famous duke of

Saxony and Bavaria. One day when several young people were calling the cat without avail, Porter said: "Let me try." He then shouted: "OH, HENRY!" To the surprise of everyone, the eccentric feline immediately responded to the summons. Porter then said:[14] "Oh, I see, O. Henry! The insult was not intentional. I failed to give you a prefix to your name, so now Mr. Duke O. Henry, I am at your service."

From that time the name "O. Henry" was applied to Porter as frequently as to the cat. When he began his literary career in New York the use of this name made it possible for his Texas friends to learn his whereabouts. He had been gone from them a long time. When Lollie Cave wrote to him and asked him why he did not explain the origin of his pseudonym and stop all the ridiculous stories which were being concocted to explain his choice of a nom-de-plume, he replied:[15]

"It's too silly; they would be calling me 'Puss, the house-cat'."

Who robbed the train at Traver? One of the men who was there that night is still alive at this writing. His secret must be kept. The reader who likes to do a little amateur sleuthing is welcome to go to work on this slight clue: Six of the men who went big-game hunting in Traver more than fifty years ago and brought down a Southern Pacific express-coach were named: Anderson, Bowers, Gramley, Johnson, Larson, and Smith. This author refuses to answer any and all further questions.

While all this tumult was taking place in the old

haunts of Chris Evans, what was he doing? Walking! He had always enjoyed this form of exercise, and now it was the only source of distraction at his disposal. Four steps to the stone wall, and four steps back to the steel door of his cell. His restless body craved motion, and so he walked back and forth, back and forth, like a caged animal, hour after hour. The hours became days, the days grew into weeks, and the weeks joined the endless procession of the months, and still he walked. Then came a break in the monotony which saved him from madness. He was assigned to work in the prison library. He loved books, and life took on a brighter hue.[16]

One day a deputy-warden was horribly slashed in the face by a negro convict. Evans volunteered to nurse the disfigured man, and thereafter had a loyal friend in this officer. Evans continued to work in the prison hospital, and became known as "the Good Samaritan." The gentle touch, soothing voice, and gracious sympathy which had endeared him to little children and wounded men in other and happier days, were likewise appreciated by hardened criminals in the days of their extremity. Chris had at least one chance to return good for evil. One of the detectives who had hounded Evans unmercifully during previous years was finally sent to Folsom himself to serve a sentence. This officer was then in a dying condition, and Chris was assigned to him as nurse. Whatever his other shortcomings may have been, Evans was never petty or vindictive. He tended his erstwhile foe tenderly, but neither medical skill nor vigilant nursing could save the life of the man who told Chris that his guilty conscience was paining him more than his physical agony. Evans did all that he could to make the officer's last days endurable, and eventually prepared the body for its burial.

Chris Evans, strangely enough, never developed any maudlin sympathy for his fellow-prisoners. He said afterwards that he believed that most of the men in the penitentiary were guilty of the crimes charged against them. Neither did he find his associates admirable persons; they were simply not his kind of people. A man who loved Nature in all of its aspects, who adored little children, and who could recite from memory long portions of Shakespeare, Swinburne, Scott, Tennyson, or the *Bible,* would have little in common with the foul-mouthed convicts from the big city slums. Nevertheless, in the name of their common humanity, he was willing to serve them when they were sick or dying.

One day Warden Aull sent for Chris Evans. He informed the latter that a visitor wanted to talk with him. This is Evans' report of that interview:[17]

"Collis P. Huntington came here one day, years ago, and Warden Aull walked me out and introduced me to Huntington. 'Chris and I used to be partners', said Huntington. But I said to myself, 'Huntington, you're a liar. Your style and mine differ. I came out in the open. You strike from behind. You're a sneak-thief. I never drove women and children from their homes. You are a vile old scoundrel, and there is nothing vile in me'. I had to keep my thoughts to myself, for this was Mr. Huntington's jail, and Aull was his superintendent."

During his spare moments Evans busied himself writing a book which he entitled *Eurasia*. This was later published by James Barry, editor of the San Francisco *Star*. In it Evans described a mythical country which had a perfect government. Chris must have dipped into the future; his book reads like a blue-print of all the reforms which were to come during the next forty years. He told about the following, none of which then existed: The CCC camps for boys; a woman Secretary of Labor (Frances Perkins); the income tax (legalized in 1913); universal military training for a short time, followed by formal education at national expense (G. I. Bill); old age pensions; the eight-hour day; accident insurance; collective bargaining; nationalization of banks (recently adopted by Great Britain's Labor Party); and a retirement of all workers at the age of sixty. Chris Evans possessed a rare prescience of things to come.

While trains were being robbed and Chris Evans was writing a book, what were the other members of the Evans family doing?

Eva Evans had secured work in a photograph gallery in Portland. She wanted to bring the rest of the family to Oregon for two reasons. She liked the state, and she believed that it would be better for the other children if they could get away from Visalia and its unhappy memories. Her big difficulty for the moment was the lack of money. One day the United States Government offered Mrs. Evans five hundred dollars for the Redwood Ranch. This was not much for a quarter section of land containing a virgin stand of cedars, sugar pines, and redwoods. However, poachers, aware that Evans could no longer defend his property, were beginning to cut his trees. So the offer was accepted, and the Evans property became a part of the Sequoia National Forest; it still is. The old home of Chris Evans is now used as a store-house at the ranger station on Redwood Mountain, about nine and a half miles east and north of Badger. The redwoods, once the pride and joy of Chris Evans, now protected by forest rangers, will remain to gladden the hearts of future generations of nature lovers.[18]

This sum of money enabled Mrs. Evans to move to Portland with her children. The Visalia episode was forever ended. Poverty was still to be their portion in life. None of the children could finish grammar school; they all had to find work. John Christopher and Louis grew to be handsome, blonde six-footers. They became truck drivers hauling high explosives to construction gangs; this was a work requiring good judgment and courage. Joe worked for a time in the Portland post-office, later as a salesman for a coffee and tea firm, and then began to gather wild flowers and ferns in the deep, dank forests of Oregon, which he shipped to eastern florists. This work was remunerative, and kept him happy; he had inherited his father's love of nature. Carl, whose back had been injured when he fell off the porch as a baby, remained frail and partially crippled; he found light work clerking at a news-stand. Ynez, a stenographer, later became Eva's partner in a photograph studio in Marshfield. All of the girls finally married.

The men who had fought Evans had left written opinions of his craft and cunning. James B. Hume, one of the best detectives in California at that time, said, after he had tangled with Evans on numerous occasions:

"Chris Evans is a remarkable man. He may always be expected to do the unexpected. That is what makes him dangerous."[19]

John Morgan, a popular chief of police at Fresno, who experienced the impact of both Evans' personality and his bullet, added his testimony:

"Evans never took a chance. He thought out every move. He was undoubtedly the brains of the partnership, and a very clever brains at that."

This was the verdict of men who must be regarded as enemies of Christopher Evans. The only other man in history who is judged solely by the verdict of his enemies is Hannibal of Carthage. All that has ever been printed about him has been drawn from Roman sources. The estimates of Chris Evans have been written chiefly by men who were his mortal foes. A few years later the judge, the jury, and most of the officers who had combined to send Chris Evans to Folsom, signed a petition to secure his parole. What gives?

In 1904 Evans' youngest daughter, Winifred, decided to move to Sacramento to work for her father's parole. She had developed into a magnificent looking woman; five feet, seven inches tall (her father's height); and was crowned with a glorious growth of deep golden hair which hung to her waist. Her personality and charm were to be used in her father's behalf. It was due to her resolution, perseverance, and strength of character that victory was finally achieved. Winifred knew that her father, a strictly out-door man, would eventually pine away and die under prison conditions. In her race against time, she had many high hurdles to overcome.

From 1904 to 1911 all the petitions for a parole were vetoed by the board and the successive governors. They all knew their master's voice, and it spoke with a Southern Pacific accent. Each time Evans appeared before the board, he was told:

"Evans, this is a penitentiary. If you will express regret for your crimes, we will be willing to consider your parole plea."

Each and every time Chris Evans replied stoutly:

"Gentlemen, I am guilty of no crimes. I killed men who were trying to kill me. That is all."

Had Evans been willing to compromise with his conscience and his ideals, he would have been freed years earlier. But he agreed with the philosophy of the man who said:

"Acceptance of authority is just the opposite of subservience to power."

Then came the organization of the Lincoln-Roosevelt League, the first steps toward which were taken in the Hotel Oakland on August 1, 1908, largely through the leadership of Chester Rowell, then editor of the Fresno *Republican*. One definite purpose of this organization was to end the domination of California politics by the Southern Pacific Railway. Hiram Johnson became the candidate of the reform groups for governor of California in 1910. The various city political machines were his sworn foes, but he toured the rural areas and received an amazing ovation. One of his innovations was the use of the automobile. Concerning this he wrote as follows to the author:[20]

"I doubt if I was the first candidate to make use of the automobile in a political campaign, but I do know that up to 1910, there had never been a more extensive use of it than I made. The machine I used was a Locomobile roadster, the motor of which possessed unusual strength, and for that day, speed."

The newspapers reported Johnson's defeat the day after election. This report was based on early city returns. The conservative factions were gleeful. But their joy was premature. His automobile had carried him into the by-ways and his speeches had proved convincing. When the returns from the rural districts began to arrive, it was apparent that a new regime stood on the threshold; Johnson's belligerent prediction, made at the conclusion of every speech: "I am going to be elected the next governor of California, and as soon as elected I am going to kick the Southern Pacific Railway out of politics," had been loudly cheered and later approved at the polls.

No one followed the campaign with more interest than Chris Evans; no one had more at stake than he, for with him it was life or death. Again Winifred presented her petition, and this time it was accepted. Johnson, too, carried scars from his battle with the

Southern Pacific, and he sympathized with the battered Evans. The date for the latter's release was set for May 1, 1911. He was met at the gates of Folsom by his daughter Winifred, and Jack Jungmeyer, a reporter for the Sacramento *Star*. The latter wrote:[21]

"Asked what had been hardest to bear, in connection with his long imprisonment, he replied instantly, 'The depravity of the majority of my fellow prisoners, particularly the obscene language.'

"Among a crew of renegades, Chris Evans stood out as a wonderfully clean man. He does not use tobacco or liquor. In three hours talk with him some days ago, I did not once hear him use an oath.

"Whatever he may have been in the past—and there are those even among the Southern Pacific officials who have told me that they believed he was as much sinned against as sinning—there is not the slightest trace of the criminal about him. He is a man I felt honored to shake by the hand."

A few days later this same paper re-printed an estimate of Evans and the Southern Pacific which had been written seventeen years before:[22]

"Taking the worst view of the case against Evans and Sontag, what was their guilt, in killing two or three Southern Pacific Railroad detectives in self-defense, compared with the crimes of such men as Stanford and Huntington, who rob every passenger on every one of their trains to the number of thousands daily; who rob all the people by refusing to pay their own taxes and stealing the public domain; who corrupt voters, buy up legislatures and prostitute the courts of justice; who murder honest settlers and innocent defenders of their firesides at Mussel Slough because they would not 'stand and deliver' their money or homes to the railroad bandits who 'claimed the earth'? Even if Evans and Sontag are criminals 'before the law', they are better men than those who placed a price upon their heads. But are the latter hunted down, and shot without warning? Oh, no! They are sent to the United States Senate, where they are hailed as philanthropists and instruct Presidents in their duties. They are a law unto themselves."

Winifred took Evans to *The Hights* in Oakland where he was entertained by Joaquin Miller. This was the first meeting between the two men, and Joaquin got up from a sick bed to be photographed with Evans. From there father and daughter went directly to Portland; the document which had set Evans free definitely stated that he had been "paroled to Oregon."

By the time Chris Evans was released from Folsom, legends had grown up about him which rivalled the "tall stories" which had been invented about Robin Hood and Joaquin Murieta. The following paragraph from a signed article in a metropolitan newspaper is inserted to show the reader how hard it was to contain the exploits of Evans within the bounds of truth. This account is supposed to tell what happened when Smith and Witty went to arrest John Sontag at the Evans home:[23]

"On the night of August 4, 1892, a posse rode down upon the Evans home at Visalia. Stealthily they surrounded the little home—the Machine's human bloodhounds. They were heavily armed, and had shackles for the arms and fetters for the feet. The quarry could choose either the chains or the lead. Softly they closed in upon the house. They knew what was inside with the man—a mother and her brood of five children. The posse battered at the door with the butt of a shotgun and called upon Evans to surrender in the name of The People.

"Chris Evans called out to the posse, telling them that they had lied like thieves in saying that they represented The People. He said that the machinery of the law of which the Sheriff was a part was but the machinery of the Machine that was grinding the souls out of The People.

"All through that flaming night the mother remained awake. Her darning needle lay idle. She worked with the cleaning rod, as did the wives of Lexington. Her dish-rag was used to cool the sweating gun. Her pitcher wet a throat that was parched by the hot smoke of powder. She prayed for the man, for the children, for all of them. Each prayer was punctured by the bark of a gun or the wheep of a bullet. Now the help of the God of rains and harvests was needed. The Machine, more blighting than the frost, the Machine more terrible than the drought, the Machine as cruel as famine, was clamoring at the door.

"The children did not sleep that night. Around their little beds the red war broke and leaped and ranged. Instead of the cradle song, they heard the singing of bullets. Into their fairy-land came hulking forms with guns that belched forth flame. The cries of the night birds were hushed by the yelping and howling of the Machine's wolves. The chirping cricket gave way to the buzzing lead. The glimmer of the firefly fled before the blaze of battle.

"For two days and two nights the Evans home was beseiged. The Machine, from a respectful distance, called him an outlaw, and the Machine's newspapers echoed the word.

"Chris Evans said, between the barks of his gun, that there was no law in California except the Machine's law, no justice except the Machine's justice.

"The People knew that Mr. Evans had spoken the truth, for this knowledge had grown in their minds even as the dank weeds grew upon the seven graves at Mussel Slough. This conviction shook their souls even as the tread of Federal troops shook the land of Tulare."

Any reader familiar with the career and exploits of Chris Evans will recognize several discrepancies in the foregoing tale. The wrong date is given for the beginning of the trouble; the number of children is incorrect; there was never any firing by a posse over their defenseless heads at any time; there are no fireflies in the valley; the wife never cooled an overheated rifle, and she never stood beside her husband on the firing-line holding a pitcher of cold water; the settlers who died at Mussel Slough at the behest of a corporate power were six in number and not seven; the officers present when the trouble started at the Evans home carried neither clanking shackles nor binding fetters; no Federal troops were present then or later; the fight did not last two days and nights; and it was manifestly impossible for Chris Evans to engage in lengthy philosophical discussions with a posse when fighting for his life. However, these minor errors made the explanation of the origin of Chris Evans' troubles with the law sound more sensational than the facts warranted, and no doubt led thousands of readers to become intense partisans of the famous outlaw.

To-day the San Joaquin Valley is one of the most peaceful regions in the world. The majority of its citizens, recent arrivals from eastern states or foreign lands, are not even aware that outlaws were once engaged in bloody battles with powerful corporations. Viewed in the light of present day conditions, it seems strange that agencies other than the state, could freely place a price on a man's head and then send private detectives out to hunt him. The individual whose scalp was wanted then automatically became an outlaw. If he resisted the hair-buyers and refused to have "his face lifted," trouble naturally ensued. The outlaw was not entirely wrong always. He pointed out by his very excesses the need for certain reforms. In time conditions were ameliorated by ballots rather than bullets. Men like Evans, Sontag, Dalton, Jennings, and Morrell possessed courage above the average, spirits that could not be broken, and abilities that made them lead ers in other fields of endeavor. Ed. Morrell became a successful author, lecturer, reformer, and sociologist. Evans wrote a book outlining the reforms that would come in subsequent decades. Al Jennings also became an author of note, as well as a lecturer, evangelist, moving picture director, and candidate for governor of Oklahoma on the Democratic ticket. Emmett Dalton went to Hollywood and won recognition as a building contractor, fame as an author, and wealth as a real-estate promoter.

In his old age Emmett Dalton attended the religious services conducted at Angelus Temple in Echo Park, Los Angeles, by Aimee Semple McPherson. This buxom, good-looking, auburn-haired lady was, in her prime, a superb orator. In her audiences could be found honest men and rogues, all huddled up together, but they all swayed to her will. When she pulled out all the stops in her magnificent, organ-like voice, and sent it careering out over the congregation, it seemed to reverberate from the far corners of the vast auditorium. Then she would tell, in an exaggerated British accent, a funny story based on her early life in Canada, and all the people would be shaken with laughter. In another moment she was tugging at their heart-strings, and soon tears would be streaming down their faces. When she asked in simple language and humble tones for an extra large offering to help defray the expenses of a trip to Europe, a tour of the Holy Land, or to help the needy and those in distress, her people would give until it hurt. She did all of these things gracefully, naturally, and with the greatest of ease:

"As effortless as woodland nooks
     Send violets up and paint them blue."

One critic of Dalton said, unkindly and unjustly, that Emmett went to hear Sister Aimee because he admired her technique. The Dalton boys, in the days of their activity, had always encountered a certain amount of sales resistance in trying to make men and their money part company. The McPherson method was less painful and far more efficient.

In 1914 the parole board granted Evans permission to leave Portland for a visit to Sacramento to ask Governor Hiram Johnson for a pardon. For reasons which have never been made clear, this plea was denied. Evans then went across the bay to San Francisco where he visited with D. E. Walker, who had moved his Visalia Saddle Works to that city one year before others had decided to move Evans to Folsom. Walker's grand-daughter wrote this about the visit:[24]

"The latter (Evans), shortly before his death in 1917, appeared at the Visalia Saddle Company store in San Francisco, crippled and partially blind, seeking to sell in a long familiar institution a book telling the story of his life that was led in the very shadow of the old Walker saddle shop. Indeed, he as well as the financially secure ranchers who owned the estimated 288,483 cattle which grazed the ranges of the California cattle country in the 1870's spent many a starry night pillowed in crude comfort by the same Walker saddle that bore him by day over the miles of range he rode."

Evans took the train to Kingsburg where he spent two weeks with Criss Tremper, the owner of a 160-acre vineyard north of that city. The latter had also seen exciting times, especially around Nome, Alaska, during the gold-rush days. His experiences in defending his diggings against claim-jumpers was the central theme in the novel entitled *The Spoilers* written by Rex Beach. Another friend of Evans, according to Constance Bigelow Mainwaring, was Thomas L. Reed; about the latter Mrs. Mainwaring wrote: "Tom Reed of Reedley was a great friend of Evans and helped him all he could."[25]

One of the things which must impress the reader is the quality of the men who befriended him. They were all men of means, responsibility, and integrity.

Evans' daughter had married Perry McCullough in 1909, and they had established a home in Southern California where her husband had become a successful realtor at Laguna Beach. Chris went to visit his oldest daughter there. His condition was bad and she took him to a doctor for treatment. One day an official looking document arrived signed by the state parole officer, Ed. H. Whyte, which read in part:[26]

"By taking the liberty to go to Los Angeles without first procuring permission, you have violated the terms of your parole, with which you are very familiar, as several copies of the rules governing your parole have been sent to you. If the book which bears your name is your composition, as you claim, I cannot understand why this office would be compelled to call your attention to the rules governing your freedom. If you recall, you informed me on your last visit to this office (at Sacramento), while you were in San Francisco, that you were going back to your family in Portland.

"I want a letter of explanation from you, and want

to be advised by whom you were granted permission to go to Los Angeles."

Evans' daughter took her father to the deputy-parole officer at Los Angeles, and asked permission to keep her old father at her home until his medical treatment had been completed. Her request was denied, and in a way which left no doubt that the sanctity of the law must always take precedence over human needs. Evans was ordered back to Portland that very afternoon, and by boat! Perhaps it was feared that he might rob another Southern Pacific train if he were allowed to approach it. He may have felt like it that afternoon, and who could have blamed him? From the vantage point of time it seems that for the authorities to treat a sick and crippled old man as if he were still a dangerous criminal was both asinine and a trifle unnecessary.

Chris Evans returned to Portland, and there a skillful surgeon removed the buckshot from his head. The headache, which had plagued him since the fight at Stone Corral, disappeared, but the palsy and partial paralysis were to remain until his final release from the worries of this world.

Now began for Chris Evans the most peaceful time of his life. His wife, Molly, devoted herself to his welfare, and developed a philosophy of life which made it possible for her to laugh merrily over the exciting episodes of their insurgent years in California. Most of their children remained in the immediate vicinity, although Eva had moved to southern California some time before this, and Winifred and Carl were eventually also to return to the state of their birth. Winifred's son, in time, was destined to go to China, where he was to represent a large American insurance firm. There he was to prove far more successful than Alice Tisdale Hobart's hero in *Oil for the Lamps of China*. His mother went to the Orient to visit him, but when she learned that a house full of servants forbade her performing any task, however light, lest the master "lose face," she returned to the more democratic United States where it was permissible to bake a lemon pie without losing her social position. Later, she, accompanied by her brother Carl, bought a ranch in the foothills of the Sierra Nevada.

Christopher Evans was approaching his allotted span of three score years and ten. As he sat palsied and trembling before the fire in life's eventide, he was charitable toward those who, with or without reason, had harmed him. However, many of Evans' friends were less forgiving than he, and took great delight in pointing out how retributive justice had come to many of his former enemies. The following tribulations were cited as evidence that "the wages of sin is death." Will Smith, the railway detective, had died from cancer in its most hideous form—his entire face had been eaten away; Perry Byrd, accused of leading Evans into the trap at Stone Corral, had been made miserable by domestic troubles; J. S. Black, who had tried to ambush Evans at Camp Badger, had been murdered in Arizona; George Witty, who had fired the first shot in the struggle, had been confronted with a charge of embezzlement, and had committed suicide; Luke Hall, who had let the posse use his trained bloodhounds to track Evans, had fallen out of his wagon when his team ran away and had been killed instantly; George Sontag, who had squealed, truthfully or untruthfully, had died of a loathesome disease which decent people usually manage to sidestep; Al Perkins had been crushed when a boulder toppled over and left only his protruding feet as a means of identification. In this last case Evans' supporters had confused Al with his older brother Elijah. The former had never done either Evans or Sontag any harm; it was Elijah whose report to the sheriff's office had led to Evans' capture. Later Elijah Perkins was to be portrayed on the stage as a low-comedy character and buffoon. Leland Stanford, one of the chief directors of the Southern Pacific, had lost his only son and would never be happy again. But Evans said nothing. To him it was all water under the bridge.[27]

His thoughts turned to his children. They had all become honest, upright citizens. They worked hard to support themselves and to make sure that their old father might have light at eventide.

No matter what his sins against society had been, Christopher Evans had through a long and stormy life so conducted himself as a father that all of his children had anchored their hearts in him. What more can any father ask when it is finished?

APPENDIX

Chapter 1:
1. Visalia *Daily Times,* August 13, 1892.
2. McCullough, Eva Evans, Personal Interview, Reedley, Sept. 23, 1940.
3. Ibid.
Chapter 2:
1. Dougherty, Willard, Personal Interview, Kingsburg, Dec. 25, 1947.
2. Perkins, Elmer, Personal Interview, Sultana, Jan. 2, 1948.
3. Patterson, Bart, Personal Interview, Dinuba, Jan. 2, 1948.
4. McCullough, Eva Evans, *An Outlaw and his Family.*
5. In 1884, one year after Evans had returned from Adelaide to Visalia, the wheat growers in the San Joaquin Valley planted 1,300,631 acres and 17,997,212 bushels were harvested. This was the peak year in wheat growing; the acreage used for this purpose began a steady decline at this time.
6. Eugene L. McCapes, who was present as a young lad when Irwin S. Wright invented the jerk-line method of controlling long strings of work stock, told me that this system had never been used prior to 1868. He also maintained that the first horse ever trained to function as a jerk-line leader was his father's strawberry roan bronco mare, Hannah. This historic animal, as well as the first factory-built Stockton plow, were both brought to Fresno county by Ransome McCapes. The plow, called a "Yankee fiddler" by the men who used it, saw service in the wheat fields of Fairview for three decades; the mare Hannah died in 1873.
7. Today many persons and places claim credit for the invention of the Fresno scraper. It remained for Ernest Nielsen of Selma to dig out the facts and prove by the Patent Office records that the first sheet-iron Fresno scraper was built by Abijah McCall and a patent secured, with Frank Dusy helping to finance the project, on June 16, 1885.
8. Associated Press Dispatches, June 13, 1893.
9. In 1887 there were 300 Houser & Haines combines in use in California; in 1888 there were 400; and in 1889 the number had been increased to 500.
10. Tapp, Jack, Personal Interview, Kingsburg, Dec. 31, 1947. Tapp worked on the old-time combines and told me that some of the sacks weighed 150 lbs.
11. Elam, William, Personal Interview, Dinuba, Dec. 20, 1947.
12. This true experience in the life of Chris Evans was to appear, only slightly altered, in *The Octopus* by Frank Norris.
13. McCullough, Eva Evans, *An Outlaw and His Family.*

Chapter 3:

1. Several years ago I was the speaker at a banquet in Selma given by the local Farm Bureau Center. I told the members about the hole in Sontag's back. After the program, an elderly woman chided me for that statement. She insisted that Sontag had no hole in his back, at least not one big enough for anyone to insert a fist into it. My reply was that Sontage had died long before I was born, and that I wouldn't know, but Eva Evans McCullough had told me about it in a personal conversation at my home. I could not resist adding: "How do you know Sontag had no hole in his back?" She sniffed and walked away in high dudgeon. Far be it from me to become involved in an argument between two ladies about the hole in a man's back. The reader may take the hole in Sontag's back or leave it. I'm taking it!

2. San Francisco *Examiner,* June 13, 1893.

3. Duxilius, C. R., Acting Chief, Land Use Division, United States Department of the Interior, Bureau of Land Management, Washington, D. C., Personal Letter, January 13, 1948. Most accounts credit the Southern Pacific with donations of ten sections of land per mile of track laid. Actually it was twice as bad as that; the government gave the corporation twenty sections per mile.

4. Louis Haas and James S. Williams operated a sheep ranch east of Kingsburg along Kings River during the Civil War period. Later this place was acquired by the famous cattleman, Crawford W. Clarke. A daughter born to Mr. and Mrs. Haas while residing along Kings River was christened Pennsylvania after their native state. The girl became noted for her striking appearance and vibrant personality. She was endowed with the body of a goddess; the complexion known as peaches and cream; a voice that was deep, throaty, and husky; and long, thick hair resembling corn silk. She was to be depicted as the heroine, Hilma Tree, in *The Octopus* written by Frank Norris. In real life she was destined to be the wife of Walter J. Crow (Buck Annixter in the novel); she was to become a widow in circumstances similar to those described in *The Octopus.*

5. Mrs. Cecil C. Cline, a daughter of James B. Flewelling and a resident of San Francisco, informed me through her lawyer, Mr. Raymond Haizlip, that Caleb Flewelling, her father's cousin, killed Walter J. Crow. The latter's son, Clarence C. Crow, was shown this letter and replied: "I did not know the name of the Flewelling mentioned in your book (*Garden of the Sun*), but from hearsay I understood that he left the vicinity immediately and went under some other name. Mrs. Cline's statement seems to verify what I have heard, and I believe her statement to be correct."

Chapter 4:

1. McCullough, Eva Evans, *An Outlaw and His Family.*

2. *Ibid.*

3. Bigelow, Henry Derby, in the San Francisco *Examiner* for Oct. 7, 1892.

4. Mr. Daniel McFadzean, a Visalia lawyer, wrote to me as follows: "In those days, the pioneers had not yet gotten over the idea that it was not in good taste to inquire into a man's past history. I do not know of anyone who would be more likely to know of the early history of the Sontags than Eva Evans. I had no intimate acquaintance with the Sontags. I simply knew who they were when I saw them on the streets. I knew Chris Evans well. At that time, his children were in the schools here, and I was one of the teachers."

5. Love, Robertus, *The Rise and Fall of Jesse James,* 191-195.

6. McClain, Andrew, Personal Interview, Reedley, Oct. 7, 1947. Mr. McClain's grandfather was present in the Visalia Saddle Works when Alsalio Herrera and John Sontag discussed "the nickels and the dimes." Mr. McClain also stated that his grandfather and John Sontag were playmates during childhood days in Aspetuck, Connecticut.

7. McCullough, Eva Evans, Personal Interview, Reedley, Sept. 17, 1940.

Chapter 5:

1. Leslie, James M., Personal Interview, Del Rey, December 23, 1947. Mr. Leslie told me that most of the old-timers were under the impression that Chris Evans did not buy Wallace's livery stable; he merely made arrangements to rent it for a certain specified time. If this is true, then the amount of money needed by Evans would have been less, and he could easily have swung the deal by securing a loan on his twenty-acre ranch. I have also run across men who have asserted that Evans set fire to the barn himself. According to these old-timers, he had proved inept in the management of the business, and sought this way out of his financial difficulties. There is no proof of this charge, and it seems preposterous. It hardly seems plausible that a horse-lover would plan to destroy fine livestock in such a cruel manner. It is decidedly not in keeping with what is known of the man's character. Yet men will do strange things for money. Evans found this out to his sorrow, when a price was put on his head, and old friends and neighbors tried to kill him. One story current in Modesto after the fire was that Jacob Claypool had learned about the lawless activities of Evans and Sontag and had been murdered to shut his mouth. The fire had then been set to cover up evidences of foul play. There is no proof of this either, but it illustrates how tongues will wag when a man gets into trouble.

2. McCullough, Eva Evans, *An Outlaw and His Family.*

Chapter 6:

1. McCullough, Eva Evans, *An Outlaw and His Family.*

2. Lyman, George, *John Marsh: Pioneer,* 27 ff.

3. Muñoz, Father Pedro, *Diario de la Expedicion Hecha por Don Gabriel Moraga a los Nuevas Descrubrimientos del Tular, September 21-November 2, 1806,* B. C., Arch. Sta. Barb. IV., 27.

4. Atherton, Gertrude, *Rezanov,* (a novel).

5. Chevigny, Hector, *Lost Empire,* 190-191.

6. Atherton, Gertrude, *Golden Gate Country,* 12.

7. *Ibid*, 13. See also Mrs. Fremont Older's *Love Stories of Old California*, (selections).

8. Chevigny, Hector, *Lost Empire*, 337.

9. Dana, Julian, *The Man Who Built San Francisco*, 293-294.

10. Atherton, Gertrude, *Golden Gate Country*, 203-204.

11. Fisher, Anne B., *The Salinas: The Upside-Down River*, 92.

12. Powers, Laura Bride, *Old Monterey: California's Adobe Capital*, 149-150.

13. Treadwell, Edward, *The Cattle King*, 26 ff.

14. Visalia *Daily Times*, August 13, 1892.

15. McCullough, Eva Evans, Personal Letter, Laguna Beach, September 26, 1940.

Chapter 7:

1. Connelly, William Elsey, *Quantrill and the Border Wars*, preface.

2. Love, Robertus, *The Rise and Fall of Jesse James*, 19.

3. Raine, William MacLeod, *Famous Sheriffs and Western Outlaws*, 207.

4. Dalton, Emmett, *When the Daltons Rode*, 17 ff.

5. Curtis, Eugene L., Personal Interview, Kingsburg, November 4, 1933.

6. Love, Robertus, *The Rise and the Fall of Jesse James*, 127-129.

7. Glasscock, Carl B., *Bandits and the Southern Pacific*, 27 ff.

8. Fresno *Expositor*, February 7, 1891.

9. Modesto *Herald*, September 5, 1891.

10. Curtis, Eugene L., Personal Interview, Kingsburg, February 2, 1931.

11. Dalton, Emmett, Personal Letter, Hollywood, October 2, 1931.

12. United States Land Commission for California, *Transcript of Proceedings in Land Case No. 357, Andreas Pico, claimant, versus the United States, defendant, for the place named "Los Moquelamos,"* San Francisco, 1852.

13. Fresno *Expositor*, September 11, 1891.

14. *Ibid*.

15. Elwood, Shirley, Personal Interview, Reedley, February 25, 1948. Miss Elwood, a student at the Reedley College, is a grand-daughter of the Burton Elwood mentioned in the text.

16. Dalton, Emmett, *When the Daltons Rode*, 127.

17. Fresno *Bee*, March 31, 1931.

Chapter 8:

1. Leslie, James M., Personal Interview, Del Rey, December 23, 1947.

2. McCullough, Eva Evans, *An Outlaw and His Family*.

3. Gillum, Scott, Personal Interview, Woodlake, January 17, 1948. For many years I was puzzled over the fact that Chris Evans shot George Witty, when it was Will Smith who had called his daughter "a damned little liar." It seemed to me impossible that a man as cool and calculating as Evans evidently was at all times, even in his supreme moments, should make a mistake and fire at the wrong man. Rumors often came to my attention that perhaps George Witty had been jealous of John Sontag, and had hated the latter as the successful rival for Eva Evans'

affections. Joaquin Miller hinted at something of this sort in his article which appeared in the San Francisco *Examiner*. One day Scott Gillum told me something which may shed light on the matter. He stated that when Will Smith spoke harshly to Eva Evans, George Witty added the foul and damaging remark: "Get out of the way, you little ———— ————; I saw John Sontag go in through the back door and I am going after him." This information Mr. Gillum received from Eva's uncle, Perry Byrd. The latter was not on very good terms with Chris Evans, but in this instance he felt that Chris had a perfect right to shoot Witty. The foregoing information was given me by Mr. Scott Gillum at Woodlake on the date listed above. Present at this interview was Mr. William Kangas of Reedley, an aviator in World War II, and a relative by marriage of the Si Lovern family of Visalia.

4. Smith, Leroy, Personal Interview, Dinuba, November 13, 1947.
5. San Francisco *Chronicle*, May 6, 1934.
6. McCullough, Eva Evans, *An Outlaw and His Family*.
7. *Ibid.*
8. Oscar Beaver was carried into the Joe Patnott house where he died.

Chapter 9:

1. Fresno *Expositor*, August 10, 1892.
2. Visalia *Daily Times*, August 12, 1892.
3. *Ibid*, August 6, 1892.
4. Jefferds, E. E., in the San Francisco *Chronicle*, August 7, 1892.
5. McCullough, Eva Evans, *An Outlaw and His Family*.
6. *Ibid.*
7. Visalia *Daily Times*, March 13, 1893.
8. Perkins, D. E., Personal Letter, Visalia, Sept. 28, 1931.
9. McCullough, Eva Evans, *An Outlaw and His Family*.
10. *Ibid.*
11. Gillum, Scott, Personal Interview, Woodlake, Jan. 17, 1948.
12. Ibid.
13. Smith, Leroy, Personal Interview, Dinuba, Dec. 13, 1947.
14. Visalia *Daily Times*, May 2, 1893.
15. McCubbin, John C., Personal Interview, Traver, April 12, 1940.
16. Elam, William, Personal Interview, Dinuba, Dec. 20, 1947.
17. *Transcript, The People of the State of California, versus George Contant, Defendant, Robbery*, 541.
18. San Francisco *Examiner*, August 19, 1939.
19. McCullough, Eva Evans, Personal Interview, Reedley, Sept. 23, 1940.
20. Ibid.
21. Williams, Samuel B., Personal Interview, Fresno, June 1, 1949.
22. San Francisco *Examiner*, August 19, 1939.
23. Morrell, Ed., *The 25th Man*, 83.
24. Dalton, Emmett, *When the Daltons Rode*, 237-261.
25. *Ibid*, 103.
26. San Francisco *Chronicle*, May 6, 1934.
27. McCullough, Eva Evans, *An Outlaw and His Family*.

Chapter 10:

1. *Transcript of the People of the State of California versus George C. Contant, Robbery,* in the Superior Court of the County of **Fresno,** State of California, Department 2, before the Honorable S. A. Holmes, Judge, and Jury, N. H. Peterson, official reporter, page 354.

2. *Ibid,* 446.
3. *Ibid,* 446.
4. Glasscock, Carl B., *Bandits and the Southern Pacific,* 116.
5. *Transcript,* 72.
6. *Ibid,* 699.
7. *Ibid,* 680.
8. *Ibid,* 543-545.
9. *Ibid,* 765.
10. *Ibid,* 714.
11. *Ibid,* 717.
12. *Ibid,* 335.
13. *Ibid,* 347-349.
14. *Ibid,* 333-334.
15. *Ibid,* 548-550.
16. *Ibid,* 555.
17. *Ibid,* 37.
18. *Ibid,* 140.
19. *Ibid,* 254.
20. *Ibid,* 235-239
21. *Ibid,* 246.
22. *Ibid,* 256.
23. *Ibid,* 262-275.
24. *Ibid,* 454.
25. *Ibid,* 601-618.
26. *Ibid,* 8.
27. *Ibid,* 558.
28. *Ibid,* 563.
29. *Ibid,* 567.
30. *Ibid,* 603-618.
31. *Ibid,* 619-636.
32. *Ibid,* 499-520.
33. *Ibid,* 661-798.

Chapter 11:

1. Glasscock, Carl B., *Bandits and the Southern Pacific,* 160 ff; and the San Francisco *Chronicle,* June 14, 1893.
2. Patterson, Bart, Personal Interview, Dinuba, January 2, 1948.
3. McCullough, Eva Evans, *An Outlaw and His Family.*
4. *Ibid.*
5. *Ibid.*

Chapter 12:

1. West, George P., "Hearst: A Psychological Note" in *The American*

Mercury for November, 1930. Quotation used by permission of Lawrence E. Spivak, publisher of *The American Mercury*.

2. Dana, Julian, *The Man Who Built San Francisco*, 292. The hatred which Ambrose Bierce felt for political graft and corrupt practices is illustrated by a poem which he wrote at this time:

A RATIONAL ANTHEM

My country, 'tis of thee,
Sweet land of felony.
 Of thee I sing——
Land where my fathers fried
Young witches and applied
Whips to the Quaker's hide
 And made him spring.

My knavish country, thee.
Land where the thief is free,
 Thy laws I love;
I love thy thieving bills
That tap the people's tills;
I love thy mob whose will's
 All laws above.

Let Federal employees
And rings rob all they please,
 The whole year long.
Let the office-holders make
Their piles and judges rake
Our coin. For Jesus' sake
 Let's *all* go wrong.

3. West, George P., "Hearst: A Psychological Note" in *The American Mercury* for November, 1930. Quotation used by permission of Lawrence E. Spivak, publisher of *The American Mercury*.

4. Sandburg, Carl, *Abraham Lincoln*, Vol. V., 249-250.

5. San Francisco *Examiner*, June 18, 1893.

6. *Ibid*, July 9, 1893.

7. Weeks, George F., *California Copy*, 283-293.

8. Bigelow, Henry Derby, San Francisco *Examiner*, October 7, 1892. While Bigelow was visiting in Fresno and Visalia, he became interested in a crime which had been committed some years before this in the San Joaquin Valley. Neither Bigelow nor other reporters who had preceded him were able to solve it. It intrigues many persons to this day and presents a challenge to all detectives, professional as well as amateur. It is known to old-timers as the Wooton murder mystery. Some time during the 1870's a woman by the name of Sanders was postmaster (the word "postmistress" is non-existent) of a little post-office across the

river due west of Reedley. This was in the days before the present city of Reedley had been founded. The locality served by this little post-office is now (1949) often referred to as the Swedish Mission Colony. The actual work in the post-office was done by Mrs. Sanders' husband, who had formerly been a commercial teacher and bookkeeper at Fresno.

A man by the name of Wooton owned a ranch several miles east of present Reedley. Today, if one takes the highway running east from Reedley, one will come to that cross-roads locality known as East Reed-ley, and there will be found the service stations and country grocery stores owned respectively by Peter Paul and Mike Baruti. If one's auto-mobile is turned north here, a drive of a few miles will bring one to the Mitchell Clark ranch. This was originally the Wooton place.

To the little post-office lying west of Kings River came innumerable packages of fancy seeds and plants addressed to Wooton, and he, in turn, mailed to many portions of the world horticultural creations of his own. Wooton was, in a small way, a forerunner of Luther Burbank as a plant wizard.

The charge was later to be made that Sanders coveted the horticultural paradise to be found on the Wooton ranch, and schemed to get it. It was further charged that he created two fictitious characters, Graves and Cavaughs, or Kavaughs, who wrote letters to Sanders, stating that they were interested in the purchase of the Wooton ranch. This correspondence continued for three or four years.

Wooton distrusted all banks. Therefore he kept his cash account with the Kutner-Goldstein general merchandise store in Fresno. When he wanted money, or wished to pay someone, he merely wrote the amount on a slip of paper and signed his name.

One day Sanders appeared at the Kutner-Goldstein emporium and pre-sented a slip of paper calling for $1,800, apparently signed by Wooton. In the meantime, Wooton, who was a respected member and faithful in attendance of the Odd Fellows Lodge at Visalia, was missed. He did not appear as was his wont, and a search was instituted. Wooton was never found. He is still missing!

Sanders was suspected in connection with the $1,800 he had drawn from the Wooton account at the Kutner-Goldstein store. He was arrested. The trial brought forth testimony from a neighbor that he had seen Sanders driving along the road from the Wooton ranch with a man sitting beside him. The charge was made that the man riding with Sanders was Wooton, who had been murdered, tied upright in the buckboard, and that Sanders was on his way to dispose of the body. Nothing was ever proved.

When Sanders was arrested, his wife went to the Kingsburg post-master, Mr. A. A. Smith, and asked him to come to her post-office and in-vestigate affairs. She wanted to be sure that everything was in order, since she had left affairs in the charge of her spouse, although she was the legal postmaster and therefore responsible in law.

Smith found letters from Graves and Cavaughs. At the trial Sanders stated that he had accompanied these two buyers to the Wooton ranch with $25,000 in gold as an inducement to Wooton to sell. A deed was also produced which showed that Wooton had sold his ranch to these two men and to Sanders' son, who was to have a one-third (⅓) share in the ranch. Sanders was a notary public and had affixed his seal to the documents. These were all in good form. So were the affairs of the post-office when examined by Smith.

Apparently a friendly lawyer had aided in the preparation of the papers. Sanders had lost the use of his right thumb some years before this and had learned to write with his left hand. Therefore it would have been impossible for him to have forged Wooton's signature over which he drew the $1,800. If Wooton's signature was a forgery then someone else must have been guilty of this part of the transaction. Suspicion pointed toward the head of a business college in Fresno. But Sanders was convicted of forgery, which was manifestly impossible. He was sent to the penitentiary, served his term, returned to Fresno, and later died in the county hospital.

When the jury was deliberating over the verdict one juror objected to convicting Sanders on circumstantial evidence, but wanted to hang him for introducing Johnson grass. This noxious weed had been offered to credulous ranchers as a luscious feed for cattle and Sanders had sold the seed to them for $1.00 a pound. By this time they had learned to rue their bargain. But it was too late. Johnson grass is still with us after lo! these many years.

Mr. A. A. Smith, the Kingsburg post-master, visited Sanders after his arrest and prior to his conviction. Sanders told Smith somewhat cryptically that he knew the authorities would never find the body of Wooton, but he feared that the prosecution might import a "stiff" and plant him and then dig him up and call him Wooton. However, this was not attempted.

About a month before Sanders was indicted, his wife told Mr. A. A. Smith's mother-in-law, one of her best friends, that her husband was suffering from unnatural nose-bleeds. The flow of blood was so copious that it frightened all the members of Sanders' family. In order to make the bleeding stop he had to run up and down along a ditch bank. As soon as Sanders was arrested his wife made a hurried visit to Smith's mother-in-law and, in great agitation, asked her to say nothing about the mysterious nose-bleeds. She feared that the prosecution might try to prove that Sanders' strange affliction was due to fear, apprehension, or a sense of guilt.

This is a perfect crime. It is a murder mystery which has never been solved. Who killed Wooton? What happened to him? Where is his body?

9. Mainwaring, Constance Bigelow, Personal Letter, Pacific Grove, December 13, 1947.

10. McCullough, Eva Evans, *An Outlaw and His Family.*

11. *Ibid.*

12. *Ibid.*

13. Wold, Edward W., Reference Room, San Francisco *Examiner,* Personal Letter, San Francisco, December 31, 1948: "The man you refer to is Edward A. Morphy. Mr. Morphy graduated from Trinity College in Dublin. He came to the San Francisco *Examiner* in the 1890's from a job as a star reporter on the New York *Telegram.* Mr. Morphy wrote "The Last of the McGintys," and served as editor of the *Argonaut.* Morphy was working for this paper at the time of Senator Hearst's death. I checked the news story relative to the funeral. Though Morphy may have written it, there was no by-line credit."

14. McCullough, Eva Evans, *An Outlaw and His Family.*

15. San Francisco *Examiner,* April 26, 1896.

16. McCullough, Eva Evans, *An Outlaw and His Family.*

17. West, George P., "Hearst: A Psychological Note" in *The American Mercury* for November, 1930.

18. Deason, Wilborn J., "A Wild Honeymoon on Horseback" in *The Western Horseman* for July-August, 1941.

19. McCullough, Eva Evans, *An Outlaw and His Family.*

20. Deason, Wilborn J., "A Wild Honeymoon on Horseback" in *The Western Horseman* for July-August, 1941.

21. *Ibid.*

22. San Francisco *Examiner,* June 4, 1893.

23. Visalia *Daily Times,* June 6, 1893.

24. Griffin, Marcus, *Fall Guys,* 26-38.

25. Young, Egerton R., *My Dogs in the Northland,* 66-124.

26. Burns, Walter Noble, *The Robin Hood of El Dorado,* 24-26.

27. McCullough, Eva Evans, *An Outlaw and His Family.*

28. San Francisco *Examiner,* July 27, 1895.

29. *Time: The Weekly Newsmagazine,* January 19, 1948. From an article entitled "The Ghost" and quoted by courtesy of *Time,* copyright *Time Inc.,* 1948.

30. Visalia *Daily Times,* December 29, 1893.

Chapter 13:

1. Visalia *Daily Times,* Nov. 30, 1892.

2. McCullough, Eva Evans, Personal Interview, Reedley, Sept. 12, 1940.

3. Ibid.

4. Glasscock, Carl B., *Bandits and the Southern Pacific,* 179-181.

5. Morrell, Ed., *The 25th Man,* 69-70.

6. Mr. and Mrs. Sam B. Kerner, Personal Interview, Dinuba, Dec. 13, 1947.

7. Elam, William, Personal Interview, Dinuba, Dec. 20, 1947.

8. Elam, Helen Foster, Personal Interview, Dinuba, Dec. 20, 1947.

9. McCullough, Eva Evans, Personal Letter, Laguna Beach, Dec. 18, 1947. Many old-timers have assured me that the prominent man who had perfected plans to make possible the escape of Evans and Sontag to a Latin American country was M. Theo. Kearney, the founder and long-time owner of the famous estate and show-place west of Fresno,

which still bears his name. I do not know what the facts in this case may be, but insert the statement for what it is worth. In May, 1906, Kearney died on board the liner *Caronia* while on his way to Germany to take the baths for his health. Chris Evans never revealed the identity of his would-be benefactor. His daughter Eva, the only other person who was cognizant of the secret plans and their planner, is under obligations to keep the faith. Hence the name of the man, who was willing to jeopardize his own position in society in order to help two men whom he felt were in need of a Good Samaritan, will probably remain unknown and unsung to the end of time. His identity will always remain a matter for conjecture.

10. "Perry Byrd was the man who betrayed my father and later received some of the blood money." From a letter to the author by Eva Evans McCullough, Laguna Beach, Dec. 18, 1947.

11. San Francisco *Chronicle,* June 13, 1893.

12. Draper, Lewis, Personal Interview, Kingsburg, Dec. 12, 1938.

13. Morrell, Ed., *The 25th Man,* 102.

14. Perkins, Elmer, Personal Interview, Sultana, Jan. 2, 1948.

15. San Francisco *Chronicle,* June 14, 1893.

16. *Ibid.*

17. *Ibid.*

18. *Ibid.*

19. San Francisco *Chronicle,* June 13, 1893.

20. McCullough, Eva Evans, *An Outlaw and His Family.*

21. Visalia *Daily Times,* June 13, 1893.

22. McCullough, Eva Evans, *An Outlaw and His Family.*

23. Visalia *Daily Times,* June 13, 1893.

24. San Francisco *Chronicle,* June 14, 1893.

25. Fresno *Republican,* July 14, 1893.

Chapter 14:

1. San Francisco *Examiner,* Sept. 19, 1893.

2. McCullough, Eva Evans, *An Outlaw and His Family.*

3. San Francisco *Examiner,* Dec. 29, 1893.

4. San Francisco *Post,* Jan. 6, 1894.

Chapter 15:

1. Parks, Norman, Personal Interview, Lazy Spur Ranch, Goshen, Dec. 31, 1937.

2. Kerner, Sam B., Personal Interview, Dinuba, Dec. 20, 1947.

3. Elam, William, Personal Interview, Dinuba, Dec. 20, 1947.

4. Bequette, Gus and Jim, brothers, and Glenn, a nephew, all of Visalia, described the two famous horses used by John Sontag on his controversial drive. I talked with these men in July, 1949, and they told me that their relative, owner of the livery stable at Visalia, was certain that his horses had been at the hold-up at Collis.

5. Nielsen, Ernest, Personal Letter, Selma, January 29, 1948.

6. Leslie, James M., Personal Interview, Del Rey, December 23, 1947.

7. Ibid.

8. Patterson, Bart, Personal Interview, Dinuba, January 2, 1948.

9. McCullough, Eva Evans, *An Outlaw and His Family.*

10. San Francisco *Examiner,* October 5, 1893.

Chapter 16:

1. *Transcript of the People of the State of California versus Christopher Evans, Murder,* in the Superior Court of the County of Fresno, State of California, Department 2, before Honorable M. K. Harris, Judge, and Jury, N. H. Peterson, official reporter, page 37.

2. *Ibid.*

3. *Ibid.*

4. *Ibid.*

5. *Ibid.*

6. *Ibid.*

7. Tolberg was one of the most picturesque highwaymen in history. He was sent to the University of Upsala, Sweden, to train for the priesthood. While there he was accused of pilfering. Another student, in danger of being caught, had placed the stolen goods in Tolberg's room. The latter was expelled. His good name was forever tarnished and his means of livelihood destroyed just prior to his graduation. The injustice of it made him bitter. He made a vow that having been unjustly branded a thief, he would become one. Like all other heroes of folk-lore, he stole from the rich and gave to the poor. He always travelled about the kingdom in a fine carriage drawn by two handsome horses. Having practically completed his studies leading to ordination as a Lutheran clergyman, he was well versed in his work. His usual method of approach was to pretend that he was a clergyman making a long journey. He would be welcomed at the parsonage where his grand manner and fine education made him delightful company. During the course of the visit he would manage to inject the remark that "the master thief, Tolberg" was in the vicinity. This was, of course, literally true. In those days, when banks were scarce, the collection money from the church members was usually kept in the parsonage. Therefore Tolberg would good-naturedly help the frightened priest of the local state church hide the money. The most common method of concealment was to place it flat on the floor under the carpet. In the morning the guest and the money would be miles away. Tolberg lived during the early 1800's; there were no railroads, telegraphs, telephones, or radios then. Therefore he was never caught. Among the common people he was considered a hero and became a living legend. We may surmise that he was not always happy, but he lived well, had many exciting and amusing experiences, and died wealthy. To the under-privileged folk of his native land he was, if not worthy of emulation, at least entitled to love and admiration. Because he was their friend and benefactor, they never betrayed him. His only son, Otto, emigrated to the United States and located in Minneapolis. There he and his descendants became pillars of the Methodist Church and prominent in civic and social service work.

8. Did Chris Evans rob the trains? Scores of old-timers have been

interrogated, and they have disagreed. James M. Leslie, who liked and admired Evans in many ways, told me that he was sure that Evans was guilty. He maintained in the presence of his wife, and my father, Mr. R. G. Smith, that when he visited Evans in the Fresno jail the latter told him that he had robbed trains to get even with the Southern Pacific for the injustice meted out to him with respect to bean shipments. This had resulted in the loss of Evans' first ranch; later he had bought the twenty acres which he mortgaged at the time he assertedly bought (some say he rented) the Modesto livery stable from Wallace. George M. (Doc) Wilson of Dunlap told me that Evans confessed to his friend, Clarke Moore, after he had escaped from the Fresno jail, that he had had a part in the Raines hanging, the robbing of trains, and the killing of Bigelow, who had written the lewd verses about his wife. Moore, who had loyally supported Evans because he had thought him innocent of all wrong doing, thereupon lost his temper and told Evans he never wanted to see him again. Evans looked at Moore for a few moments without saying anything, and then said quietly "All right." Evans walked out on Moore and never saw his old friend again. When I repeated this story to Mr. and Mrs. Howard R. McGee, also of Dunlap, they laughed heartily and thought Wilson's account very funny. They explained it this way: Moore had become angry with Evans over some minor matter relative to the mine at Sampson's Flat, and then had lied about Evans in order to get even with him. Other persons who assured me that Evans was guilty were: Leroy Smith, a Dinuba attorney and a former schoolmate of Eva Evans at Visalia; William Elam, also of Dinuba and at one time a member of Vernon C. Wilson's posse; and Constance Bigelow Mainwaring, who wrote to me as follows: "Sontag (John) was an old hand at train robbery, and had been at it on the East Coast, so Eva Evans told me. She (Eva Evans) gave me a ring which he (John) had stolen back east. They (Evans and Sontag) could not have gotten much out of the Goshen hold-up, for the Evans family was very poor. Evans and Sontag would have starved in the mountains if it had not been for Clarke Moore and others who fed and sheltered them." Scott Gillum of Woodlake, whose wife was a daughter of Tiburcio Vasquez's sister, took an entirely opposite view of the whole matter. He was sure that Evans was innocent, and told me that the money bags dug up by the railway detectives in the Evans backyard had been planted there. Howard R. McGee of Dunlap went much further and said those money bags had not even been planted there; they had never been near the Evans yard. He asserted that it was the consensus of opinion at that time that the train robbers, whoever they were, had shortly after the hold-up ascertained that two of the bags contained relatively worthless Peruvian coins, and had thrown them away near the scene of the robbery. Officers had picked them up and had stated later that they had been found in Evans' backyard at Visalia. Thus their previous attempts to kill Evans and Sontag would apparently be justified. Other friends of Evans, still very much alive at this writing (1949), are Mrs. Maggie

Crosse, a daughter of Bill Downing, and her cousin, Mrs. Clara Moelke, both of Badger; Walter Robison, a rancher at the same place; several members of the Barton family, also at Badger; and Mrs. Jane Bierer, residing between Elderwood and Woodlake. When I first travelled the roads surrounding Badger the natives met me with true mountain reserve amounting at times to hostility. Questions concerning Chris Evans were not welcomed. I was accused of being a detective and a seeker after buried treasure. The intercession of mutual friends, Mrs. Carol Backus of Visalia, and Mrs. Virginia Stapp, of Badger, secured a hearing for me. As a stranger I was told that Chris Evans was a pure, old man innocent of all the charges against him; as an acquaintance vouched for by persons trusted in the community, I was informed that Chris had rightfully punished the Southern Pacific for its iniquities by robbing its trains, and had buried his loot on his Redwood Ranch. In subsequent years members of his family, so I was told, periodically visited their former home to withdraw cash on deposit. The people in the mountains have two sets of stories to relate. God only knows which is the true account, and He is not telling. The story which best serves the purpose of the moment is the one presented. One of them is false, but which one? Circumstantial evidence is heavily in favor of Evans' guilt, but proof was lacking in his time. It is still lacking. Sam B. Williams, an old-timer well known in Fresno, spent two days with Evans just prior to the famous battle at Young's cabin. Evans took a liking to the big, handsome youngster, fresh out of Tennessee, and warned him against a life of sin and crime. Williams told me that Evans gave him a lurid account of his various robberies, not only in California, but in eastern states as well. Elmer Perkins, a resident of Sultana, whose aunt was the wife of Perry Byrd, had no reason to like or defend Evans. Yet he told me that he doubted that Chris had ever successfully robbed a train. His argument was based on the fact that Evans was always poor and in need of money during the years when huge sums of money were supposedly being stolen from the express coaches. On two occasions Evans was forced to borrow money from Elmer Perkins' grandmother. However, Perkins admitted that Chris hated the Southern Pacific with good reason, and had the resolution and physical courage to hold up a train if it had suited his purpose. He merely doubted that Evans had ever felt so inclined. Perkins thought it barely possible that Evans might have been involved in unsuccessful attempts, especially those at Ceres and Alila, where no money was taken. Since neither the Southern Pacific nor Wells, Fargo ever brought charges against Evans for robbery, they must have thought that the evidence against him was somewhat shaky. Neither the judge nor the jury was required to render an official verdict in the matter. Public opinion is as divided now as it was among Evans' contemporaries. Did Chris Evans rob the trains? I do not know.

9. McGee, Howard R., Personal Interview, Dunlap, March 7, 1948.
10. Fresno *Expositor,* December 1, 1893.
11. Visalia *Daily Times,* December 14, 1893.

12. *Ibid.*

Chapter 17:

1. San Francisco *Chronicle*, May 6, 1934.
2. White, Stewart Edward, *Folded Hills*, 431.
3. Morrell, Ed., *The 25th Man*, 360-361.
4. Fresno *Expositor*, December 29, 1893.
5. Glasscock, Carl B., *Bandits and the Southern Pacific*, 229 ff.
6. McCullough, Eva Evans, *An Outlaw and His Family.*
7. *Ibid.*
8. Glasscock, Carl B., *Bandits and the Southern Pacific*, 259-262.
9. Nielsen, Ernest, in Fresno *Bee* for July 20, 1932.
10. San Jose *Mercury*, December 29, 1893.
11. Visalia *Daily Times*, December 31, 1893.
12. Perkins, Elmer, Personal Interview, Sultana, January 2, 1948.
13. Mainwaring, Constance Bigelow, Personal Letter, Pacific Grove, December 13, 1947.
14. Glasscock, Carl B., *Bandits and the Southern Pacific*, 255-257.
15. Fresno *Expositor*, January 16, 1894.
16. San Francisco *Chronicle*, January 8, 1894.
17. Morrell, Ed., *The 25th Man*, 172-174.
18. *Ibid*, 175.
19. *Ibid*, 188-189.
20. *Ibid*, 224.
21. McCullough, Eva Evans, Personal Interview, Reedley, Sept. 23, 1940.
22. Mainwaring, Constance Bigelow, Personal Letter, Pacific Grove., December 13, 1947.
23. Ibid, January 7, 1948.
24. Morrell, Ed., *The 25th Man*, 227-228.
25. Los Angeles *Times*, February 22, 1894. Mrs. Jane Bierer told me that J. V. Brighton asked Mrs. Chris Evans if he and his wife could rent her house as he was homeless, poor, and in need of work. His wife was engaged to care for the small Evans children while the mother and oldest daughter were away with the show. Brighton was hired to chop wood in the Visalia oak forest for the various householders in the vicinity. He often complained about the work being too hard, and seemed to crave sympathy.
26. San Francisco *Chronicle*, May 6, 1934.
27. Morris, Kathleen, Personal Interview, Reedley, March 10, 1948. Miss Morris, a student at the Reedley college, told me about her uncle's experiences as an eight-year-old boy in 1894.
28. Morrell, Ed., *The 25th Man*, 245-249.
29. *Transcript of the People of the State of California versus Christopher Evans, Murder*, in the Superior Court of the County of Fresno, State of California, Department 2, before Honorable M. K. Harris, Judge, and Jury, N. H. Peterson, official reporter, page 196.
30. San Francisco *Chronicle*, May 6, 1934.

31. Sacramento *Star,* May 1, 1911.

Chapter 18:

1. Kerner, Sam B., Personal Interview, Dinuba, February 22, 1948.
2. McCubbin, John C., "The Rise and the Fall of Traver" in the Fresno *Republican,* March 6, 1923.
3. *Ibid,* March 5, 1923.
4. McCubbin, John C., Personal Letter, Los Angeles, Jan. 23, 1948.
5. Ibid.
6. Gillum, Scott, Personal Interview, Woodlake, Jan. 17, 1948.
7. The information regarding Si Loverin was given to me by Ellsworth (Bud) Loverin, a well-known honor student and football player at Fresno State College, and a grandson of Wesley Loverin mentioned in the text. He granted me permission to tell the facts as related, and also furnished the photograph of Chris Evans taken at Millwood in 1893.
8. McCubbin, John C., Personal Letter, Los Angeles, Jan. 23, 1948.
9. Wilson, Lollie Cave, *Hard to Forget,* 195-205.
10. Jennings, Al, *Through the Shadows with O. Henry,* 80-96.
11. McGuigin, Robert, Personal Interview, Traver, Jan. 20, 1938.
12. Draper, Lewis, Personal Interview, Kingsburg, June 11, 1938.
13. Jennings, Al, *Through the Shadows With O. Henry,* 80-96.
14. Wilson, Lollie Cave, *Hard to Forget,* 68-73.
15. *Ibid.*
16. McCullough, Eva Evans, *An Outlaw and His Family.*
17. McConnell, Thomas, "Chris Evans, Original Insurgent" in San Francisco *Bulletin,* May 6, 1911.
18. McCullough, Eva Evans, *An Outlaw and His Family.*
19. San Francisco *Chronicle,* June 14, 1893.
20. Johnson, Hiram, United States Senator from California, Personal Letter, Washington, D. C., Oct. 9, 1931.
21. Sacramento *Star,* May 1, 1911.
22. *Ibid,* May 20, 1911.
23. McConnell, Thomas, "Chris Evans, Original Insurgent" in San Francisco *Bulletin,* May 6, 1911.
24. Bergen, Yvonne, "Saddle Saga" in *The Western Horseman* for March-April, 1940.
25. Mainwaring, Constance Bigelow, Personal Letter, Pacific Grove, Dec. 13, 1947.
26. McCullough, Eva Evans, *An Outlaw and His Family.*
27. Christopher Evans died in Oregon at 9:15 in the evening of February 9th, 1917. He thus lacked eleven days of being seventy years of age. Four sons served as pall-bearers and lowered their father's body into the grave.

SPECIAL NOTE

Mrs. Sam Ellis, a resident of Fresno at this writing, has a vivid recollection of the Evans and Sontag visit. Her account differs somewhat from the foregoing. Mrs. Ellis had been sick in bed for several days, and neighbors had taken turns sitting up with her nights. This particular Sunday her house was filled with children, guests, friends, and relatives. Her mother, Mrs. W. C. Cortner, and a married sister, were preparing a chicken dinner. Sam, her husband, and Freeman Thomas, a half-brother, although there were no slot machines in those days, were achieving the same results out in the backyard pitching ten dollar gold pieces at a hole in the ground. Their game was interrupted by the breathless announcement of the small Ellis boys that two bearded and heavily armed men, screened by live oaks growing in some rocks in the adjacent mountain, were peering intently down at the Ellis home. The men adjourned to the house for a council of war. Belle Ellis, a sister of Sam, solved the problem by following the Ellis boys to the outlaw hide-out and inviting Evans and Sontag to dinner.

As the group approached the house, Ellis walked out to meet them. His father-in-law, W. C. Cortner, placed himself beside the window in the front room with a rifle in his hands. Ellis offered to shake hands with Evans, and the latter said:

"Sam, you ——— ——— ———, I ought to kill you. You have hunted me without any cause. You and I have been friends for years. We slept in the same bed when on the road in the mountains, and now you are hunting me. If you promise never to do so again, I will shake hands with you."

Mrs. Ellis was to say later that Sam was smart when he went out to meet Evans that Sunday, but much smarter when he promised never to hunt him again.

All the men present that day sat down in the shade of the pump house and engaged in small talk; nothing was said about outlaws or man-hunters. Finally Ellis said:

"Chris, my wife has been sick for several days, and she is worried to death about your coming here. Will you go in and talk to her?"

Evans, perfectly agreeable, took off his belt and revolver, laid his rifle beside them, went into the house, greeted Mrs. Cortner, and walked into the room where Mrs. Ellis was confined to her bed.

"Hello, Janie, feeling much better?"

"Chris, I feel much better seeing you here. Worry over my husband's safety while hunting you has kept my nerves in such a state I am almost crazy. I'll be all right now. How are Molly and the children?"

Evans replied that they were fine, but showed that he did not want to talk about his own troubles. He picked up the Ellis girl, then a baby barely able to crawl about the floor, chucked her under the chin, while Mrs. Ellis continued:

"I was just thinking yesterday about our school days at Auckland. Molly and I were chums. I can see her now, a slender little tyke, twelve years old, blond pig-tails down her back, dreamy blue eyes, dressed in a simple calico dress so short that her garter tips, holding up her woollen stockings, were visible. We tripped hand in hand down the road to the old Auckland school. The Byrds were fine folks, Chris. You got a mighty nice girl when you married Molly. Old Jesse Byrd was respected by everyone. Their home was the social center of the community."

Mrs. Ellis and Evans laughed over the current feud between Fielding Bacon and William Ham, whose droves of hogs were ranging in disputed oak forests. The two men finally decided that a fight between "bacon" and "ham" would be silly. They also talked about George Stanwood, a devout Quaker and a marvelous violinist, who would play imitations of hill-billy fiddling, and then play the same selection as a concert artist would render it. Stanwood was to say later that Evans and Sontag had come to his cabin one night, had brought out two beautiful little redwood treasure chests, had laid out tray after tray of gold coins, had divided the money equally, and that Evans had buried his share in the grave of his little son at Redwood Ranch. Mrs. Ellis went on to talk about the old days in the mountains:

"Half the weddings in the old hill country were held in the Byrd home. I remember how nervous you were at your own wedding, Chris. I have never seen you show any fear until the day you married Molly Byrd. You kept shifting from one foot to the other as if it took all your weight to keep the shivers out of one knee. Molly was a picture that night; more beautiful than any painted by an artist. As she came into the living room for the service, leaning on your arm, I felt a hush come over the guests, and then there was the rustle of whispers, all saying how beautiful she looked in her black taffeta dress, trimmed in pink ribbons."

Mrs. Ellis stopped short with a gulp, shocked by the memory of her mother's prediction. The latter had also been married in black taffeta and pink, and had told her daughter that this meant bad luck. Mrs. Cortner had buried two husbands and all but five of her fourteen children; she had said that Molly Byrd's marriage would turn out disastrously. Now Chris Evans was an outlaw with a price on his head; what would the end be?

Fortunately Mrs. Cortner appeared at this embarrassing moment to announce dinner. Evans went into the dining room, and Mrs. Ellis was left alone to worry over the two small, motherless children of William C. Russell, who had placed them in her care. The latter, a deputy serving under Sheriff Kay at Visalia, always came to visit his small daughters on Sundays. He was a fearless, reckless man, endowed with more courage than discretion. Evans was warned, but merely remarked:

"If Billy comes, we will capture him."

Finally Freeman Thomas received permission from Evans to go home and do his chores. He met a young Dutch boy hunting doves, and told him of the presence of Evans and Sontag at the Ellis home. Shortly thereafter this boy intercepted Russell, who returned to Visalia to inform the posse.

Ellis owned a fast trotting horse, Tony, which he used on his long drives to Visalia when obliged to attend meetings of the board of supervisors. Evans borrowed this sorrel horse and a Petaluma cart, and Sontag and he left the Ellis home about seven o'clock that evening.

About three o'clock the next morning the Ellis family saw lights in their front-yard and realized the posse had arrived. The man-hunters camped there until daybreak, and then followed their Indian guide along the trail of the hunted men into the mountains.

AFTERWORD

S COUR the history books of any place or time, and it will be difficult—and probably impossible—to find a series of events which parallel the Evans and Sontag saga. While the spate of train robberies, the fights with lawmen, the flight into the Sierra and the battle of Stone Corral amount to a compelling-enough story, it bursts well beyond those limits. Before the final scenes played out, who would have expected that George Contant would attempt a spectacular break out of Folsom State Prison; that Evans family members would eventually portray themselves on stage, in a "great train robbery drama"; and that the half-blind, one-armed Chris Evans would make a final break for freedom and bedevil the state's peace officers for two more months? The audacity of the tale seems to argue for its truthfulness. What imagination could have invented such a chain of circumstances?

Unsurprisingly, the bandits have provided fodder for hundreds of newspaper and magazine articles over the years, and several full-length studies. Hu Maxwell's *Evans and Sontag*, an imaginary dialogue-laden account, appeared in 1893, when interest in the story was at its peak (and, in fact, before it had concluded). It was followed by Carl B. Glasscock's not-always-reliable *Bandits and the Southern Pacific*, in 1929. *Prodigal Sons*, which was published two decades after Glasscock's opus, represented a significant departure from the previous efforts. As a college professor and Ph.D., Smith had the good sense to investigate printed, manuscript and oral historical materials, and compare them in an attempt to reach the truth. He was fortunate in that a number of people with firsthand knowledge of Evans and Sontag were alive while he was conducting his research. Most fortuitously—and, in some ways, unfortunately—Eva Evans was available, and provided more information than any other source.

Most readers will detect a noticeable tilt toward the cause of Evans and Sontag in Smith's narrative. Note how he says, toward the end of the book: "The estimates of Chris Evans have been written chiefly by men who were his mortal foes. A few years later the judge, the jury, and most of the officers who had combined to send Chris Evans to Folsom, signed a petition to secure his parole. What gives?" The implication is that Evans was a better man than history's verdict would otherwise indicate. In this, and other complimentary passages, we can see the influence of Eva Evans—an unswerving defender of her father throughout her entire lifetime.

Yet in spite of his partisanship, Smith's academic training came to the fore, and he did recite certain facts uncomplimentary to the bandits—such as the unearthing of the Collis train robbery loot in Evans' yard. While he tried to downplay this incident by saying that only lawmen were present at the time, and could have planted the evidence, there is no good reason to believe this happened. In this instance, he seems to have been navigating between fidelity to the established record, and loyalty to Eva Evans. Nor, sagely, did Smith issue a blanket exoneration of Evans and Sontag for involvement in the train robberies.

Since Smith felt obligated to construct an account honest on one hand, and sympathetic to Eva on the other, the results are not always accurate or consistent—and seem to have displeased his principal source greatly. In the wake of

Prodigal Sons' publication, Eva threatened Smith with a lawsuit, which was withdrawn when he produced copious evidence of her intent to collaborate freely on the project. Significantly, however, Smith presented a broader array of facts than any of his predecessors in the Evans and Sontag field, and few major details of their exploits have come to light since he concluded his research. It also helps that his work, relying as it does on much first-person information, is quite readable.

Reissued once by Frank Foster's California History Books in 1973, *Prodigal Sons* has now been out of print for some years, and has remained a sought-after book for its unique perspectives and lucid style. This new edition reprints Smith's text verbatim, with the addition of an index and a few new photographs. For the added benefit of readers, some notes follow which amplify and correct portions of the narrative:

Evans' early history: His birthdate was February 19, not February 20, as Smith reports incorrectly much later in the narrative. He was one of nine children, not eight, and his mother (Mary Ann Switzer) was Irish; thus, his ancestry was altogether Irish and not Irish-German. Investigation into available records has failed to find any proof of Evans' service in the Civil War or, for that matter, his naturalization as an American citizen. The 1878-1882 time frame for his residence in San Luis Obispo county is inaccurate, as he was involved in Visalia land transactions during 1880 and 1882, and once stated that he was residing there during the former year. His son, Joseph, was two years old in 1887, not three as stated by Smith.

It was the Grangers' Bank of California which employed Evans as a warehouseman, rather than the Bank of California. His Visalia properties were never mortgaged, as Smith asserts repeatedly. He did sell his land in town to John Sontag, who later conveyed it to Eva Evans.

Sontag/Contant early history: John Sontag was born in Mankato in 1862; there is no need to consider the alternate birthplaces given by Smith. Sontag's stepfather was Martin Contant, not John. The James-Younger gang members who appeared in Mankato during Sontag's youth numbered five (Jesse and Frank James, Jim Younger and Clell Miller), not eight, as reported by Smith.

The Mussel Slough tragedy: Evans' narration of the story is, of course, a dramatic reconstruction. Depending on the source, the death toll was either seven or eight, with (contrary to Smith's statement) no railroad representatives being killed. Mills Hartt is the correct spelling of the tragedy victim's name. None of the authorities are precisely certain as to the action that took place during the fight, though it is likely Harris fired the first shot; and Crow's killing of Knutson is disputed. Smith recites the counts against the Mussel Slough defendants incorrectly; they were charged with obstructing federal officers and conspiracy to obstruct the same. There were a total of six defendants who served nine months in jail,

The Pixley robbery: In the prelude to this episode, Smith has outlaw Tiburcio Vasquez attempting to stop a train with logs piled on the tracks; instead, he tried to derail it. Peter Bollenger (not Boelenger) was the locomotive engineer's name. He was ordered to take the train two miles south of town and stop there, as opposed to stopping immediately.

Smith adds the characters of "Anscon" and James Symington to the story. What seems to have happened is that Ed Bentley and Charles Gobart were suspicious of the train's stopping, and when they went to investigate, Gobart was killed by one of the robbers. The actual robbery take was $400, not $5000.

The Goshen robbery: Its actual date was January 22, 1890, and Smith transposed the fireman's initials (G.W. Lovejoy). The express car was rifled, but the strongbox was not thrown out, and the robbery's total take seems to have been less than the $25,000-$40,000 figure reported at the time.

The Evans-Sontag stable: While operated by the pair, it was leased from Thomas Wallace and not owned by them. The Goshen robbery money was probably applied to the lease payments. When the stable burned down, Wallace collected on an insurance policy, but the lessees were not covered by it and their loss was total. Jacob Claypool, the fire victim, was sixteen years old at the time of his demise, not eighteen.

The Dalton gang: The story of the outlaw brothers' coming to California is not entirely accurate. While Bob Dalton (not Grattan) did have his pay as a U.S. marshal withheld, the "shooting scrape" story is apocryphal. What seems to have brought the boys to California was their father's involvement in the Golden State's horse racing circuit, and the ranching activities of William and Littleton Dalton.

"William McElhanie," cited as a Dalton gang associate by Smith in several instances, was in fact Emmett Dalton's alias. Grattan Dalton was arrested by railroad detective Bill Hickey in Fresno—not by Will Smith—and was convicted and awaiting sentence at the time of the Ceres robbery, as opposed to awaiting trial. Joe Middleton was pressured by officers to inform on Grat Dalton and Riley Dean, and did not travel to Reedley and speak to them there, as Smith reports.

Bill Dalton's trial was in late 1891, so he was not incarcerated during the Coffeyville raid, dated by Smith in one place as October 4, 1892 (it occurred on October 5). His account of the raid has the position of the men reversed; Bob and Emmett Dalton led the way, with Grat, Powers and Broadwell behind. The bank vault time-lock ruse was that it would open in "about ten minutes," not three.

Smith knew Emmett Dalton personally, and appears to have felt obligated to present his denials of all Dalton involvement in the California train robberies, but the research of other authors (notably Frank F. Latta, in Dalton Gang Days, and Nancy Samuelson in The Dalton Gang Story) argue convincingly for the opposite position.

The Alila robbery: The locomotive fireman's name was Radcliffe, with an "e" at the end. Tulare County Sheriff Eugene Kay followed the bandits' trail to Huron; Sheriff Borgaerdt of Kern County was conducting a reconnaissance of Tulare Lake at that time.

The Ceres robbery attempt: The fireman's name was Wallace, not Lewis, and it seems that no defective bomb was lobbed at him during the incident. Southern Pacific Detective Len Harris was the first to shoot, with the bandits returning fire and hitting him in the neck with buckshot, instead of a bullet.

The Collis robbery: In it, the bandits did not bid the engineer and fireman to light cigars, but attempted to blow open the express car door with a bomb—whose fuse was lit by a cigar. They also damaged the engine with a bomb, which was not reported by Smith. The total take was estimated at $15,000, rather than $50,000. Contant later confessed that $500 in silver dollars, $500 in gold and two sacks of Peruvian coins were stolen.

Confrontation at Visalia: Toward the end of the book Smith says this event took place on August 4, 1892; it happened on August 5. Significantly, Witty was not the first to fire during the incident at Evans' house; Evans and Sontag got the drop on the officers, and they ran. Smith was hit between the shoulder blades and in the hand, and was not shot in the posterior while stuck in a fence, per Smith's claim. During the outlaws' late-night escape, in which Oscar Beaver was killed, both horses were wounded and one died later, but both did not expire at the scene.

Flight: None of the other major accounts of Evans and Sontag refer to the pair being almost cornered by Sam Ellis' posse. The outlaws did visit the Ellis ranch northeast of Visalia on September 8, 1892 (not September 4, as Smith says), and left when they were told authorities had been notified of their presence.

Clark Moore, the guardian angel of Evans and Sontag, lacked the "e" Smith sometimes added to his first name. The William Garton who Moore referred to in court testimony actually spelled his surname Garten.

The apparent timing of Evans and Sontag's near-apprehension outside Visalia is faulty. Smith seems to place it before the Young's cabin battle, but it happened on April 19, 1893, a short time before the Stone Corral fight.

Young's cabin: Smith says the posse totaled thirteen men; other accounts list it as eight. Young was not present when Evans and Sontag appropriated the cabin, so it seems more likely that Ed Mainwaring walked in on the outlaws, rather than responding to Young's call to fix the pair breakfast. The exchange between Evans and Andy McGinnis during the gunbattle is apocryphal and unlikely; he seems to have shot McGinnis at close range, minus any comment.

George Contant: Before being taken in for questioning, Contant took the train to Reedley on July 22 (not July 23). George Witty was the officer responsible for detaining Contant, and was not assisted by Will Smith. After it was decided to incarcerate him, he attempted a jailbreak on August 13, 1892 (not August 12) and was caught while it was in progress, not during the following morning, as per Smith.

Whether Evans hatched the plot to break Contant out of Folsom is debatable, as is Si Lovern's claim that the weapons used in the attempt were stolen from his Visalia saloon. Lovern was suspected of laundering train robbery loot for Evans and Sontag, and his involvement in the later Tagus train robbery makes his story look even more dubious.

Smith dates the furtive Folsom break at June 27, but it actually happened a day later. There is some confusion as to who among the prisoners wielded weapons, and what weapons were used; not only were firearms called into play, but also a rock drill-bit and a knife. The inmates who overpowered Briare were Dalton, Williams, Henry (not Ben) Wilson, and Charles Abbott (sometimes given by Smith as Abbot). Warden Aull denied using Gatling guns to quell the escape, as was claimed, since they would risk harming innocent parties. Smith's death count for the incident is off slightly, as Thomas Schell (not Schill) died of his wounds; and Contant was wounded in the thigh, shin and abdomen, not in the shoulder.

Smith has John Sontag as a partner in the Kasota train robbery; he was back in California at the time. Also, the dramatic statement that Contant's wife died just prior to his 1908 release from prison is incorrect. She passed away nine years earlier.

Chase in the Sierra: Henry Bigelow's interview with Evans took place at the John Coffee cabin, a point Bigelow was unable to make at the time his story was published. The rancher who provided assistance to Evans and Sontag was Emil Treeton (not Tretton), and he lived on Mill Creek, not in Squaw Valley. The Indian trackers, Pelon and Camino, stayed with the posse after the Young's cabin gunbattle, contrary to Smith's account. They progressed from Sampson Flat to the home of Sands Baker, then to Davis Flat, the J.F. Crabtree home and thence to Mill Creek, where Treeton lived. Smith calls Samuel Black "J.S. Black."

Stone Corral: The posse led by Gard consisted, initially, of the four members named by Smith (Gard, Rapelje, Burns and Jackson). The Saturday Smith refers to fell on June 10, not June 11. The "third rig" mentioned by Smith held deputy sheriffs Ed Fudge and John Broder, with no correspondents being noted as present with them. It was Eli, not Al, Perkins who convinced Evans to surrender.

After he was wounded, Jackson was taken to Visalia by Rapelje, Charles Norden, and J.S. Van Noy; Rapelje then returned to Stone Corral with George Witty, William English, Robert Johnson and Samuel Stingley. A third party scouting the area was made up of reporters Jo P. (not "Joe") Carroll and Harry Stuart, along with Visalia photographer E.M. Davidson. The presence of Jud Elwood, George Stanley and William Stack is uncertain.

Smith's identifications for the men standing behind John Sontag, in the famous photo taken at Stone Corral, are not altogether accurate. Left to right, they are: Stingley, Rapelje, Hall, Witty, English, Burns, Gard, Carroll, Stuart. Sontag was later brought down to Visalia in Hall's wagon.

Contrary to Smith's claim, the reward sums paid out on behalf of Evans and Sontag are known. Gard and Jackson each received $1000, Burns and Rapelje each got $500, and Hall, Witty and Eli Perkins split a pot of $2000.

Smith's chronology of the events surrounding the amputation of Evans' arm is off; he quotes from newspaper accounts dated June 13, while the surgery was performed on the 14th.

Train Robbery Drama: Grandmother Byrd was portrayed by Julia Bane, not Julia Blanc, and the last act of Evans and Sontag featured four scenes, not seven.

Evans' Murder Trial: Alva Snow, later mayor of Fresno, was also on the prosecution team.

Final Flight: Ed Morrell (not Morrel, as Smith sometimes has it) worked for the Quinby House Restaurant in Fresno, not Stock's. Morrell's own account of his nativity, as opposed to James Hume's, is correct; he was born in Schuykill County, Pennsylvania.

The escape buggy slated for use by Evans and Morrell was indeed rented by Jim Hutchinson from the Woy and Shields livery stable. Molly Evans was not held at the jail for "fainting," as Smith states (perhaps wanting to be gracious to Eva Evans). Instead, she was arrested for complicity, but the charge was later dropped due to insufficient evidence.

The betrayal of Evans and Morrell by Walter Kirkland is not certain, and it seems unlikely the duo committed the robbery at Fowler on January 10 (not January 11, as Smith reports). The constable involved in the robbery was Oaks, not Ochs.

Morrell's extravagant tales of the booby-trapped hideout, plotting escape to the south Pacific and Mexico, and seeing Eva Evans on stage in the train robbery drama, are highly embroidered at best and likely false.

Evans and Morrell obtained aid from other mountain residents, including D.H. Caldwell of Squaw Valley and John C. March of Stokes Mountain. As Indian numbers in the area were depleted, and most of those remaining had attached themselves to ranches, it seems unlikely they were assisted by any Yokuts—as Smith claims.

The St. Clair house shootout took place in Squaw Valley, not Camp Badger. Officer Boyd went up to the house in a cart, not a buckboard, and both Evans and Morrell exchanged shots with the lawmen; Eva Evans' claim her father was uninvolved is not true.

The posse which pursued Evans and Morrell was larger than Smith indicates. Its members included P.F. Peck, C.M. Boyd, Fred Smart, P.J. Mead, and Thomas Burns and Hi Rapelje of Stone Corral fame.

Final Capture and Sentencing: J.V. Brighton was a detective hired by Gard to obtain federal evidence against Evans; both stories Smith tells about Brighton are, thus, true in part.

Evans and Morrell arrived in Visalia on February 17 at 8 p.m., not at daybreak. Smith garbles the message sequence used during the capture. The first was a ploy, telling Mrs. Brighton her husband had been arrested and the house had to be evacuated. The message Smith labels as the first was actually the second, delivered by Beeson to Evans, and the second was the third, delivered by Joseph Evans to his father.

Gard was also in the party that escorted Evans and Morrell to jail. Later, Morrell was not convicted of "highway robbery" of Bennie Cochran's horse and cart, but of armed robbery. Smith has his incarceration terms wrong; Morrell spent two years at Folsom and twelve years at San Quention, not five and four respectively.

The Tagus robbery: Smith dates this incident incorrectly (on April 19, 1896, instead of March 19) and inexplicably splits it in two; the "Johnny Keener" of the first story is Dan McCall of the second. Jim Lee, Joe Anderson and the Johnson brothers were not involved, and the deputy at the robbery was Earl Daggett, not "Draggett."

Britt fired at McCall accidentally while they were walking toward Goshen, not while they were atop the railroad coaches. Later, there was a brief gunbattle between McCall, Reed and Daggett, and McCall was not totally surprised by it (contrary to Smith). McCall was wounded badly in the abdomen and killed; Daggett was hit in the chest, and Reed in the shoulder.

The Cross Creek robbery: A total of two dynamite charges were used during its commission. Smith errs a bit when he says the robbers were never caught; they were the Johnson boys, Dudley and Benjamin, who fled to Orange City, Florida afterward and were cornered by peace officers there. Dudley was killed and Benjamin escaped and disappeared.

Evans' later years: Smith's resume of Eurasia is essentially correct, except that Evans advocated retirement at age seventy, not sixty.

It appears that Smith was, again, taking Eva Evans' side when he averred that Chris Evans asserted his innocence to all. To his parole committee, he once said: "I am not innocent of wrong doing, for if I had not violated the law, I would not be in prison, but they were errors of the head, not of the heart."

Smith also suggests that the rise of the Lincoln-Roosevelt League and anti-railroad sentiment in California played a role in Evans' release. The facts are that his family and a number of other individuals lobbied heavily for his release over a nine-year period, beginning before the progressive political tide rose, and the parole board was at last swayed by their diligence.

There is no evidence Evans visited Sacramento to attempt obtaining a pardon in 1914, and Eva Evans' story that her father was harrassed while attempting to market Eurasia is false. In 1916, the parole board gave him blanket travel permission throughout the state so he could peddle the book.

The operation performed not long before Evans' death removed a bullet from his brain, not buckshot.

The litany of men given by Smith who pursued Evans, Sontag and Morrell—and who all met dire fates—is, once again, representing wishful thinking, perhaps on the part of Eva Evans. A number of them (Gard, Rapelje, Jackson and Brighton) all passed away quietly and with their boots off.

Those wishing to know more of Evans and Sontag's turbulent times are directed toward two recent, and generally excellent, studies: Harold L. Edwards' Train Robbers and Tragedies, and John J. Koblas' Robbers of the Rails: The Sontag Boys of Minnesota. Both were of invaluable help in researching this Afterword.

—WILLIAM B. SECREST, JR.

INDEX

Q

Quantrill, William Clarke,
guerrilla leader, 98–99

R

Radcliff [brakeman], killed,
107, 340
Rafferty, John, mentioned, 102
Ralston, William C., banks of,
85
Rapelje, Hi
confronts Evans and Sontag,
270
mentioned, 282
recovers Sontag, 286, 287
testifies, 272
Reed, Thomas L., befriends
Evans, 412
Reed, Vic, shoots robber, 381
Reynolds, T. A., wounded, 175
Rezanov, Nicolai Petrovich,
betroths Concha, 85–86
Richards, Lowell A., develops
gang plow, 35
Rivers, Jim, frees Loverin,
389–90
Roberts, George D.
testifies, 191–92, 328–29
wounded, 123, 340
Robison brothers, recount Slick
Rock, 364–65
Rucker, Maggie
profiled, 114–15
succours Evans and Sontag,
261
Ruggles, John and Charles,
hanged, 381

S

San Joaquin Valley, agricultural
development of, 53–54
Sayle and Coldwell, defend
George Sontag, 181
Scott, Ben, "releases" Evans,
347, 349–51
Scott, Jay
complains reward, 284–85
loses Evans, 349–51
Scrapers, Fresno, 37
Smith, Leroy, mentioned,
155–56
Smith, Will
and Collis robbery, 129,
130–31
curses Eva, 130
and Daltons, 110
dies, 414
in Evans pursuit, 141, 263–65
flees, 132–33
in posse, 166
reputation of, 141–43
testifies, 333, 335
Sontag, George
arrested, 178–80
and Collis robbery, 128–29
confession of, cross-
examined, 325–26
convicted, 200
dies, 415
early life of, 90–91, 94
at Evans' trial, 332
history of, 126
jailbreak plan for, 203–14
sells confession, 310–24
testifies, 200
tried, 181–201
wounded, 340

ized audiences. The Society, under Maxwell's leadership, published seven issues of *The Trans-Allegheny Historical Magazine* during a two-year span. The record clearly demonstrates his commitment to historical scholarship.

Readers not familiar with the "gee whiz" style of writing of the 1890s may feel that Maxwell exaggerated his characterizations. . His portrayal of Will Smith almost succeeds in making him the villain. Contemporaries would agree with Maxwell, for Smith bungled his job and so did the other officers. It was generally conceded that local officers could have handled the entire affair much more efficiently if they had not had to contend with so much outside help.

This book was written prior to October 1893, only a few weeks' after the Battle at Stone Corral. Maxwell used his newspaper articles for the framework so the story is substantially correct. It was written for an avid public. There are minor errors and his description of some of Evans's friends as Judases is highly questionable. The Perkins family did not betray Chris for reward money. His physical conditon was so poor that they knew he had to have medical attention to survive. Evans's own message that he would surrender if his wife got the reward money was the message carried to Visalia. (Who got the reward money is one of the real mysteries in the story. Mrs. Evans did not get it.)

Even the most reliable reporters are subject to occasional slips, and Maxwell was no exception. His description of the Indian trackers if perhaps unfair and misleading, whatever its accuracy in reflecting popular sentiment. According to all of the available evidence, the men were intelligent and well-trained, and performed admirably.

Like Chris Evans's friends and neighbors, Maxwell cannot seem to make up his mind to judge Chris as a hero or as a villain. Wisely, he does not try to answer the question. The reader, like Chris Evans's friends, will have to decide if Evans and Sontag were bandits or men who set out to harm a hated corporation and became enmeshed in a situation they could not control. Perhaps Chris gave his answer when Maxwell has him say, "Act on the impulse of the moment. A man can think more, decide more in one moment of impulse than in days of sober planning."

Annie R. Mitchell
Visalia, California

xiv

sheriffs announced that the holdups were solved. Grat was convicted largely on his past reputation and circumstantial evidence but Bill Dalton was acquitted. While Grat was in the Tulare County Jail awaiting sentence, the Ceres holdup took place and embarrassed officers were faced with the question, "If the Daltons did not rob the trains, who did?" Bill Dalton was re-arrested. Meantime, Grat embarrassed officers much more, for he walked out of Tulare County's fine new jail with the help of keys provided by his friends. Unfortunately, he rode back east and with his brother Bob was killed at Coffeyville.

Evans and the Sontags were busy in Minnesota where on July 2, 1891, a train was robbed at Kasota and in November there was a holdup at Western Junction. Express company detectives trailed George Sontag to Fresno and were rather positive they knew who the other two bandits were when the Collis robbery proved them right.

Hu Maxwell, who wrote this book, was a daily observer of the manhunt. For two and a half years, starting in 1891, he was city editor of the *Fresno Expositor*. For the next two and a half years he was city editor of the *Fresno Republican*. He wrote special articles for the *San Francisco Chronicle* and was its field correspondent during the long search for the bandits. With this background it is easy to see why he emphasized the role of the Fresno County officers rather than the work done by Tulare County lawmen.

Maxwell himself was as notable a figure as the subjects he so assiduously followed. A meticulous writer, he comfortably called upon several voices. The Hu Maxwell of Section One is a synthesizer, a reporter whose grasp of facts and sense of place enabled him to weave a saga enthralling enough to rival the best of the period's popular fiction. It is relaxed storytelling, but riveting nonetheless.

The Maxwell we encounter in Section Two is the journeyman journalist, the chronicler of the moment—a writer who knew well his audience and catered to its appetite for the sensational. Yet Maxwell's strength was and continues to be his credibility; stripped of hyperbole, his dispatches have endured as the most faithful account of a volatile time.

Maxwell left the San Joaquin Valley after Evans's imprisonment, laying down roots in West Virginia. In that state, he helped revive the dormant West Virginia Historical Society, completing five county histories and another eight volumes geared to special-